W. B. Yeats
Selected Criticism

" the religion of the wilderness
— the only religion possible
to poetry today."

W. B. Yeats
Selected Criticism

edited with an introduction and notes by A. Norman Jeffares
Professor of English Literature, University of Leeds

Pan Books in association with
Macmillan London

This selection first published 1964 by Macmillan and Co Ltd
This edition published 1976 by
Pan Books Ltd, Cavaye Place, London SW10 9PG,
in association with Macmillan London
Selection and editorial matter © A. Norman Jeffares 1964
Select bibliography © A. Norman Jeffares 1970
ISBN 0 330 24619 4

Printed and bound in England by
Richard Clay (The Chaucer Press) Ltd, Bungay, Suffolk

CONTENTS

Acknowledgments   6
Introduction   7

The Irish National Literary Society   17
from William Blake and his Illustrations to the Divine Comedy   22
A Symbolic Artist and the Coming of Symbolic Art   33
The Autumn of the Body   38
The Symbolism of Poetry   43
The Philosophy of Shelley's Poetry   53
from Magic   80
from At Stratford-on-Avon   95
from Edmund Spenser   106
from The Happiest of the Poets   122
The Galway Plains   127
Samhain: 1904. First Principles   130
from Discoveries   150
from Poetry and Tradition   160
Anima Hominis   165
A People's Theatre   181
The Irish Dramatic Movement   195
Introduction to Fighting the Waves   207
On D. H. Lawrence   215
from the Introduction to The Oxford Book of Modern Verse   217
Modern Poetry: A Broadcast   238
A General Introduction for my Work   255
from Ireland after the Revolution   270

Notes   273
Select Bibliography   287

ACKNOWLEDGMENTS

THE editor and publishers wish to acknowledge their indebtedness to the following, who have kindly given permission for the use of copyright material: the Clarendon Press, Oxford, for the extract from the introduction to *The Oxford Book of Modern Verse*; Rupert Hart-Davis Ltd., for the letter from *The Letters of W. B. Yeats*, edited by Allan Wade; and Harvard University Press, for 'The Irish National Literary Society', from *Letters to the New Island*.

INTRODUCTION

W. B. YEATS grew up in a stimulating atmosphere, for his father, the artist J. B. Yeats, was an admirable conversationalist, full of ideas and ready with arguments, questioning, enthusiastic, and, above all, unconventional. He scorned an essay set on the theme 'Men may rise on stepping-stones of their dead selves to higher things', suggesting indignantly that his son should write instead on Shakespeare's lines, 'To thine own self be true, and it must follow, as the night the day, thou canst not then be false to any man'. Sometimes he would attack the concept of duty with equal vehemence. All of this was exciting to a youth in his teens, but Yeats later looked back with some regret upon this formative period of his life. The Yeats family were living in Howth, and father and son travelled by train to Dublin, walked through the city and breakfasted together in the painter's studio in York Street before the son went to his school in Harcourt Street nearby:

> All he said was, I now believe, right, but he should have taken me away from school. He would have taught me nothing but Greek and Latin, and I would now be a properly educated man, and would not have to look in useless longing at books that have been, through the poor mechanism of translation, the builders of my soul, nor face authority with the timidity born of excuse and evasion. Evasion and excuse were in the event as wise as the house-building instinct of the beaver.

J. B. Yeats read passages from the poets over breakfast, choosing the most passionate moments in play or poem

because he felt contemplative men overrated their state of life.
A Pre-Raphaelite in his literary tastes as well as in his painting,
he disliked the Victorian poetry of ideas and taught his son
to admire Balzac and to set some passages from Shakespeare
above all else in literature. He held that all valuable education
'was but a stirring up of the emotions', and thought that his
friend Edward Dowden, Professor of English Literature at
Trinity College, Dublin, believed too much in the intellect.
Yeats described his father as 'living in a free world accustomed
to the gay exaggeration of the talk of equals, of men who talk
and write to discover truth, and not for popular instruction'.

The influence of J. B. Yeats, a rationalist follower of John
Stuart Mill and a Home Ruler in his politics, lessened as his
son became interested in psychical research and mystical
philosophy, and began to develop strong nationalist views.
John O'Leary, the old Fenian, had introduced him to a new
world of Irish writing, and, partially in order to convince
Maud Gonne, with whom he had fallen in love at twenty-
three, that he possessed truly patriotic fervour, he began to
develop ideas of creating a new kind of Irish literature:

> I had noticed that Irish Catholics among whom had been
> born so many political martyrs had not the good taste, the
> household courtesy and decency of the Protestant Ireland I
> had known, yet Protestant Ireland seemed to think of
> nothing but getting on in the world. I thought we might
> bring the halves together if we had a national literature that
> made Ireland beautiful in the memory, and yet had been
> freed from provincialism by an exacting criticism, a
> European pose.

This ambition prompted many of Yeats's activities after
J. B. Yeats and his family moved to London in 1887. Apart
from writing about Irish subjects in his own poetry, trying his

hand at Irish subject-matter in novel form in *John Sherman and Dhoya* (1891) and in dramatic form in *The Countess Cathleen* (1892), he selected and edited *Fairy and Folk Tales of the Irish Peasantry* (1888), *Stories from Carleton* (1889), *Representative Irish Tales* (1891), and *Irish Fairy Tales* (1892). In 1895 he selected poems for *A Book of Irish Verse*. His views on the inter-relationship of nationalism and literature were put forward in critical and journalistic articles written for various journals from 1886 onwards. Many of these pieces dealt with the work of Irish writers: between 1886 and 1896, for instance, he wrote about Sir Samuel Ferguson, R. D. Joyce, James Clarence Mangan, William Allingham, John Todhunter, William Carleton, the Banim brothers, Jeremiah Curtin, Lady Wilde, Douglas Hyde, Rose Kavanagh, Ellen O'Leary, Oscar Wilde, Standish O'Grady, William Larminie, AE, Thomas Davis and John Eglinton. He also wrote about the aims and activities of Irish writers in London, of the London Irish Literary Society and the National Literary Society (see p. 17); he joined in controversies in support of the new literary movement and wrote articles in *The Bookman* on Irish national literature, beginning with Callanan and Carleton and bringing the survey up to the work of his contemporaries.

These critical articles were at first simply written and enthusiastic, filled with a gentle missionary zeal. Later, just as his poetry changed from local subjects to legends, from folk-lore to symbolism, so his criticism altered its scope and style. In 1894 he praised a Parisian performance of *Axel*; between 1895 and 1897 he reviewed books by Arthur Symons and by Maeterlinck, and wrote on Verlaine and on Blake.

His interest in symbolism and in the occult had an effect on his mannered, decorative style, influenced as it was by Pater and by Wilde also. His prose became, like his poetry, more occupied with an elaboration which is almost ritualistic and incantatory. 'The Autumn of the Body', written in 1898 (see p. 38), reflects this: 'Man has wooed and won the world, and has fallen weary, and not, I think, for a time but with a weariness that will not end until the last autumn, when the stars shall be blown away like withered leaves. . . . The arts are, I believe, about to take upon their shoulders the burdens that have fallen from the shoulders of priests, and to lead us back upon our journey by filling our thoughts with the essences of things, and not with things.' This essay reveals his interest in the European movement of symbolism which suited the wistful Pre-Raphaelite melancholia of his own defeatist love poetry, itself earlier affected by Indian quietism. He had learned about the French symbolists through his friendship with Arthur Symons, and this added to what he had learned about technique from the English poets (though many of them were 'Celts'), who met in the Cheshire Cheese, a public house in Fleet Street, to discuss their work. He wrote of 'The Symbolism of Poetry' in 1900 (see p. 43), asserting that

> With this change of substance, this return to imagination, this understanding that the laws of art, which are the hidden laws of the world, can alone bind the imagination, would come a change of style, and we would cast out of serious poetry those energetic rhythms, as of a man running, which are the invention of the will with its eyes always on something to be done or undone; and we would seek out those wavering, meditative organic rhythms, which are the embodiment of the imagination, that neither desires nor hates, because it has done with time and only wishes to gaze upon some reality, some beauty; nor would it be any longer possible for anybody to deny the importance of

form, in all its kinds, for although you can expound an opinion or describe a thing, when your words are not quite well chosen you cannot give a body to something that moves beyond the senses, unless your words are as subtle, as complex, as full of mysterious life, as the body of a flower or of a woman.

In another essay of 1900 on 'The Philosophy of Shelley's Poetry' (see p. 53), he again explored the technique of symbolism, probing into Shelley's successful use of continually repeated symbols, a thing he had not yet mastered himself in his own poetry written in the 'nineties.

The change that came over his own writing after the turn of the century, after the shock of Maud Gonne's marriage in 1903, after he had been brought back into contact with the speech of the peasantry by Lady Gregory, was not as clear cut in his prose as in his verse.

His older critical interests continued to occupy him, and he became readier to write more openly and strongly about them. In an essay on Magic of 1901 (see p. 80) he nailed his colours to the mast, asserting that the conscious use of symbols by the 'masters of magic' was continued in the half-conscious use of them by poets, musicians and artists. His restriction of his poetry to subjects of beauty in the 'nineties gave way to realistic, bitter, sometimes even prosaic poetry. His prose began to gain a corresponding strength and became simpler and more direct. In commenting on Spenser, in an introduction to an edition of 1906 (see p. 106), and on Shakespeare, in an essay on Stratford-on-Avon (see p. 95), he developed an air of confidence, a sensitive feeling for the relationship of both poets to the English tradition, both medieval and Elizabethan. These pieces engage the reader's sympathy more easily than Yeats's earlier writing; they convey a fresh and lively appreciation, the stronger for its more direct attitude. He was, however, attacking on a wide front. Various essays, on 'The Galway Plains' (see p. 127) and 'Dust hath closed Helen's Eye', showed the emergent effect of Lady Gregory on his prose style. He had developed a more positive sense of what he thought was an authentic Irish note. The Irish literary revival was now coming to be accepted as a fact, and the struggle to establish an Irish national theatre was challenging.

This difficult task produced some of Yeats's most original criticism. He was deeply committed to the ideal of recreating Ireland's image of itself, and his essay 'First Principles' of 1904 conveys his sense that the tide was rising, that instead of the sorrow of life portrayed in pictorial poetry the energy of life was now expressing itself through the imagination of personality, the vital force of drama.

For ten years, from 1899 to 1909, Yeats expressed his views on drama in essays included in *Beltaine*, *Samhain*, and *The Arrow*, occasional publications issued by the Abbey Theatre. These essays show his increasing awareness of his audience; they demonstrate the benefits he gained from his experience of 'theatre business, management of men'. He wrote with an element of realism and practicality supporting his ideas. The energy which had gone into his devotion to Maud Gonne's beauty now had a new object. Though he complained in 'The Fascination of What's Difficult' that his Pegasus was dragging road-metal, he was strengthening and testing his convictions. His sensitive, generous praise of Synge, for instance, in the prefaces he wrote to the volumes of Synge's work and in the essay on 'J. M. Synge and the Ireland of his Time', has a discerning authority about it.

Yet the Abbey Theatre did not go the way he had hoped. 'A People's Theatre' (see p. 181) weighed up in 1919 the results of the Irish theatrical movement, and this was done with a detachment made possible, in fact, by his new interest in writing plays for smaller, more select audiences. 'The Irish Dramatic Movement', a lecture delivered in Sweden when he was awarded the Nobel Prize in 1923 (see p. 195), reverts to what seemed to him the great achievement of the Abbey Theatre, and presents, along with this celebration, a reminder of the political and financial difficulties which had to be overcome in its creation. This is interpretative criticism, which can base its interpretations upon intimate knowledge of the aims and the actions of the three playwrights:

> John Synge, I and Augusta Gregory, thought
> All that we did, all that we said or sang
> Must come from contact with the soil, from that
> Contact everything Antaeus-like grew strong.
> We three alone in modern times had brought
> Everything down to that sole test again,
> Dream of the noble and the beggar-man.

Throughout the first decade of the century Yeats was slowly piecing together the ideas, many of them developed from his reading in the occult writers, which he included in *Per Amica Silentia Lunae*. These essays are critical in that they reveal much of his thinking about the nature of literary art; they contain the subjective meditation which built the framework of much of his later poetry, the ideas of the mask, the self and anti-self, the Daimon (see p. 165). They are full of memorable rhetorical phrases, some of them later glossed in *A Vision*: 'The poet finds and makes his mask in disappointment, the hero in defeat', or, 'A poet when he is growing old will ask himself if he cannot keep his mask and his vision without new bitterness, new disappointment', or again the simple and

moving description (later echoed in the poem 'Vacillation')
of happiness:

> At certain moments, always unforeseen, I became happy,
> most commonly when at hazard I have opened some book
> of verse. Sometimes it is my own verse when, instead of dis-
> covering new technical flaws, I read with all the excite-
> ment of the first writing. Perhaps I am sitting in some
> crowded restaurant, the open book beside me, or closed,
> my excitement having overbrimmed the page. I look at the
> strangers near as if I had known them all my life, and it
> seems strange that I cannot speak to them: everything fills
> me with affection, I have no longer any fears or needs;
> I do not even remember that this happy mood must come
> to an end. It seems as if the vehicle had suddenly grown
> pure and far extended and so luminous that the images from
> *Anima Mundi*, embodied there and drunk with that sweet-
> ness, would, like a country drunkard who has thrown a
> wisp into his own thatch, burn up time.

In the nineteen-twenties the writing of *A Vision*, 'getting it
all in order', involved him in fresh reading of history and
philosophy. His letters convey some of the excitement this
reading aroused in him; his introduction to the Hone and
Rossi *Bishop Berkeley* (1931) and his introductions to the plays
in *Wheels and Butterflies* (1934) also recapture this lively period
of speculation, this arresting arrangement of human experience into a mixture of decorative pattern and dramatic
design. In the process he rediscovered his Anglo-Irish heritage:

> I declare this tower is my symbol; I declare
> This winding, gyring, spiring treadmill of a stair is my
>   ancestral stair;

That Goldsmith and the Dean, Berkeley and Burke have
  travelled here.

This heritage was important to him. Now that the family
line was assured by the birth of his son Michael Butler Yeats
in 1921, he could also delight in having extended a personal
sense of continuity to a larger community. His critical exami-
nation of the Anglo-Irish writers reinforced his predilection,
formed as a result of his own earlier experience of revolutionary movements in literature and politics, for forthright
speech. Now as a Senator of the Irish Free State he felt it his
duty to speak out:

> We are one of the great stocks of Europe. We are the
> people of Burke; we are the people of Grattan; we are the
> people of Swift, the people of Emmet, the people of
> Parnell. We have created the most of the modern literature
> of this country. We have created the best of its political
> intelligence.

The Senate speeches on copyright (March 11 and May 4,
1927), his speech to the Irish Literary Society on 'The Child
and the State' (*Irish Statesman*, December 1925) and his
article on 'The Irish Censorship' (*The Spectator*, September
29, 1928) illustrated his concern with the role of literature in
society. They are direct; they are written in a prose which is
arresting because it gives the effect of thought in action. And
Yeats had reached a clarity, a strength of thought which no
longer needed to rely upon the hammered gold and gold
enamelling of names, allusive and decorative, of knowledge
recondite and cryptic. He no longer needed to face authority
with the timidity born of excuse and evasion. We realise
when we read his 'General Introduction for my Work',
written in 1937 (see p. 255) that he had himself achieved

authority; this was an authority which could permit him to face his own evasions:

> 'The work is done,' grown old he thought,
> 'According to my boyish plan;
> Let the fools rage, I swerved in naught,
> Something to perfection brought';
> But louder sang that ghost, '*What then?*'

THE IRISH NATIONAL LITERARY SOCIETY

YOUR Celt has written the greater bulk of his letters from the capitol of the enemy, but he is now among his own people again, and no longer The Celt in London, but The Celt in Ireland. At this moment he is sitting writing, or trying to write, in the big, florid new National Library with its stone balcony, where nobody is allowed to walk, and its numberless stone niches, in which there will never be any statues. He is sitting dreaming much, and writing a little from time to time, watching the people come and go, and wondering what shall be born of the new generation that is now so very busy reading endless scholasticisms along the five rows of oak tables. An old fairy tale which exists in many forms in many countries tells of a giant whose life was hidden away in an egg, which was in its turn hid in the mouth of a fish, or some such unlikely place. The library is just such an egg, for it hides under its white curved ceiling a good portion of the scholastic life of student Dublin. Here they come to read for examinations, and to work up their various subjects. At my left hand is a man reading some registers of civil service or other examinations; opposite me an ungainly young man with a puzzled face is turning over the pages of a trigonometry work; and a little beyond him a medical student is deep in anatomical diagrams. On all sides men are studying the things that are to get them bodily food, but no man among them is searching for the imaginative and spiritual food to be got out of great literature. Nobody, with the exception of a few ladies, perhaps, ever seems to do any disinterested reading in this library, or indeed anywhere else in

Ireland. Every man here is grinding at the mill wherein he grinds all things into pounds and shillings, and but few of them will he get when all is done. Ireland, half through her own fault and half through circumstances over which she has no control, is not a reading nation, nor has she been so for many a long day. A single town in Scotland is said to buy more books than all Ireland put together, and surely nowhere out of Ireland will you find a great library like this given over completely to the student cramming for examinations.

Can we find a remedy? Can we not unite literature to the great passion of patriotism and ennoble both thereby? This question has occupied a good many of us this spring. We think that a national literary society and a series of national books like Duffy's Library of Ireland may do something, and have accordingly founded such a society and planned out, with the help of a number of well known men of letters, such a national series. Our task should not, after all, be so difficult. These very students will do for the love of Ireland what they would not do for the love of literature. When literature comes to them, telling of their own country and of its history and of its legends, they will listen gladly enough. The people of Ireland have ever honoured intellect, although they have no intellectual life themselves. I have heard a drunken fisherman tell a man that he was no gentleman 'because nobody is a gentleman who has not been educated at Trinity College Dublin'. The people of Ireland have created perhaps the most beautiful folk-lore in the world, and have made a wild music that is the wonder of all men, and yet to-day they have turned aside from imaginative arts. Can we bring them to care once more for the things of the mind? Well, we are going to do our best to bring books to their doors and music, too, perhaps. Thomas of Erceldoune foretold the day when the gray goose quill would rule the world; and may not we men of the pen hope to move some Irish hearts and make them beat true to manhood and to Ireland? Will not the day come when we shall have again in Ireland men who will not lie for any party advantage, or traffic away eternal principles for any expediency however urgent — men like the men of '48, who lived by the light of noble books and the great traditions of the past? Amidst the clash of party against party we have tried to put forward a nationality that is above party, and amid the oncoming roar of a general election we have tried to assert those everlasting principles of love of truth and love of country that speak to men in solitude and in the silence of the night. So far all has gone well with us, for men who are saddened and disgusted with the turn public affairs have taken have sought in our society occasion to do work for Ireland that will bring about assured good, whether that good be great or small. We have met more support than we ventured to hope for, and there is no sign of its falling off.

The committee represents all parties and opinions which have any claim to be considered national. The Reverend T. A. Finlay of the Catholic University, Mr. John O'Leary, Sir Charles Gavan Duffy, Dr. Douglas Hyde, Dr Sigerson, Count Plunkett, Miss Katharine Tynan, Miss Maud Gonne, so well known for her oratory and her beauty, and Mr. Richard Ashe King, the novelist, are among the best known. Books have been offered upon all manner of national epochs and events from the Ossianic days to our own time.

Apart from the literary society altogether, things are not looking so badly for the future of our literature. Mr. Standish O'Grady, for instance, is doing better and better work. He has on hand an historical romance dealing with the invasions of Strongbow, and is contributing also from time to time

singularly moving and picturesque little stories on events
in Irish history to the Dublin papers. He will doubtless collect
them into a volume before long. He has also written for Fisher
Unwin's Children's Library a book called *Finn and His Companions*, which gives the most vivid pictures of the Ossianic
age I ever hope to see. Caoilte, having survived to the
time of St. Patrick by enchantment, describes to the saint
the life of the Fenians, and tells numbers of the old tales
out of the bardic poems in English both powerful and
beautiful.

Dr. Douglas Hyde has also a book on the legendary age in
progress. It will give translations of bardic stories, and will be,
I believe, but the first of a series if Dr. Hyde meets with
proper support. It is impossible to overrate the importance of
such books, for in them the Irish poets of the future will in all
likelihood find a good portion of their subject matter. From
that great candle of the past we must all light our little
tapers.

In England I sometimes hear men complain that the old
themes of verse and prose are used up. Here in Ireland the
marble block is waiting for us almost untouched, and the
statues will come as soon as we have learned to use the chisel.
Our history is full of incidents well worthy of drama, story
and song. And they are incidents involving types of character
of which this world has not yet heard. If we can but put those
tumultuous centuries into tale or drama, the whole world will
listen to us and sit at our feet like children who hear a new
story. Nor is this new thing we have to say in our past alone.
The very people who come and go in this library where I
write are themes full of new wisdom and new mystery, for in
them is that yet uncultured thing — Irish character. And if
history and the living present fail us, do there not lie hid
among those spear heads and golden collars over the way in

the New Museum, suggestions of that age before history when the art legends and wild mythology of earliest Ireland rose out of the void? There alone is enough of the stuff that dreams are made on to keep us busy a thousand years.

November 19, 1892

WILLIAM BLAKE AND HIS ILLUSTRATIONS TO THE DIVINE COMEDY

I. HIS OPINIONS UPON ART

WILLIAM BLAKE was the first writer of modern times to preach the indissoluble marriage of all great art with symbol. There had been allegorists and teachers of allegory in plenty, but the symbolic imagination, or, as Blake preferred to call it, 'vision', is not allegory, being 'a representation of what actually exists really and unchangeably'. A symbol is indeed the only possible expression of some invisible essence, a transparent lamp about a spiritual flame; while allegory is one of many possible representations of an embodied thing, or familiar principle, and belongs to fancy and not to imagination: the one is a revelation, the other an amusement. It is happily no part of my purpose to expound in detail the relations he believed to exist between symbol and mind, for in doing so I should come upon not a few doctrines which, though they have not been difficult to many simple persons, ascetics wrapped in skins, women who had cast away all common knowledge, peasants dreaming by their sheepfolds upon the hills, are full of obscurity to the man of modern culture; but it is necessary to just touch upon these relations, because in them was the fountain of much of the practice and of all the precept of his artistic life.

If a man would enter into 'Noah's rainbow', he has written, and 'make a friend' of one of 'the images of wonder' which dwell there, and which always entreat him 'to leave mortal things', 'then would he arise from the grave and meet the Lord in the air'; and by this rainbow, this sign of a covenant granted to him who is with Shem and Japhet, 'painting, poetry and music', 'the three powers in man of conversing with Paradise which the flood "of time and space" did not sweep away', Blake represented the shapes of beauty haunting our moments of inspiration: shapes held by most for the frailest of ephemera, but by him for a people older than the world, citizens of eternity, appearing and reappearing in the minds of artists and of poets, creating all we touch and see by casting distorted images of themselves upon 'the vegetable glass of nature'; and because beings, none the less symbols, blossoms, as it were, growing from invisible immortal roots, hands, as it were, pointing the way into some divine labyrinth. If 'the world of imagination' was 'the world of eternity', as this doctrine implied, it was of less importance to know men and nature than to distinguish the beings and substances of imagination from those of a more perishable kind, created by the fantasy, in uninspired moments, out of memory and whim; and this could best be done by purifying one's mind, as with a flame, in study of the works of the great masters, who were great because they had been granted by divine favour a vision of the unfallen world from which others are kept apart by the flaming sword that turns every way; and by flying from the painters who studied 'the vegetable glass' for its own sake, and not to discover there the shadows of imperishable beings and substances, and who entered into their own minds, not to make the unfallen world a test of all they heard and saw and felt with the senses, but to cover the naked spirit with 'the rotten rags of memory' of older sensations. The struggle of the first part of his life had been to distinguish between these two schools, and to cleave always to the Florentine, and so to escape the fascination of those who seemed to him to offer the sleep of nature to a spirit weary

with the labours of inspiration; but it was only after his return
to London from Felpham in 1804 that he finally escaped from
'temptations and perturbations' which sought to destroy 'the
imaginative power' at 'the hands of Venetian and Flemish
Demons'. 'The spirit of Titian' — and one must always remember that he had only seen poor engravings, and what his
disciple, Palmer, has called 'picture-dealers' Titians' — 'was
particularly active in raising doubts concerning the possibility
of executing without a model; and when once he had raised the
doubt it became easy for him to snatch away the vision time
after time'; and Blake's imagination 'weakened' and 'darkened' until a 'memory of nature and of pictures of various
schools possessed his mind, instead of appropriate execution'
flowing from the vision itself. But now he wrote, 'O glory,
and O delight! I have entirely reduced that spectrous fiend to
his station' — he had overcome the merely reasoning and
sensual portion of the mind — 'whose annoyance has been
the ruin of my labours for the last passed twenty years of my
life. . . . I speak with perfect confidence and certainty of the
fact which has passed upon me. Nebuchadnezzar had seven
times passed over him, I have had twenty; thank God I was
not altogether a beast as he was. . . . Suddenly, on the day
after vising the Truchsessian Gallery of pictures' — this was a
gallery containing pictures by Albert Dürer and by the great
Florentines — 'I was again enlightened with the light I enjoyed in my youth, and which has for exactly twenty years
been closed from me, as by a door and by window-shutters.
. . . Excuse my enthusiasm, or rather madness, for I am really
drunk with intellectual vision whenever I take a pencil or
graver into my hand, even as I used to be in my youth.'

This letter may have been the expression of a moment's
enthusiasm, but was more probably rooted in one of those
intuitions of coming technical power which every creator

feels, and learns to rely upon; for all his greatest work was done, and the principles of his art were formulated, after this date. Except a word here and there, his writings hitherto had not dealt with the principles of art except remotely and by implication; but now he wrote much upon them, and not in obscure symbolic verse, but in emphatic prose, and explicit if not very poetical rhyme. He explained spiritual art, and praised the painters of Florence and their influence and cursed all that has come of Venice and Holland in his *Descriptive Catalogue*, in the *Address to the Public*, in the notes on Sir Joshua Reynolds, in *The Book of Moonlight* — of which some not very dignified rhymes alone remain — in beautiful detached passages of his *MS. Book*. The limitation of his view was from the very intensity of his vision; he was a too literal realist of imagination, as others are of nature; and because he believed that the figures seen by the mind's eye, when exalted by inspiration, were 'external existences', symbols of divine essences, he hated every grace of style that might obscure their lineaments. To wrap them about in reflected lights was to do this, and to dwell over-fondly upon any softness of hair or flesh was to dwell upon that which was least permanent and least characteristic, for 'The great and golden rule of art, as well as of life, is this: that the more distinct, sharp and wiry the bounding line, the more perfect the work of art; and the less keen and sharp, the greater is the evidence of weak imitation, plagiarism and bungling'. Inspiration was to see the permanent and characteristic in all forms, and if you had it not, you must needs imitate with a languid mind the things you saw or remembered, and so sink into the sleep of nature where all is soft and melting. 'Great inventors in all ages knew this. Protogenes and Apelles knew each other by this line. Raphael and Michelangelo and Albert Dürer are known by this and this alone. . . . How do we distinguish the oak from the beech, the horse from the ox, but by the bounding outline? How do we distinguish one face or countenance from another, but by the bounding outline and its infinite inflections and movements? What is it that builds a house and plants a garden, but the definite and determinate? What is it that distinguishes honesty from knavery, but the hard and wiry line of rectitude and certainty in the actions and intentions? Leave out this line and you leave out life itself; all is chaos again, and the line of the Almighty must be drawn out upon it before man or beast can exist.' He even insisted that 'colouring does not depend upon where the colours are put, but upon where the lights and darks are put, and all depends on form or outline' — meaning, I suppose, that a colour gets its brilliance or its depth from being in light or in shadow. He does not mean by outline the bounding line dividing a form from its background, as one of his commentators has thought, but the line that divides it from surrounding space, and unless you have an overmastering sense of this you cannot draw true beauty at all, but only 'the beauty that is appended to folly', a beauty of mere voluptuous softness, 'a lamentable accident of the mortal and perishing life', for 'the beauty proper for sublime art is lineaments, or forms and features that are capable of being the receptacles of intellect', and 'the face or limbs that alter least from infancy to old age are the face and limbs of greatest beauty and perfection'. His praise of a severe art had been beyond price had his age rested a moment to listen, in the midst of its enthusiasm for Correggio and the later Renaissance, for Bartolozzi and for Stothard. What matter if in his visionary realism, in his enthusiasm for what, after all, is perhaps the greatest art, he refused to admit that he who wraps the vision in lights and shadows, in irridescent or glowing colour, until form be half lost in pattern, may, as did Titian in his *Bacchus and Ariadne*, create a talisman as powerfully charged with intellectual virtue as though it were a jewel-studded door of the city seen on Patmos?

To cover the imperishable lineaments of beauty with shadows and reflected lights was to fall into the power of his 'Vala', the indolent fascination of Nature, the woman divinity who is so often described in the 'Prophetic Books' as 'sweet pestilence', and whose children weave webs to take the souls of men; but there was a yet more lamentable chance, for Nature has also a 'masculine portion' or 'spectre' which kills instead of taking prisoner, and is continually at war with inspiration. To 'generalise' forms and shadows, to 'smooth out' spaces and lines in obedience to 'laws of composition', and of painting; founded not upon imagination, which always thirsts for variety and delights in freedom, but upon reasoning from sensation, which is always seeking to reduce everything to a lifeless and slavish uniformity; as the popular art of Blake's day had done, and as he understood Sir Joshua Reynolds to advise, was to fall into 'Entuthon Benithon', or 'the Lake of Udan Adan', or some other of those regions where the imagination and the flesh are alike dead, that he names by so many resonant fantastical names. 'General knowledge is remote knowledge,' he wrote; 'it is in particulars that wisdom consists, and happiness too. Both in art and life general masses are as much art as a pasteboard man is human. Every man has eyes, nose and mouth; this every idiot knows. But he who enters into and discriminates most minutely the manners and intentions, the characters in all their branches, is the alone wise or sensible man, and on this discrimination all art is founded. . . . As poetry admits not a letter that is insignificant, so painting admits not a grain of sand or a blade of grass insignificant, much less an insignificant blot or blur.'

Against another desire of his time, derivative also from what

he has called 'corporeal reason', the desire for 'a tepid modera-
tion', for a lifeless 'sanity in both art and life', he had protested years before with a paradoxical violence. 'The road-
way of excess leads to the palace of wisdom', and we must
only 'bring out weight and measure in time of dearth'. This
protest, carried, in the notes on Sir Joshua Reynolds, to the
point of dwelling with pleasure on the thought that 'The
Lives of the Painters say that Raphael died of dissipation',
because dissipation is better than emotional penury, seemed
as important to his old age as to his youth. He taught it to his
disciples, and one finds it in its purely artistic shape in a diary
written by Samuel Palmer, in 1824: 'Excess is the essential
vivifying spirit, vital spark, embalming spice of the finest art.
There are many mediums in the *means* — none, oh, not a jot,
not a shadow of a jot, in the *end* of great art. In a picture
whose merit is to be excessively brilliant, it can't be too
brilliant, but individual tints may be too brilliant. . . . We
must not begin with medium, but think always on excess and
only use medium to make excess more abundantly excessive.'

These three primary commands, to seek a determinate outline, to avoid a generalised treatment, and to desire always
abundance and exuberance, were insisted upon with vehe-
ment anger, and their opponents called again and again
'demons' and 'villains', 'hired' by the wealthy and the idle;
but in private, Palmer has told us, he could find 'sources of
delight throughout the whole range of art', and was ever
ready to praise excellence in any school, finding, doubtless,
among friends, no need for the emphasis of exaggeration.
There is a beautiful passage in *Jerusalem* in which the merely
mortal part of the mind, 'the spectre', created 'pyramids of
pride', and 'pillars in the deepest hell to reach the heavenly
arches', and seeks to discover wisdom in 'the spaces between
the stars', not 'in the stars', where it is, but the immortal

part makes all his labours vain, and turns his pyramids to 'grains of sand', his 'pillars' to 'dust on the fly's wing', and makes of 'his starry heavens a moth of gold and silver mocking his anxious grasp'. So when man's desire to rest from spiritual labour, and his thirst to fill his art with mere sensation and memory, seem upon the point of triumph, some miracle transforms them to a new inspiration; and here and there among the pictures born of sensation and memory is the murmuring of a new ritual, the glimmering of new talismans and symbols.

It was during and after the writing of these opinions that Blake did the various series of pictures which have brought him the bulk of his fame. He had already completed the illustrations to Young's *Night Thoughts* — in which the great sprawling figures, a little wearisome even with the luminous colours of the original water-colour, became nearly intolerable in plain black and white — and almost all the illustrations to the 'Prophetic Books', which have an energy like that of the elements, but are rather rapid sketches taken while some phantasmic procession swept over him, than elaborate compositions, and in whose shadowy adventures one finds not merely, as did Dr. Garth Wilkinson, 'the hells of the ancient people, the Anakim, the Nephalim, and the Rephaim . . . gigantic petrifications from which the fires of lust and intense selfish passion have long dissipated what was animal and vital'; not merely the shadows cast by the powers who had closed the light from him as 'with a door and window-shutters', but the shadows of those who gave them battle. He did now, however, the many designs to Milton, of which I have only seen those to *Paradise Regained*; the reproductions of those to *Comus*, published, I think, by Mr. Quaritch; and the three or four to *Paradise Lost*, engraved by Bell Scott — a series of designs which one good judge considers his greatest work; the illustrations to Blair's *Grave*, whose gravity and passion struggled with the mechanical softness and trivial smoothness of Schiavonetti's engraving; the illustrations to Thornton's *Virgil*, whose influence is manifest in the work of the little group of landscape-painters who gathered about him in his old age and delighted to call him master. The member of the group whom I have already so often quoted has alone praised worthily these illustrations to the first Eclogue: 'There is in all such a misty and dreamy glimmer as penetrates and kindles the inmost soul and gives complete and unreserved delight, unlike the gaudy daylight of this world. They are like all this wonderful artist's work, the drawing aside of the fleshly curtain, and the glimpse which all the most holy, studious saints and sages have enjoyed, of the rest which remains to the people of God.' Now, too, he did the great series, the crowning work of his life, the illustrations to *The Book of Job* and the illustrations to the *Divine Comedy*. Hitherto he had protested against the mechanical 'dots and lozenges' and 'blots and blurs' of Woollett and Strange,[1] but had himself used both 'dot and lozenge', 'blot and blur', though always in subordination 'to a firm and determinate outline'; but in Marc Antonio, certain of whose engravings he was shown by Linnell, he found a style full of delicate lines, a style where all was living and energetic, strong and subtle. And almost his last words, a letter written upon his death-bed, attack the 'dots and lozenges' with even more than usually quaint symbolism, and praise expressive lines. 'I know too well that the majority of Englishmen are fond of the infinite . . . a line is a line in its minutest subdivisions,

---

[1] Woollett and Strange had established names when Blake began to draw, and must have seemed to Blake in certain moods the types of all triumphant iniquity. Woollett used to fire a cannon from the roof of his house whenever he finished an important plate.

straight or crooked. It is itself, not intermeasurable by anything else . . . but since the French Revolution' — since the
reign of reason began, that is —'Englishmen are all intermeasurable by one another; certainly a happy state of agreement, in which I for one do not agree.' The Dante series
occupied the last years of his life; even when too weak to get
out of bed he worked on, propped up with the great drawing-
book before him. He sketched a hundred designs, but left
nearly all incomplete, some greatly so, and partly engraved
seven plates, of which the 'Francesca and Paolo' is the most
finished. It is not, I think, inferior to any but the finest in *Job*,
if indeed to them, and shows in its perfection Blake's mastery
over elemental things, the swirl in which the lost spirits are
hurried, 'a watery flame' he would have called it, the haunted
waters and the huddling shapes. In the illustrations of Purga-
tory there is a serene beauty, and one finds his Dante and
Virgil climbing among the rough rocks under a cloudy sun,
and in their sleep upon the smooth steps towards the summit,
a placid, marmoreal, tender, starry rapture.

All in this great series are in some measure powerful and
moving, and not, as it is customary to say of the work of
Blake, because a flaming imagination pierces through a cloudy
and indecisive technique, but because they have the only
excellence possible in any art, a mastery over artistic expression. The technique of Blake was imperfect, incomplete, as is
the technique of wellnigh all artists who have striven to
bring fires from remote summits; but where his imagination
is perfect and complete, his technique has a like perfection, a
like completeness. He strove to embody more subtle rap-
tures, more elaborate intuitions than any before him; his
imagination and technique are more broken and strained
under a great burden than the imagination and technique of
any other master. 'I am,' wrote Blake, 'like others, just equal

in invention and execution.' And again, 'No man can improve an original invention; nor can an original invention exist without execution, organised, delineated and articulated either by God or man . . . I have heard people say, "Give me the ideas; it is no matter what words you put them into"; and others say, "Give me the design; it is no matter for the execution". . . . Ideas cannot be given but in their minutely appropriate words, nor can a design be made without its minutely appropriate execution.' Living in a time when technique and imagination are continually perfect and complete, because they no longer strive to bring fire from heaven, we forget how imperfect and incomplete they were in even the greatest masters, in Botticelli, in Orcagna, and in Giotto.

The errors in the handiwork of exalted spirits are as the more fantastical errors in their lives; as Coleridge's opium cloud; as Villiers de l'Isle-Adam's candidature for the throne of Greece; as Blake's anger against causes and purposes he but half understood; as that veritable madness an Eastern scripture thinks permissible among the saints; for he who half lives in eternity endures a rending of the structures of the mind, a crucifixion of the intellectual body.

[1896]

A SYMBOLIC ARTIST AND THE COMING
OF SYMBOLIC ART

The only two powers that trouble the deeps are religion and love, the others make a little trouble upon the surface. When I have written of literature in Ireland, I have had to write again and again about a company of Irish mystics, who have taught for some years a religious philosophy which has changed many ordinary people into ecstatics and visionaries. Young men, who were, I think, apprentices or clerks, have told me how they lay awake at night hearing miraculous music, or seeing forms that made the most beautiful painted or marble forms seem dead and shadowy. This philosophy has changed its symbolism from time to time, being now a little Christian, now very Indian, now altogether Celtic and mythological; but it has never ceased to take a great part of its colour and character from one lofty imagination. I do not believe I could easily exaggerate the direct and indirect influences which 'A. E.' (Mr. George Russell), the most subtle and spiritual poet of his generation, and a visionary who may find room beside Swedenborg and Blake, has had in shaping to a definite conviction the vague spirituality of young Irish men and women of letters. I know that Miss Althea Gyles, in whose work I find so visionary a beauty, does not mind my saying that she lived long with this little company, who had once a kind of conventual house; and that she will not think I am taking from her originality when I say that the beautiful lithe figures of her art, quivering with a life half mortal tragedy, half immortal ecstasy, owe something of their inspiration to this little company. I indeed believe that I see in them a beginning of what may become a new manner in the arts of the modern world; for there are tides in the imagination of the world, and a motion in one or two minds may show a change of tide.

Pattern and rhythm are the road to open symbolism, and the arts have already become full of pattern and rhythm. Subject pictures no longer interest us, while pictures with patterns and rhythms of colour, like Mr. Whistler's, and drawings with patterns and rhythms of line, like Mr. Beardsley's in his middle period, interest us extremely. Mr. Whistler and Mr. Beardsley have sometimes thought so greatly of these patterns and rhythms, that the images of human life have faded almost perfectly; and yet we have not lost our interest. The arts have learned the denials, though they have not learned the fervours of the cloister. Men like Sir Edward Burne-Jones and Mr. Ricketts have been too full of the emotion and the pathos of life to let its images fade out of their work, but they have so little interest in the common thoughts and emotions of life, that their images of life have delicate and languid limbs that could lift no burdens, and souls vaguer than a sigh; while men like Mr. Degas, who are still interested in life, and life at its most vivid and vigorous, picture it with a cynicism that remind one of what ecclesiastics have written in old Latin about women and about the world.

Once or twice an artist has been touched by a visionary energy amid his weariness and bitterness, but it has passed away. Mr. Beardsley created a visionary beauty in *Salome with the Head of John the Baptist*, but because, as he told me, 'beauty is the most difficult of things', he chose in its stead the satirical grotesques of his later period. If one imagine a flame burning in the air, and try to make one's mind dwell on it, that it may continue to burn, one's mind strays immediately to other images; but perhaps, if one believed that it was a divine flame, one's mind would not stray. I think that I would find this visionary beauty also in the work of some of the younger French artists, for I have a dim memory of a little statue in ebony and ivory. Certain recent French writers, like Villiers de l'Isle Adam, have it, and I cannot separate art and literature in this, for they have gone through the same change, though in different forms. I have certainly found it in the poetry of a young Irish Catholic who was meant for the priesthood, but broke down under the strain of what was to him a visionary ecstasy; in some plays by a new Irish writer; in the poetry of 'A. E.'; in some stories of Miss Macleod's; and in the drawings of Miss Gyles; and in almost all these a passion for symbol has taken the place of the old interest in life. These persons are of very different degrees and qualities of power, but their work is always energetic, always the contrary of what is called 'decadent'. One feels that they have not only left the smoke of human hearths and come to The Dry Tree, but that they have drunk from The Well at the World's End.

Miss Gyles' images are so full of abundant and passionate life that they remind one of William Blake's cry, 'Exuberance is Beauty', and Samuel Palmer's command to the artist 'Always seek to make excess more abundantly excessive'. One finds in them what a friend, whose work has no other passion, calls 'the passion for the impossible beauty'; for the beauty which cannot be seen with the bodily eyes, or pictured otherwise than by symbols. Her own favourite drawing, which unfortunately cannot be printed here, is *The Rose of God*, a personification of this beauty as a naked woman, whose hands are stretched against the clouds, as upon a cross, in the traditional attitude of the Bride, the symbol of the microcosm in the Kabala; while two winds, two destinies, the one full of white and the other full of red rose petals, personifying all purities and all passions, whirl about her and descend upon a fleet of ships and a walled city, personifying the wavering and the fixed powers, the masters of the world in the alchemical symbolism. Some imperfect but beautiful verses accompany the drawing, and describe her as for 'living man's delight and his eternal revering when dead'.

I have described this drawing because one must understand Miss Gyles' central symbol, the Rose, before one can understand her dreamy and intricate *Noah's Raven*. The ark floats upon a grey sea under a grey sky, and the raven flutters above the sea. A sea nymph, whose slender swaying body drifting among the grey waters is a perfect symbol of a soul untouched by God or by passion, coils the fingers of one hand about his feet and offers him a ring, while her other hand holds a shining rose under the sea. Grotesque shapes of little fishes flit about the rose, and grotesque shapes of larger fishes swim hither and thither. Sea nymphs swim through the windows of a sunken town and reach towards the rose hands covered with rings; and a vague twilight hangs over all. The story is woven out of as many old symbols as if it were a mystical story in 'The Prophetic Books'. The raven, who is, as I understand him, the desire and will of man, has come out of the ark, the personality of man, to find if the Rose is anywhere above the flood, which is here, as always, the flesh, 'the flood of the five senses'. He has found it and is returning with it to the ark, that the soul of man may sink into the ideal and pass away; but the sea nymphs, the spirits of the senses, have bribed him with a ring taken from the treasures of the kings of the world, a ring that gives the mastery of the world, and he has given them the Rose. Henceforth man will seek for the ideal in the flesh, and the flesh will be full of illusive beauty, and the spiritual beauty will be far away.

The Knight upon the Grave of his Lady tells much of its meaning to the first glance; but when one has studied for a time, one discovers that there is a heart in the bulb of every hyacinth, to personify the awakening of the soul and of love out of the grave. It is now winter, and beyond the knight, who lies in the abandonment of his sorrow, the trees spread their leafless boughs against a grey winter sky; but spring will come, and the boughs will be covered with leaves, and the hyacinths will cover the ground with their blossoms, for the moral is not the moral of the Persian poet: 'Here is a secret, do not tell it to anybody. The hyacinth that blossomed yesterday is dead.' The very richness of the pattern of the armour, and of the boughs, and of the woven roots, and of the dry bones, seems to announce that beauty gathers the sorrows of man into her breast and gives them eternal peace.

It is some time since I saw the original drawing of *Lilith*, and it has been decided to reproduce it in this number of *The Dome* too late for me to have a proof of the engraving; but I remember that Lilith, the ever-changing phantasy of passion, rooted neither in good nor evil, half crawls upon the ground, like a serpent before the great serpent of the world, her guardian and her shadow; and Miss Gyles reminds me that Adam, and things to come, are reflected on the wings of the serpent; and that beyond, a place shaped like a heart is full of thorns and roses. I remember thinking that the serpent was a little confused, and that the composition was a little lacking in rhythm, and upon the whole caring less for this drawing than for others, but it has an energy and a beauty of its own. I believe that the best of these drawings will live, and that if Miss Gyles were to draw nothing better, she would still have won a place among the few artists in black and white whose work is of the highest intensity. I believe, too, that her inspiration is a wave of a hidden tide that is flowing through many minds in many places, creating a new religious art and poetry.

[December, 1898]

THE AUTUMN OF THE BODY

OUR thoughts and emotions are often but spray flung up from hidden tides that follow a moon no eye can see. I remember that when I first began to write I desired to describe outward things as vividly as possible, and took pleasure, in which there was, perhaps, a little discontent, in picturesque and declamatory books. And then quite suddenly I lost the desire of describing outward things, and found that I took little pleasure in a book unless it was spiritual and unemphatic. I did not then understand that the change was from beyond my own mind, but I understand now that writers are struggling all over Europe, though not often with a philosophic understanding of their struggle, against that picturesque and declamatory way of writing, against that 'externality' which a time of scientific and political thought has brought into literature. This struggle has been going on for some years, but it has only just become strong enough to draw within itself the little sinner world which alone seeks more than amusement in the arts. In France, where movements are more marked, because the people are pre-eminently logical, *The Temptation of Saint Anthony*, the last great dramatic invention of the old romanticism, contrasts very plainly with *Axël*, the first great dramatic invention of the new; and Maeterlinck has followed Count Villiers de l'Isle-Adam. Flaubert wrote unforgettable descriptions of grotesque, bizarre, and beautiful scenes and persons, as they show to the ear and to the eye, and crowded them with historical and ethnographical details; but Count Villiers de l'Isle-Adam swept together, by what seemed a sudden energy, words behind which glimmered a spiritual and passionate mood, as the flame glimmers behind the dusky blue and red glass in an Eastern lamp; and created persons from whom has fallen all even of personal characteristic except a thirst for that hour when all things shall pass away like a cloud, and a pride like that of the Magi following their star over many mountains; while Maeterlinck has plucked away even this thirst and this pride and set before us faint souls, naked and pathetic shadows already half vapour and sighing to one another upon the border of the last abyss. There has been, as I think, a like change in French painting, for one sees everywhere, instead of the dramatic stories and picturesque moments of an older school, frail and tremulous bodies unfitted for the labour of life, and landscape where subtle rhythms of colour and of form have overcome the clear outline of things as we see them in the labour of life.

There has been a like change in England, but it has come more gradually and is more mixed with lesser changes than in France. The poetry which found its expression in the poems of writers like Browning and Tennyson, and even of writers who are seldom classed with them, like Swinburne, and like Shelley in his earlier years, pushed its limits as far as possible, and tried to absorb into itself the science and politics, the philosophy and morality of its time; but a new poetry, which is always contracting its limits, has grown up under the shadow of the old. Rossetti began it, but was too much of a painter in his poetry to follow it with a perfect devotion; and it became a movement when Mr. Lang and Mr. Gosse and Mr. Dobson devoted themselves to the most condensed of lyric poems, and when Mr. Bridges, a more considerable poet, elaborated a rhythm too delicate for any but an almost bodiless emotion, and repeated over and over the most ancient notes of poetry, and none but these. The poets who

followed have either, like Mr. Kipling, turned from serious
poetry altogether, and so passed out of the processional
order, or speak out of some personal or spiritual passion in
words and types and metaphors that draw one's imagination
as far as possible from the complexities of modern life and
thought. The change has been more marked in English
painting, which, when intense enough to belong to the processional order, began to cast out things, as they are seen by
minds plunged in the labour of life, so much before French
painting that ideal art is sometimes called English art upon the
Continent.

I see, indeed, in the arts of every country those faint lights
and faint colours and faint outlines and faint energies which
many call 'the decadence', and which I, because I believe
that the arts lie dreaming of things to come, prefer to call the
autumn of the body. An Irish poet whose rhythms are like
the cry of a sea-bird in autumn twilight has told its meaning in
the line, 'The very sunlight's weary, and it's time to quit the
plough'. Its importance is the greater because it comes to us at
the moment when we are beginning to be interested in many
things which positive science, the interpreter of exterior law,
has always denied: communion of mind with mind in
thought and without words, foreknowledge in dreams and in
visions, and the coming among us of the dead, and of much
else. We are, it may be, at a crowning crisis of the world, at
the moment when man is about to ascend, with the wealth he
has been so long gathering upon his shoulders, the stairway he
has been descending from the first days. The first poets, if
one may find their images in the *Kalevala*, had not Homer's
preoccupation with things, and he was not so full of their
excitement as Virgil. Dante added to poetry a dialectic
which, although he made it serve his laborious ecstasy, was
the invention of minds strained by the labour of life, by a

traffic among many things, and not a spontaneous expression of an interior life; while Shakespeare shattered the symmetry of verse and of drama that he might fill them with things and their accidental relations to one another.

Each of these writers had come further down the stairway than those who had lived before him, but it was only with the modern poets, with Goethe and Wordsworth and Browning, that poetry gave up the right to consider all things in the world as a dictionary of types and symbols and began to call itself a critic of life and an interpreter of things as they are. Painting, music, science, politics, and even religion, because they have felt a growing belief that we know nothing but the fading and flowering of the world, have changed in numberless elaborate ways. Man has wooed and won the world, and has fallen weary, and not, I think, for a time, but with a weariness that will not end until the last autumn, when the stars shall be blown away like withered leaves. He grew weary when he said, 'These things that I touch and see and hear are alone real', for he saw them without illusion at last, and found them but air and dust and moisture. And now he must be philosophical above everything, even about the arts, for he can only return the way he came, and so escape from weariness, by philosophy. The arts are, I believe, about to take upon their shoulders the burdens that have fallen from the shoulders of priests, and to lead us back upon our journey by filling our thoughts with the essences of things, and not with things. We are about to substitute once more the distillation of alchemy for the analyses of chemistry and for some other sciences; and certain of us are looking everywhere for the perfect alembic that no silver or golden drop may escape. Mr. Symons has written lately on Mallarmé's method, and has quoted him as saying that we should 'abolish the pretension, aesthetically an error, despite its dominion over almost all the masterpieces, to enclose within the subtle paper other than — for example — the horror of the forest or the silent thunder in the leaves, not the intense dense wood of the trees', and as desiring to substitute for 'the old lyric afflatus or the enthusiastic personal direction of the phrase' words 'that take light from mutual reflection, like an actual trail of fire over precious stones', and 'to make an entire word hitherto unknown to the language' 'out of many vocables'. Mr. Symons understands these and other sentences to mean that poetry will henceforth be a poetry of essences, separated one from another in little and intense poems. I think there will be much poetry of this kind, because of an ever more arduous search for an almost disembodied ecstasy, but I think we will not cease to write long poems, but rather that we will write them more and more as our new belief makes the world plastic under our hands again. I think that we will learn again how to describe at great length an old man wandering among enchanted islands, his return home at last, his slow-gathering vengeance, a flitting shape of a goddess, and a flight of arrows, and yet to make all of these so different things 'take light from mutual reflection, like an actual trail of fire over precious stones', and become 'an entire word', the signature or symbol of a mood of the divine imagination as imponderable as 'the horror of the forest or the silent thunder in the leaves'.

1898

THE SYMBOLISM OF POETRY

SYMBOLISM, as seen in the writers of our day, would have no value if it were not seen also, under one 'disguise or another, in every great imaginative writer', writes Mr. Arthur Symons in *The Symbolist Movement in Literature*, a subtle book which I cannot praise as I would, because it has been dedicated to me; and he goes on to show how many profound writers have in the last few years sought for a philosophy of poetry in the doctrine of symbolism, and how even in countries where it is almost scandalous to seek for any philosophy of poetry, new writers are following them in their search. We do not know what the writers of ancient times talked of among themselves, and one bull is all that remains of Shakespeare's talk, who was on the edge of modern times; and the journalist is convinced, it seems, that they talked of wine and women and politics, but never about their art, or never quite seriously about their art. He is certain that no one who had a philosophy of his art, or a theory of how he should write, has ever made a work of art, that people have no imagination who do not write without forethought and afterthought as he writes his own articles. He says this with enthusiasm, because he has heard it at so many comfortable dinner-tables, where someone had mentioned through carelessness, or foolish zeal, a book whose difficulty had offended indolence, or a man who had not forgotten that beauty is an accusation. Those formulas and generalisations, in which a hidden sergeant has drilled the ideas of journalists and through them the ideas of all but all the modern world, have created in their turn a forgetfulness like that of soldiers in battle, so that journalists and their readers have forgotten, among many like events, that Wagner spent seven years arranging and explaining his ideas before he began his most characteristic music; that opera, and with it modern music, arose from certain talks at the house of one Giovanni Bardi of Florence; and that the Pléiade laid the foundations of modern French literature with a pamphlet. Goethe has said, 'a poet needs all philosophy, but he must keep it out of his work', though that is not always necessary; and almost certainly no great art, outside England, where journalists are more powerful and ideas less plentiful than elsewhere, has arisen without a great criticism, for its herald or its interpreter and protector, and it may be for this reason that great art, now that vulgarity has armed itself and multiplied itself, is perhaps dead in England.

All writers, all artists of any kind, in so far as they have had any philosophical or critical power, perhaps just in so far as they have been delicate artists at all, have had some philosophy, some criticism of their art; and it has often been this philosophy, or this criticism, that has evoked their most startling inspiration, calling into outer life some portion of the divine life, or of the buried reality, which could alone extinguish in the emotions what their philosophy or their criticism would extinguish in the intellect. They had sought for no new thing it may be, but only to understand and to copy the pure inspiration of early times, but because the divine life wars upon our outer life, and must needs change its weapons and its movements as we change ours, inspiration has come to them in beautiful startling shapes. The scientific movement brought with it a literature which was always tending to lose itself in externalities of all kinds, in opinion, in declamation, in picturesque writing, in word-painting, or in what Mr. Symons has called an attempt 'to build in brick and mortar inside the covers of a book'; and now writers have begun to dwell upon the element of evocation, of suggestion, upon what we call the symbolism in great writers.

II

In 'Symbolism in Painting', I tried to describe the element of symbolism that is in pictures and sculpture, and described a little the symbolism in poetry, but did not describe at all the continuous indefinable symbolism which is the substance of all style.

There are no lines with more melancholy beauty than these by Burns:

> The white moon is setting behind the white wave,[1]
> And Time is setting with me, O!

and these lines are perfectly symbolical. Take from them the whiteness of the moon and of the wave, whose relation to the setting of Time is too subtle for the intellect, and you take from them their beauty. But, when all are together, moon and wave and whiteness and setting Time and the last melancholy cry, they evoke an emotion which cannot be evoked by any other arrangement of colours and sounds and forms. We may call this metaphorical writing, but it is better to call it symbolical writing, because metaphors are not profound enough to be moving, when they are not symbols, and when they are symbols they are the most perfect of all, because the most subtle, outside of pure sound, and through them one can best find out what symbols are. If one begins the reverie with any beautiful lines that one can remember, one finds they are like those by Burns. Begin with this line by Blake:

[1] [Burns actually wrote:

'The wan moon is setting ayont the white wave,'

but Yeats's version has been retained for the sake of his comments.]

The gay fishes on the wave when the moon sucks up the dew;

or these lines by Nash:

> Brightness falls from the air,
> Queens have died young and fair,
> Dust hath closed Helen's eye;

or these lines by Shakespeare:

> Timon hath made his everlasting mansion
> Upon the beached verge of the salt flood;
> Who once a day with his embossed froth
> The turbulent surge shall cover;

or take some line that is quite simple, that gets its beauty from its place in a story, and see how it flickers with the light of the many symbols that have given the story its beauty, as a sword-blade may flicker with the light of burning towers.

All sounds, all colours, all forms, either because of their preordained energies or because of long association, evoke indefinable and yet precise emotions, or, as I prefer to think, call down among us certain disembodied powers, whose footsteps over our hearts we call emotions; and when sound, and colour, and form are in a musical relation, a beautiful relation to one another, they become, as it were, one sound, one colour, one form, and evoke an emotion that is made out of their distinct evocations and yet is one emotion. The same relation exists between all portions of every work of art, whether it be an epic or a song, and the more perfect it is, and the more various and numerous the elements that have flowed into its perfection, the more powerful will be the emotion, the power, the god it calls among us. Because an emotion does not exist, or does not become perceptible and active among us, till it has found its expression, in colour or in sound or in form, or in all of these, and because no two modulations or arrangements of these evoke the same emotion, poets and painters and musicians, and in a less degree because their effects are momentary, day and night and cloud and shadow, are continually making and unmaking mankind. It is indeed only those things which seem useless or very feeble that have any power, and all those things that seem useful or strong, armies, moving wheels, modes of architecture, modes of government, speculations of the reason, would have been a little different if some mind long ago had not given itself to some emotion, as a woman gives herself to her lover, and shaped sounds or colours or forms, or all of these, into a musical relation, that their emotion might live in other minds. A little lyric evokes an emotion, and this emotion gathers others about it and melts into their being in the making of some great epic; and at last, needing an always less delicate body, or symbol, as it grows more powerful, it flows out, with all it has gathered, among the blind instincts of daily life, where it moves a power within powers, as one sees ring within ring in the stem of an old tree. This is maybe what Arthur O'Shaughnessy meant when he made his poets say they had built Nineveh with their sighing; and I am certainly never sure, when I hear of some war, or of some religious excitement, or of some new manufacture, or of anything else that fills the ear of the world, that it has not all happened because of something that a boy piped in Thessaly. I remember once telling a seeress to ask one among the gods who, as she believed, were standing about her in their symbolic bodies, what would come of a charming but seeming trivial labour of a friend, and the form answering, 'the devastation of peoples and the overwhelming of cities'. I doubt indeed if the crude circumstance of the world, which seems to create all our emotions, does more than reflect, as in multiplying mirrors, the emotions that have come to solitary men

in moments of poetical contemplation; or that love itself
would be more than an animal hunger but for the poet and
his shadow the priest, for unless we believe that outer things
are the reality, we must believe that the gross is the shadow of
the subtle, that things are wise before they become foolish,
and secret before they cry out in the market-place. Solitary
men in moments of contemplation receive, as I think, the
creative impulse from the lowest of the Nine Hierarchies, and
so make and unmake mankind, and even the world itself, for
does not 'the eye altering alter all'?

> Our towns are copied fragments from our breast;
> And all man's Babylons strive but to impart
> The grandeurs of his Babylonian heart.

III

The purpose of rhythm, it has always seemed to me, is to
prolong the moment of contemplation, the moment when
we are both asleep and awake, which is the one moment of
creation, by hushing us with an alluring monotony, while it
holds us waking by variety, to keep us in that state of perhaps
real trance, in which the mind liberated from the pressure of
the will is unfolded in symbols. If certain sensitive persons
listen persistently to the ticking of a watch, or gaze persistently on the monotonous flashing of a light, they fall into
the hypnotic trance; and rhythm is but the ticking of a watch
made softer, that one must needs listen, and various, that one
may not be swept beyond memory or grow weary of listening; while the patterns of the artist are but the monotonous
flash woven to take the eyes in a subtler enchantment. I have
heard in meditation voices that were forgotten the moment
they had spoken; and I have been swept, when in more profound meditation, beyond all memory but of those things

that came from beyond the threshold of waking life. I was writing once at a very symbolical and abstract poem, when my pen fell on the ground; and as I stooped to pick it up, I remembered some fantastic adventure that yet did not seem fantastic, and then another like adventure, and when I asked myself when these things had happened, I found that I was remembering my dreams for many nights. I tried to remember what I had done the day before, and then what I had done that morning; but all my waking life had perished from me, and it was only after a struggle that I came to remember it again, and as I did so that more powerful and startling life perished in its turn. Had my pen not fallen on the ground and so made me turn from the images that I was weaving into verse, I would never have known that meditation had become trance, for I would have been like one who does not know that he is passing through a wood because his eyes are on the pathway. So I think that in the making and in the understanding of a work of art, and the more easily if it is full of patterns and symbols and music, we are lured to the threshold of sleep, and it may be far beyond it, without knowing that we have ever set our feet upon the steps of horn or of ivory.

IV

Besides emotional symbols, symbols that evoke emotions alone, — and in this sense all alluring or hateful things are symbols, although their relations with one another are too subtle to delight us fully, away from rhythm and pattern, — there are intellectual symbols, symbols that evoke ideas alone, or ideas mingled with emotions; and outside the very definite traditions of mysticism and the less definite criticism of certain modern poets, these alone are called symbols. Most things belong to one or another kind, according to the way we speak of them and the companions we give them, for symbols, associated with ideas that are more than fragments of the shadows thrown upon the intellect by the emotions they evoke, are the playthings of the allegorist or the pedant, and soon pass away. If I say 'white' or 'purple' in an ordinary line of poetry, they evoke emotions so exclusively that I cannot say why they move me; but if I bring them into the same sentence with such obvious intellectual symbols as a cross or a crown of thorns, I think of purity and sovereignty. Furthermore, innumerable meanings, which are held to 'white' or to 'purple' by bonds of subtle suggestion, and alike in the emotions and in the intellect, move visibly through my mind, and move invisibly beyond the threshold of sleep, casting lights and shadows of an indefinable wisdom on what had seemed before, it may be, but sterility and noisy violence. It is the intellect that decides where the reader shall ponder over the procession of the symbols, and if the symbols are merely emotional, he gazes from amid the accidents and destinies of the world; but if the symbols are intellectual too, he becomes himself a part of pure intellect, and he is himself mingled with the procession. If I watch a rushy pool in the moonlight, my emotion at its beauty is mixed with memories of the man that I have seen ploughing by its margin, or of the lovers I saw there a night ago; but if I look at the moon herself and remember any of her ancient names and meanings, I move among divine people, and things that have shaken off our mortality, the tower of ivory, the queen of waters, the shining stag among enchanted woods, the white hare sitting upon the hilltop, the fool of Faery with his shining cup full of dreams, and it may be 'make a friend of one of these images of wonder', and 'meet the Lord in the air'. So, too, if one is moved by Shakespeare, who is content with emotional symbols that he may come the nearer to our sympathy, one is mixed with the whole spectacle of the world; while if one is moved by Dante, or by the myth of Demeter, one is mixed into the shadow of God or of a goddess. So, too, one is furthest from symbols when one is busy doing this or that, but the soul moves among symbols and unfolds in symbols when trance, or madness, or deep meditation has withdrawn it from every impulse but its own. 'I then saw,' wrote Gérard de Nerval of his madness, 'vaguely drifting into form, plastic images of antiquity, which outlined themselves, became definite, and seemed to represent symbols of which I only seized the idea with difficulty.' In an earlier time he would have been of that multitude whose souls austerity withdrew, even more perfectly than madness could withdraw his soul, from hope and memory, from desire and regret, that they might reveal those processions of symbols that men bow to before altars, and woo with incense and offerings. But being of our time, he has been like Maeterlinck, like Villiers de l'Isle-Adam in *Axël*, like all who are preoccupied with intellectual symbols in our time, a foreshadower of the new sacred book, of which all the arts, as somebody has said, are beginning to dream. How can the arts overcome the slow dying of men's hearts that we call the progress of the world, and lay their hands upon men's heartstrings again, without becoming the garment of religion as in old times?

V

If people were to accept the theory that poetry moves us because of its symbolism, what change should one look for in the manner of our poetry? A return to the way of our fathers, a casting out of descriptions of nature for the sake of nature, of the moral law for the sake of the moral law, a casting out of all anecdotes and of that brooding over scientific opinion that so often extinguished the central flame in Tennyson, and of that vehemence that would make us do or not do certain things; or, in other words, we should come to understand that the beryl stone was enchanted by our fathers that it might unfold the pictures in its heart, and not to mirror our own excited faces, or the boughs waving outside the window. With this change of substance, this return to imagination, this understanding that the laws of art, which are the hidden laws of the world, can alone bind the imagination, would come a change of style, and we would cast out of serious poetry those energetic rhythms, as of a man running, which are the invention of the will with its eyes always on something to be done or undone; and we would seek out those wavering, meditative, organic rhythms, which are the embodiment of the imagination, that neither desires nor hates, because it has done with time, and only wishes to gaze upon some reality, some beauty; nor would it be any longer possible for anybody to deny the importance of form, in all its kinds, for although you can expound an opinion, or describe a thing, when your words are not quite well chosen, you cannot give a body to something that moves beyond the senses, unless your words are as subtle, as complex, as full of mysterious life, as the body of a flower or of a woman. The form of sincere poetry, unlike the form of the 'popular poetry', may indeed be sometimes obscure, or ungrammatical as in some of the best of the *Songs of Innocence and Experience*, but it must have the perfections that escape analysis, the subtleties that have a new meaning every day, and it must have all this whether it be but a little song made out of a moment of dreamy indolence, or some great epic made out of the dreams of one poet and of a hundred generations whose hands were never weary of the sword.

1900

THE PHILOSOPHY OF SHELLEY'S POETRY

I. HIS RULING IDEAS

WHEN I was a boy in Dublin I was one of a group who rented a room in a mean street to discuss philosophy. My fellow-students got more and more interested in certain modern schools of mystical belief, and I never found anybody to share my one unshakable belief. I thought that whatever of philosophy has been made poetry is alone permanent, and that one should begin to arrange it in some regular order, rejecting nothing as the make-believe of the poets. I thought, so far as I can recollect my thoughts after so many years, that if a powerful and benevolent spirit has shaped the destiny of this world, we can better discover that destiny from the words that have gathered up the heart's desire of the world, than from historical records, or from speculation, wherein the heart withers. Since then I have observed dreams and visions very carefully, and am now certain that the imagination has some way of lighting on the truth that the reason has not, and that its commandments, delivered when the body is still and the reason silent, are the most binding we can ever know. I have re-read *Prometheus Unbound*, which I had hoped my fellow-students would have studied as a sacred book, and it seems to me to have an even more certain place than I had thought among the sacred books of the world. I remember going to a learned scholar to ask about its deep meanings, which I felt more than understood, and his telling me that it was Godwin's *Political Justice* put into rhyme, and that Shelley was a crude revolutionist, and believed that the overturning

of kings and priests would regenerate mankind. I quoted the
lines which tell how the halcyons ceased to prey on fish, and
how poisonous leaves became good for food, to show that he
foresaw more than any political regeneration, but was too
timid to push the argument. I still believe that one cannot help
believing him, as this scholar I know believes him, a vague
thinker, who mixed occasional great poetry with a fantastic
rhetoric, unless one compares such passages, and above all
such passages as describe the liberty he praised, till one has discovered the system of belief that lay behind them. It should
seem natural to find his thought full of subtlety, for Mrs.
Shelley has told how he hesitated whether he should be a
metaphysician or a poet, and has spoken of his 'huntings after
the obscure' with regret, and said of that *Prometheus Unbound*,
which so many for three generations have thought *Political
Justice* put into rhyme, 'It requires a mind as subtle and pene-
rating as his own to understand the mystic meanings scattered
throughout the poem. They elude the ordinary reader by
their abstraction and delicacy of distinction, but they are far
from vague. It was his design to write prose metaphysical
essays on the nature of Man, which would have served to
explain much of what is obscure in his poetry; a few scattered
fragments of observations and remarks alone remain. He
considered these philosophical views of Mind and Nature to
be instinct with the intensest spirit of poetry.' From these
scattered fragments and observations, and from many passages
read in their light, one soon comes to understand that his
liberty was so much more than the liberty of *Political Justice*
that it was one with Intellectual Beauty, and that the regeneration he foresaw was so much more than the regeneration
many political dreamers have foreseen, that it could not come
in its perfection till the Hours bore 'Time to his tomb in
eternity'. In *A Defence of Poetry*, he will have it that the poet

and the lawgiver hold their station by the right of the same
faculty, the one uttering in words and the other in the forms of
society his vision of the divine order, the Intellectual Beauty.
'Poets, according to the circumstances of the age and nation in
which they appeared, were called in the earliest epoch of the
world legislators or prophets, and a poet essentially com-
prises and unites both these characters. For he not only beholds intensely the present as it is, and discovers those laws
according to which present things are to be ordained, but he
beholds the future in the present, and his thoughts are the
germs of the flowers and the fruit of latest time.' 'Language,
colour, form, and religious and civil habits of action are all the
instruments and materials of poetry.' Poetry is 'the creation of
actions according to the unchangeable process of human
nature as existing in the mind of the creator, which is itself
the image of all other minds'. 'Poets have been challenged to
resign the civic crown to reasoners and merchants. . . . It is
admitted that the exercise of the imagination is the most
delightful, but it is alleged that that of reason is the more
useful. . . . Whilst the mechanist abridges and the political
economist combines labour, let them be sure that their speculations, for want of correspondence with those first principles
which belong to the imagination, do not tend, as they have in
modern England, to exasperate at once the extremes of
luxury and want. . . . The rich have become richer, the poor
have become poorer, . . . such are the effects which must ever
flow from an unmitigated exercise of the calculating faculty.'
The speaker of these things might almost be Blake, who held
that the Reason not only created Ugliness, but all other evils.
The books of all wisdom are hidden in the cave of the Witch
of Atlas, who is one of his personifications of beauty, and
when she moves over the enchanted river that is an image of
all life, the priests cast aside their deceits, and the king crowns

an ape to mock his own sovereignty, and the soldiers gather about the anvils to beat their swords to ploughshares, and lovers cast away their timidity, and friends are united; while the power which, in *Laon and Cythna*, awakens the mind of the reformer to contend, and itself contends, against the tyrannies of the world, is first seen as the star of love or beauty. And at the end of the *Ode to Naples*, he cries out to 'the spirit of beauty' to overturn the tyrannies of the world, or to fill them with its 'harmonising ardours'. He calls the spirit of beauty liberty, because despotism, and perhaps, as 'the man of virtuous soul commands not, nor obeys', all authority, pluck virtue from her path towards beauty, and because it leads us by that love whose service is perfect freedom. It leads all things by love, for he cries again and again that love is the perception of beauty in thought and things, and it orders all things by love, for it is love that impels the soul to its expressions in thought and in action, by making us 'seek to awaken in all things that are, a community with what we experience within ourselves'. 'We are born into the world, and there is something within us which, from the instant that we live, more and more thirsts after its likeness.' We have 'a soul within our soul that describes a circle around its proper paradise which pain and sorrow and evil dare not overleap', and we labour to see this soul in many mirrors, that we may possess it the more abundantly. He would hardly seek the progress of the world by any less gentle labour, and would hardly have us resist evil itself. He bids the reformers in the *Philosophical Review of Reform* receive 'the onset of the cavalry', if it be sent to disperse their meetings, 'with folded arms', and 'not because active resistance is not justifiable, but because temperance and courage would produce greater advantages than the most decisive victory'; and he gives them like advice in *The Masque of Anarchy*, for liberty, the poem cries, 'is love', and can make the rich man kiss its feet, and, like those who followed Christ, give away his goods and follow it throughout the world.

He does not believe that the reformation of society can bring this beauty, this divine order, among men without the regeneration of the hearts of men. Even in *Queen Mab*, which was written before he had found his deepest thought, or rather perhaps before he had found words to utter it, for I do not think men change much in their deepest thought, he is less anxious to change men's beliefs, as I think, than to cry out against that serpent more subtle than any beast of the field, 'the cause and the effect of tyranny'. He affirms again and again that the virtuous, those who have 'pure desire and universal love', are happy in the midst of tyranny, and he fore-sees a day when the 'Spirit of Nature', the Spirit of Beauty of his later poems, who has her 'throne of power unappeal-able' in every human heart, shall have made men so virtuous that 'kingly glare will lose its power to dazzle', and 'silently pass by', and, as it seems, commerce, 'the venal interchange of all that human art or nature yield; which wealth should purchase not', come as silently to an end.

He was always, indeed in chief, a witness for that 'power unappealable'. Maddalo, in *Julian and Maddalo*, says that the soul is powerless, and can only, like a 'dreary bell hung in a heaven-illumined tower, toll our thoughts and our desires to meet below round the rent heart and pray'; but Julian, who is Shelley himself, replies, as the makers of all religions have replied:

> Where is the love, beauty, and truth we seek
> But in our mind? And if we were not weak,
> Should we be less in deed than in desire?

while *Mont Blanc* is an intricate analogy to affirm that the soul has its sources in 'the secret strength of things which governs thought, and to the infinite dome of heaven is as a law'. He even thought that men might be immortal were they sinless, and his Cythna bids the sailors be without remorse, for all that live are stained as they are. It is thus, she says, that time marks men and their thoughts for the tomb. And the 'Red Comet', the image of evil in *Laon and Cythna*, when it began its war with the star of beauty, brought not only 'Fear, Hatred, Fraud and Tyranny', but 'Death, Decay, Earthquake, and Blight and Madness pale'.

When the Red Comet is conquered, when Jupiter is overthrown by Demogorgon, when the prophecy of Queen Mab is fulfilled, visible Nature will put on perfection again. Shelley declares, in one of the notes to *Queen Mab*, that 'there is no great extravagance in presuming . . . that there should be a perfect identity between the moral and physical improvement of the human species', and thinks it 'certain that wisdom is not compatible with disease, and that, in the present state of the climates of the earth, health, in the true and comprehensive sense of the word, is out of the reach of civilised man'. In *Prometheus Unbound* he sees, as in the ecstasy of a saint, the ships moving among the seas of the world without fear of danger —

>   by the light
> Of wave-reflected flowers, and floating odours,
> And music soft,

and poison dying out of the green things, and cruelty out of all living things, and even the toads and efts becoming beautiful, and at last Time being borne 'to his tomb in eternity'.

This beauty, this divine order, whereof all things shall become a part in a kind of resurrection of the body, is already visible to the dead and to souls in ecstasy, for ecstasy is a kind of death. The dying Lionel hears the song of the nightingale, and cries:

> Heardst thou not sweet words among
> That heaven-resounding minstrelsy?
> Heardst thou not, that those who die
> Awake in a world of ecstasy?
> That love, when limbs are interwoven,
> And sleep, when the night of life is cloven,
> And thought, to the world's dim boundaries clinging,
> And music, when one beloved is singing,
> Is death? Let us drain right joyously
> The cup which the sweet bird fills for me.

And in the most famous passage in all his poetry he sings of Death as of a mistress. 'Life, like a dome of many-coloured glass, stains the white radiance of Eternity.' 'Die, if thou wouldst be with that which thou dost seek'; and he sees his own soon-coming death in a rapture of prophecy, for 'the fire for which all thirst' beams upon him, 'consuming the last clouds of cold mortality'. When he is dead he will still influence the living, for though Adonais has fled 'to the burning fountain whence he came', and 'is a portion of the Eternal which must glow through time and change, unquenchably the same', and has 'awakened from the dream of life', he has not gone from the 'young Dawn', or the caverns and the forests, or the 'faint flowers and fountains'. He has been 'made one with Nature', and his voice is 'heard in all her music', and his presence is felt wherever 'that Power may move which has withdrawn his being to its own', and he bears 'his part' when it is compelling mortal things to their appointed forms, and he overshadows men's minds at their supreme moments, for —

> when lofty thought
> Lifts a young heart above its mortal lair,
> And love and life contend in it for what
> Shall be its earthly doom, the dead live there,
> And move like winds of light on dark and stormy air.

'Of his speculations as to what will befall this inestimable spirit when we appear to die,' Mrs. Shelley has written, 'a mystic ideality tinged these speculations in Shelley's mind; certain stanzas in the poem of *The Sensitive Plant* express, in some degree, the almost inexpressible idea, not that we die into another state, when this state is no longer, from some reason, unapparent as well as apparent, accordant with our being — but that those who rise above the ordinary nature of man, fade from before our imperfect organs; they remain in their "love, beauty, and delight", in a world congenial to them, and we, clogged by "error, ignorance, and strife", see them not till we are fitted by purification and improvement to their higher state.' Not merely happy souls, but all beautiful places and movements and gestures and events, when we think they have ceased to be, have become portions of the Eternal.

> In this life
> Of error, ignorance and strive,
> Where nothing is, but all things seem,
> And we the shadows of the dream,
>
> It is a modest creed, and yet
> Pleasant, if one considers it,
> To own that death itself must be,
> Like all the rest, a mockery.
>
> That garden sweet, that lady fair,
> And all sweet shapes and odours there,

> In truth have never past away;
> 'Tis we, 'tis ours, are changed, not they.

> For love, and beauty, and delight
> There is no death nor change; their might
> Exceeds our organs, which endure
> No light, being themselves obscure.

He seems in his speculations to have lit on that memory of Nature the visionaries claim for the foundation of their knowledge; but I do not know whether he thought, as they do, that all things good and evil remain for ever, 'thinking the thought and doing the deed', though not, it may be, self-conscious; or only thought that 'love and beauty and delight' remain for ever. The passage where Queen Mab awakes 'all knowledge of the past', and the good and evil 'events of old and wondrous times', was no more doubtless than a part of the machinery of the poem, but all the machineries of poetry are parts of the convictions of antiquity, and readily become again convictions in minds that brood over them with visionary intensity.

Intellectual Beauty has not only the happy dead to do her will, but ministering spirits who correspond to the Devas of the East, and the Elemental Spirits of mediaeval Europe, and the Sidhe of ancient Ireland, and whose too constant presence, and perhaps Shelley's ignorance of their more traditional forms, give some of his poetry an air of rootless fantasy. They change continually in his poetry, as they do in the visions of the mystics everywhere and of the common people in Ireland, and the forms of these changes display, in an especial sense, the flowing forms of his mind when freed from all impulse not out of itself or out of supersensual power. These are 'gleams of a remoter world which visit us in sleep', spiritual essences whose shadows are the delights of all the senses, sounds 'folded in cells of crystal silence', 'visions swift, and sweet, and quaint', which lie waiting their moment 'each in its thin sheath, like a chrysalis', 'odours' among 'ever-blooming Eden-trees', 'liquors' that can give 'happy sleep', or can make tears 'all wonder and delight'; 'the golden genii who spoke to the poets of Greece in dreams'; 'the phantoms' which become the forms of the arts when 'the mind, arising bright from the embrace of beauty', 'casts on them the gathered rays which are reality'; 'the guardians' who move in 'the atmosphere of human thought', as 'the birds within the wind, or the fish within the wave', or man's thought itself through all things; and who join the throng of the happy Hours when Time is passing away —

> As the flying-fish leap
> From the Indian deep,
> And mix with sea-birds half asleep.

It is these powers which lead Asia and Panthea, as they would lead all the affections of humanity, by words written upon leaves, by faint songs, by eddies of echoes that draw 'all spirits on that secret way', by the 'dying odours' of flowers and by 'the sunlight of the spherèd dew', beyond the gates of birth and death to awake Demogorgon, eternity, that 'the painted veil called life' may be 'torn aside'.

There are also ministers of ugliness and all evil, like those that came to Prometheus:

> As from the rose which the pale priestess kneels
> To gather for her festal crown of flowers
> The aërial crimson falls, flushing her cheek,
> So from our victim's destined agony
> The shade which is our form invests us round;
> Else we are shapeless as our mother Night.

Or like those whose shapes the poet sees in *The Triumph of Life*, coming from the procession that follows the car of life, as 'hope' changes to 'desire', shadows 'numerous as the dead leaves blow in autumn evening from a poplar-tree'; and resembling those they come from, until, if I understand an obscure phrase aright, they are 'wrapt' round 'all the busy phantoms that were there as the sun shapes the clouds'. Some to sit 'chattering like restless apes', and some like 'old anatomies' 'hatching their bare broods under the shade of demon wings', laughing 'to reassume the delegated power' they had given to the tyrants of the earth, and some 'like small gnats and flies' to throng 'about the brow of lawyers, statesmen, priest and theorist', and some 'like discoloured flakes of snow' to fall 'on fairest bosoms and the sunniest hair', to be 'melted by the youthful glow which they extinguished', and many to 'fling shadows of shadows, yet unlike themselves', shadows that are shaped into new forms by that 'creative ray' in which all move like motes.

These ministers of beauty and ugliness were certainly more than metaphors or picturesque phrases to one who believed the 'thoughts which are called real or external objects' differed but in regularity of recurrence from 'hallucinations, dreams, and the ideas of madness', and lessened this difference by telling how he had dreamed 'three several times, between intervals of two or more years, the same precise dream', and who had seen images with the mind's eye that left his nerves shaken for days together. Shadows that were —

> as when there hovers
> A flock of vampire-bats before the glare
> Of the tropic sun, bringing, ere evening,
> Strange night upon some Indian isle,

could not but have had more than a metaphorical and

picturesque being to one who had spoken in terror with an image of himself, and who had fainted at the apparition of a woman with eyes in her breasts, and who had tried to burn down a wood, if we can trust Mrs. Williams' account, because he believed a devil, who had first tried to kill him, had sought refuge there.

It seems to me, indeed, that Shelley had reawakened in himself the age of faith, though there were times when he would doubt, as even the saints have doubted, and that he was a revolutionist, because he had heard the commandment, 'If ye know these things, happy are ye if ye do them'. I have re-read his *Prometheus Unbound* for the first time for many years, in the woods of Drim-na-Rod, among the Echtge hills, and sometimes I have looked towards Slieve ná nOg where the country people say the last battle of the world shall be fought till the third day, when a priest shall lift a chalice, and the thousand years of peace begin. And I think this mysterious song utters a faith as simple and as ancient as the faith of those country people, in a form suited to a new age, that will understand with Blake that the Holy Spirit is 'an intellectual fountain', and that the kinds and degrees of beauty are the images of its authority.

II. HIS RULING SYMBOLS

At a comparatively early time Shelley made his imprisoned Cythna become wise in all human wisdom through the contemplation of her own mind, and write out this wisdom upon the sands in 'signs' that were 'clear elemental shapes, whose smallest change' made 'a subtler language within language', and were 'the key of truths which once were dimly taught in old Crotona'. His early romances and much throughout his poetry show how strong a fascination the traditions of magic and of the magical philosophy had cast over his mind, and one can hardly suppose that he had not brooded over their doctrine of symbols or signatures, though I do not find anything to show that he gave it any deep study. One finds in his poetry, besides innumerable images that have not the definiteness of symbols, many images that are certainly symbols, and as the years went by he began to use these with a more and more deliberately symbolic purpose. I imagine that when he wrote his earlier poems he allowed the subconscious life to lay its hands so firmly upon the rudder of his imagination that he was little conscious of the abstract meaning of the images that rose in what seemed the idleness of his mind. Anyone who has any experience of any mystical state of the soul knows how there float up in the mind profound symbols,[1] whose meaning, if indeed they do not delude one into the dream that they are meaningless, one does not perhaps understand for years. Nor I think has any one, who has known that experience with any constancy, failed to find some day, in some old book or on some old monument, a strange or intricate image that had floated up before him, and to grow perhaps dizzy with the sudden conviction that our little memories are but a part of some great Memory that renews the world and men's thoughts age after age, and that our thoughts are not, as we suppose, the deep, but a little foam upon the deep. Shelley understood this, as is proved by what he says of the eternity of beautiful things and of the influence of the dead, but whether he understood that the great Memory is also a dwelling-house of symbols, of images that are living souls, I cannot tell. He had certainly experience of all but the most profound of the mystical states, and had known that union with created things

---

[1] *Marianne's Dream* was certainly copied from a real dream of somebody's, but like images come to the mystic in his waking state.

which assuredly must precede the soul's union with the un-created spirit. He says, in his fragment of an essay 'On Life', mistaking a unique experience for the common experience of all: 'Let us recollect our sensations as children . . . we less habitually distinguished all that we saw and felt from our-selves. They seemed as it were to constitute one mass. There are some persons who in this respect are always children. Those who are subject to the state called reverie, feel as if their nature were resolved into the surrounding universe or as if the surrounding universe were resolved into their being', and he must have expected to receive thoughts and images from beyond his own mind, just in so far as that mind trans-cended its preoccupation with particular time and place, for he believed inspiration a kind of death; and he could hardly have helped perceiving that an image that has transcended par-ticular time and place becomes a symbol, passes beyond death, as it were, and becomes a living soul.

When Shelley went to the Continent with Godwin's daughter in 1814 they sailed down certain great rivers in an open boat, and when he summed up in his preface to *Laon and Cythna* the things that helped to make him a poet, he spoke of these voyages: 'I have sailed down mighty rivers, and seen the sun rise and set, and the stars come forth, whilst I have sailed night and day down a rapid stream among mountains.'

He may have seen some cave that was the bed of a rivulet by some river-side, or have followed some mountain stream to its source in a cave, for from his return to England rivers and streams and wells, flowing through caves or rising in them, came into every poem of his that was of any length, and always with the precision of symbols. Alastor passed in his boat along a river in a cave; and when for the last time he felt the presence of the spirit he loved and followed, it was when he watched his image in a silent well; and when he died

it was where a river fell into 'an abysmal chasm'; and the
Witch of Atlas in her gladness, as he in his sadness, passed in
her boat along a river in a cave, and it was where it bubbled
out of a cave that she was born; and when Rousseau, the
typical poet of *The Triumph of Life*, awoke to the vision that
was life, it was where a rivulet bubbled out of a cave; and the
poet of *Epipsychidion* met the evil beauty 'by a well, under
blue nightshade bowers'; and Cythna bore her child imprisoned in a great cave beside 'a fountain round and vast, in
which the wave, imprisoned, boiled and leaped perpetually';
and her lover Laon was brought to his prison in a high column
through a cave where there was 'a putrid pool', and when he
went to see the conquered city he dismounted beside a polluted fountain in the market-place, foreshadowing thereby
that spirit who at the end of *Prometheus Unbound* gazes at a re-
generated city from 'within a fountain in the public square';
and when Laon and Cythna are dead they awake beside a
fountain and drift into Paradise along a river; and at the end
of things Prometheus and Asia are to live amid a happy world
in a cave where a fountain 'leaps with an awakening sound';
and it was by a fountain, the meeting-place of certain unhappy lovers, that Rosalind and Helen told their unhappiness
to one another; and it was under a willow by a fountain that
the enchantress and her lover began their unhappy love;
while his lesser poems and his prose fragments use caves and
rivers and wells and fountains continually as metaphors. It
may be that his subconscious life seized upon some passing
scene, and moulded it into an ancient symbol without help
from anything but that great Memory; but so good a
Platonist as Shelley could hardly have thought of any cave as
a symbol, without thinking of Plato's cave that was the world;
and so good a scholar may well have had Porphyry on 'the
Cave of the Nymphs' in his mind. When I compare

Porphyry's description of the cave where the Phaeacian boat
left Odysseus, with Shelley's description of the cave of the
Witch of Atlas, to name but one of many, I find it hard to
think otherwise. I quote Taylor's translation, only putting
Mr. Lang's prose for Taylor's bad verse. 'What does Homer
obscurely signify by the cave in Ithaca which he describes in
the following verses? "Now at the harbour's head is a long-
leaved olive-tree, and hard by is a pleasant cave and shadowy,
sacred to the nymphs, that are called Naiads. And therein are
mixing-bowls and jars of stone, and there moreover do bees
hide. And there are great looms of stone, whereon the nymphs
weave raiment of purple stain, a marvel to behold; and there
are waters welling evermore. Two gates there are to the
cave, the one set towards the North wind, whereby men may
go down, but the portals towards the South pertain rather to
the gods, whereby men may not enter: it is the way of the
immortals."' He goes on to argue that the cave was a temple
before Homer wrote, and that 'the ancients did not establish
temples without fabulous symbols', and then begins to interpret Homer's description in all its detail. The ancients, he
says, 'consecrated a cave to the world' and held 'the flowing
waters' and the 'obscurity of the cavern' 'apt symbols of what
the world contains', and he calls to witness Zoroaster's cave
with fountains; and often caves are, he says, symbols of 'all
invisible power; because as caves are obscure and dark, so the
essence of all these powers is occult', and quotes a lost hymn to
Apollo to prove that nymphs living in caves fed men 'from
intellectual fountains'; and he contends that fountains and
rivers symbolise generation, and that the word nymph 'is
commonly applied to all souls descending into generation',
and that the two gates of Homer's cave are the gate of
generation and the gate of ascent through death to the gods,
the gate of cold and moisture, and the gate of heat and fire.

Cold, he says, causes life in the world, and heat causes life among the gods, and the constellation of the Cup is set in the heavens near the sign Cancer, because it is there that the souls descending from the Milky Way receive their draught of the intoxicating cold drink of generation 'The mixing-bowls and jars of stone' are consecrated to the Naiads, and are also, as it seems, symbolical of Bacchus, and are of stone because of the rocky beds of the rivers. And 'the looms of stone' are the symbols of the 'souls that descend into generation'. 'For the formation of the flesh is on or about the bones, which in the bodies of animals resemble stones,' and also because 'the body is a garment' not only about the soul, but about all essences that become visible, for 'the heavens are called by the ancients a veil, in consequence of being as it were the vestments of the celestial gods'. The bees hive in the mixing-bowls and jars of stone, for so Porphyry understands the passage, because honey was the symbol adopted by the ancients for 'pleasure arising from generation'. The ancients, he says, called souls not only Naiads but bees, 'as the efficient cause of sweetness'; but not all souls 'proceeding into generation' are called bees, 'but those who will live in it justly and who after having performed such things as are acceptable to the gods will again return (to their kindred stars). For this insect loves to return to the place from whence it came and is eminently just and sober.' I find all these details in the cave of the Witch of Atlas, the most elaborately described of Shelley's caves, except the two gates, and these have a far-off echo in her summer journeys on her cavern river and in her winter sleep in 'an inextinguishable well of crimson fire'. We have for the mixing-bowls, and jars of stone full of honey, those delights of the senses, 'sounds of air' 'folded in cells of crystal silence', 'liquors clear and sweet' 'in crystal vials', and for the bees, visions 'each in its thin sheath like a chrysalis', and for 'the looms of stone' and 'raiment of purple stain' the Witch's spinning and embroidering; and the Witch herself is a Naiad, and was born from one of the Atlantides, who lay in a 'chamber of grey rock' until she was changed by the sun's embrace into a cloud.

When one turns to Shelley for an explanation of the cave and fountain one finds how close his thought was to Porphyry's. He looked upon thought as a condition of life in generation and believed that the reality beyond was something other than thought. He wrote in his fragment *On Life*: 'That the basis of all things cannot be, as the popular philosophy alleges, mind, is sufficiently evident. Mind, as far as we have any experience of its properties, and beyond that experience how vain is argument, cannot create, it can only perceive'; and in another passage he defines mind as existence. Water is his great symbol of existence, and he continually meditates over its mysterious source. In his prose he tells how 'thought can with difficulty visit the intricate and winding chambers which it inhabits. It is like a river, whose rapid and perpetual stream flows outward. . . . The caverns of the mind are obscure and shadowy; or pervaded with a lustre, beautiful and bright indeed, but shining not beyond their portals.' When the Witch has passed in her boat from the caverned river, that is doubtless her own destiny, she passes along the Nile 'by Moeris and the Mareotid lakes', and sees all human life shadowed upon its waters in shadows that 'never are erased but tremble ever'; and in 'many a dark and subterranean street under the Nile' — new caverns — and along the bank of the Nile; and as she bends over the unhappy, she compares unhappiness to the strife that 'stirs the liquid surface of man's life'; and because she can see the reality of things she is described as journeying 'in the calm depths' of 'the wide lake' we journey over unpiloted.

Alastor calls the river that he follows an image of his mind, and thinks that it will be as hard to say where his thought will be when he is dead as where its waters will be in ocean or cloud in a little while. In *Mont Blanc*, a poem so overladen with descriptions in parentheses that one loses sight of its logic, Shelley compares the flowing through our mind of 'the universe of things', which are, he has explained elsewhere, but thoughts, to the flowing of the Arve through the ravine, and compares the unknown sources of our thoughts, in some 'remoter world' whose 'gleams' 'visit the soul in sleep', to Arve's sources among the glaciers on the mountain heights. Cythna, in the passage where she speaks of making signs 'a subtler language within language' on the sand by the 'fountain' of sea water in the cave where she is imprisoned, speaks of the 'cave' of her mind which gave its secrets to her, and of 'one mind, the type of all' which is a 'moveless wave' reflecting 'all moving things that are'; and then passing more completely under the power of the symbol, she speaks of growing wise through contemplation of the images that rise out of the fountain at the call of her will. Again and again one finds some passing allusion to the cave of man's mind, or to the caves of his youth, or to the cave of mysteries we enter at death, for to Shelley as to Porphyry it is more than an image of life in the world. It may mean any enclosed life, as when it is the dwelling-place of Asia and Prometheus, or when it is 'the still cave of poetry', and it may have all meanings at once, or it may have as little meaning as some ancient religious symbol enwoven from the habit of centuries with the patterns of a carpet or a tapestry.

As Shelley sailed along those great rivers and saw or imagined the cave that associated itself with rivers in his mind, he saw half-ruined towers upon the hilltops, and once at any rate a tower is used to symbolise a meaning that is the

contrary to the meaning symbolised by caves. Cythna's lover
is brought through the cave where there is a polluted fountain to a high tower, for being man's far-seeing mind, when
the world has cast him out he must to the 'towers of thought's
crowned powers'; nor is it possible for Shelley to have forgotten this first imprisonment when he made men imprison
Lionel in a tower for a like offence; and because I know how
hard it is to forget a symbolical meaning, once one has found
it, I believe Shelley had more than a romantic scene in his
mind when he made Prince Athanase follow his mysterious
studies in a lighted tower above the sea, and when he made the
old hermit watch over Laon in his sickness in a half-ruined
tower, wherein the sea, here doubtless, as to Cythna, 'the one
mind', threw 'spangled sands' and 'rarest sea shells'. The
tower, important in Maeterlinck, as in Shelley, is, like the
sea, and rivers, and caves with fountains, a very ancient
symbol, and would perhaps, as years went by, have grown
more important in his poetry. The contrast between it and the
cave in *Laon and Cythna* suggests a contrast between the mind
looking outward upon men and things and the mind looking
inward upon itself, which may or may not have been in
Shelley's mind, but certainly helps, with one knows not how
many other dim meanings, to give the poem mystery and
shadow. It is only by ancient symbols, by symbols that have
numberless meanings besides the one or two the writer lays
an emphasis upon, or the half-score he knows of, that any
highly subjective art can escape from the barrenness and
shallowness of a too conscious arrangement, into the abundance and depth of Nature. The poet of essences and pure
ideas must seek in the half-lights that glimmer from symbol
to symbol as if to the ends of the earth, all that the epic and
dramatic poet finds of mystery and shadow in the accidental
circumstances of life.

The most important, the most precise of all Shelley's symbols, the one he uses with the fullest knowledge of its meaning, is the Morning and Evening Star. It rises and sets for ever over the towers and rivers, and is the throne of his genius. Personified as a woman it leads Rousseau, the typical poet of *The Triumph of Life*, under the power of the destroying hunger of life, under the power of the sun that we shall find presently as a symbol of life, and it is the Morning Star that wars against the principle of evil in *Laon and Cythna*, at first as a star with a red comet, here a symbol of all evil as it is of disorder in *Epipsychidion*, and then as a serpent with an eagle — symbols in Blake too and in the Alchemists; and it is the Morning Star that appears as a winged youth to a woman, who typifies humanity amid its sorrows, in the first canto of *Laon and Cythna*; and it is invoked by the wailing women of *Hellas*, who call it 'lamp of the free' and 'beacon of love' and would go where it hides flying from the deepening night among those 'kingless continents sinless as Eden', and 'mountains and islands' 'prankt on the sapphire sea' that are but the opposing hemispheres to the senses, but, as I think, the ideal world, the world of the dead, to the imagination; and in the *Ode to Liberty*, Liberty is bid lead wisdom out of the inmost cave of man's mind as the Morning Star leads the sun out of the waves. We know too that had *Prince Athanase* been finished it would have described the finding of Pandemos, the Star's lower genius, and the growing weary of her, and the coming of its true genius Urania at the coming of death, as the day finds the Star at evening. There is hardly indeed a poem of any length in which one does not find it as a symbol of love, or liberty, or wisdom, or beauty, or of some other expression of that Intellectual Beauty which was to Shelley's mind the central power of the world; and to its faint and fleeting light he offers up all desires, that are as —

> The desire of the moth for the star,
>   Of the night for the morrow,
> The devotion to something afar
>   From the sphere of our sorrow.

When its genius comes to Rousseau, shedding dew with one hand, and treading out the stars with her feet, for she is also the genius of the dawn, she brings him a cup full of oblivion and love. He drinks and his mind becomes like sand 'on desert Labrador' marked by the feet of deer and a wolf. And then the new vision, life, the cold light of day moves before him, and the first vision becomes an invisible presence. The same image was in his mind too when he wrote:

> Hesperus flies from awakening night
> And pants in its beauty and speed with light,
> Fast fleeting, soft and bright.

Though I do not think that Shelley needed to go to Porphyry's account of the cold intoxicating cup, given to the souls in the constellation of the Cup near the constellation Cancer, for so obvious a symbol as the cup, or that he could not have found the wolf and the deer and the continual flight of his Star in his own mind, his poetry becomes the richer, the more emotional, and loses something of its appearance of idle fantasy when I remember that these are ancient symbols, and still come to visionaries in their dreams. Because the wolf is but a more violent symbol of longing and desire than the hound, his wolf and deer remind me of the hound and deer that Oisin saw in the Gaelic poem chasing one another on the water before he saw the young man following the woman with the golden apple; and of a Galway tale that tells how Niamh, whose name means brightness or beauty, came to Oisin as a deer; and of a vision that a friend of mine saw when gazing at a dark-blue curtain. I was with a number of Hermetists, and one of them said to another, 'Do you see something in the curtain?' The other gazed at the curtain for a while and saw presently a man led through a wood by a black hound, and then the hound lay dead at a place the seer knew was called, without knowing why, 'the Meeting of the Suns', and the man followed a red hound, and then the red hound was pierced by a spear. A white fawn watched the man out of the wood, but he did not look at it, for a white hound came and he followed it trembling, but the seer knew that he would follow the fawn at last, and that it would lead him among the gods. The most learned of the Hermetists said, 'I cannot tell the meaning of the hounds or where the Meeting of the Suns is, but I think the fawn is the Morning and Evening Star'. I have little doubt that when the man saw the white fawn he was coming out of the darkness and passion of the world into some day of partial regeneration, and that it was the Morning Star and would be the Evening Star at its second coming. I have little doubt that it was but the story of Prince Athanase and what may have been the story of Rousseau in *The Triumph of Life*, thrown outward once again from that great Memory, which is still the mother of the Muses, though men no longer believe in it.

It may have been this memory, or it may have been some impulse of his nature too subtle for his mind to follow, that made Keats, with his love of embodied things, of precision of form and colouring, of emotions made sleepy by the flesh, see Intellectual Beauty in the Moon; and Blake, who lived in that energy he called eternal delight, see it in the Sun, where his personification of poetic genius labours at a furnace. I think there was certainly some reason why these men took so deep a pleasure in lights that Shelley thought of with weariness and trouble. The Moon is the most changeable of symbols, and not merely because it is the symbol of change. As mistress of the waters she governs the life of instinct and the generation of things, for, as Porphyry says, even 'the apparition of images' in the 'imagination' is through 'an excess of moisture'; and, as a cold and changeable fire set in the bare heavens, she governs alike chastity and the joyless idle drifting hither and thither of generated things. She may give God a body and have Gabriel to bear her messages, or she may come to men in their happy moments as she came to Endymion, or she may deny life and shoot her arrows; but because she only becomes beautiful in giving herself, and is no flying ideal, she is not loved by the children of desire.

Shelley could not help but see her with unfriendly eyes. He is believed to have described Mary Shelley at a time when she had come to seem cold in his eyes, in that passage of *Epipsychidion* which tells how a woman like the Moon led him to her cave and made 'frost' creep over the sea of his mind, and so bewitched Life and Death with 'her silver voice' that they ran from him crying, 'Away, he is not of our crew'. When he describes the Moon as part of some beautiful scene he can call her beautiful, but when he personifies, when his words come under the influence of that great Memory or of some mysterious tide in the depth of our being, he grows unfriendly or not truly friendly or at the most pitiful. The Moon's lips 'are pale and waning', it is 'the cold Moon', or 'the frozen and inconstant Moon', or it is 'forgotten' and 'waning', or it 'wanders' and is 'weary', or it is 'pale and grey', or it is 'pale for weariness', and 'wandering companionless' and 'ever changing', and finding 'no object worth' its 'constancy', or it is like a 'dying lady' who 'totters' 'out of her chamber led by the insane and feeble wanderings of her fading brain', and even when it is no more than a star, it casts an evil influence that makes the lips of lovers 'lurid' or pale. It only becomes a thing of delight when Time is being borne to his tomb in eternity, for then the spirit of the Earth, man's procreant mind, fills it with his own joyousness. He describes the spirit of the Earth and of the Moon, moving above the rivulet of their lives, in a passage which reads like a half-understood vision. Man has become 'one harmonious soul of many a soul' and 'all things flow to all' and 'familiar acts are beautiful through love', and an 'animation of delight' at this change flows from spirit to spirit till the snow 'is loosened' from the Moon's 'lifeless mountains'.

Some old magical writer, I forget who, says if you wish to be melancholy hold in your left hand an image of the Moon made out of silver, and if you wish to be happy hold in your right hand an image of the Sun made out of gold.[1] The Sun is the symbol of sensitive life, and of belief and joy and pride and energy, of indeed the whole life of the will, and of that beauty which neither lures from far off, nor becomes beautiful in giving itself, but makes all glad because it is beauty. Taylor quotes Proclus as calling it 'the Demiurgos of everything sensible'. It was therefore natural that Blake, who was always praising energy, and all exalted overflowing of oneself, and who thought art an impassioned labour to keep men from doubt and despondency, and woman's love an evil, when it would trammel man's will, should see the poetic genius not in a woman star but in the Sun, and should rejoice throughout his poetry in 'the Sun in his strength'. Shelley, however, except when he uses it to describe the peculiar beauty of Emilia Viviani, who was like 'an incarnation of the Sun when light is changed to love', saw it with less friendly eyes. He seems to have seen it with perfect happiness only when

[1] Wilde told me that he had read this somewhere. He had suggested it to Burne-Jones as a subject for a picture. 1924.

veiled in mist, or glimmering upon water, or when faint enough to do no more than veil the brightness of his own Star; and in *The Triumph of Life*, the one poem in which it is part of the avowed symbolism, its power is the being and the source of all tyrannies. When the woman personifying the Morning Star has faded from before his eyes, Rousseau sees a 'new vision' in 'a cold bright car' with a rainbow hovering over her, and as she comes the shadow passes from 'leaf and stone' and the souls she has enslaved seem 'in that light, like atomies to dance within a sunbeam', or they dance among the flowers that grow up newly in 'the grassy vesture of the desert', unmindful of the misery that is to come upon them. These are 'the great, the unforgotten', all who have worn 'mitres and helms and crowns, or wreaths of light', and yet have not known themselves. Even 'great Plato' is there, because he knew joy and sorrow, because life that could not subdue him by gold or pain, by 'age, or sloth, or slavery', subdued him by love. All who have ever lived are there except Christ and Socrates and the 'sacred few' who put away all life could give, being doubtless followers throughout their lives of the forms borne by the flying ideal, or who, 'as soon as they had touched the world with living flame, fled back like eagles to their native noon'.

In ancient times, it seems to me that Blake, who for all his protest was glad to be alive, and ever spoke of his gladness, would have worshipped in some chapel of the Sun, but that Shelley, who hated life because he sought 'more in life than any understood', would have wandered, lost in a ceaseless reverie, in some chapel of the Star of infinite desire.

I think too that as he knelt before an altar where a thin flame burnt in a lamp made of green agate, a single vision would have come to him again and again, a vision of a boat drifting down a broad river between high hills where there were caves and towers, and following the light of one Star; and that voices would have told him how there is for every man some one scene, some one adventure, some one picture that is the image of his secret life, for wisdom first speaks in images, and that this one image, if he would but brood over it his life long, would lead his soul, disentangled from unmeaning circumstance and the ebb and flow of the world, into that far household where the undying gods await all whose souls have become simple as flame, whose bodies have become quiet as an agate lamp.

But he was born in a day when the old wisdom had vanished and was content merely to write verses, and often with little thought of more than verses.

1900

MAGIC

I

I BELIEVE in the practice and philosophy of what we have agreed to call magic, in what I must call the evocation of spirits, though I do not know what they are, in the power of creating magical illusions, in the visions of truth in the depths of the mind when the eyes are closed; and I believe in three doctrines, which have, as I think, been handed down from early times, and been the foundations of nearly all magical practices. These doctrines are:

(1) That the borders of our mind are ever shifting, and that many minds can flow into one another, as it were, and create or reveal a single mind, a single energy.

(2) That the borders of our memories are as shifting, and that our memories are a part of one great memory, the memory of Nature herself.

(3) That this great mind and great memory can be evoked by symbols.

I often think I would put this belief in magic from me if I could, for I have come to see or to imagine, in men and women, in houses, in handicrafts, in nearly all sights and sounds, a certain evil, a certain ugliness, that comes from the slow perishing through the centuries of a quality of mind that made this belief and its evidences common over the world.

II

Some ten or twelve years ago, a man with whom I have since quarrelled for sound reasons, a very singular man who

had given his life to studies other men despised, asked me and
an acquaintance, who is now dead, to witness a magical work.
He lived a little way from London, and on the way my
acquaintance told me that he did not believe in magic, but
that a novel of Bulwer Lytton's had taken such a hold upon
his imagination that he was going to give much of his time
and all his thought to magic. He longed to believe in it, and
had studied, though not learnedly, geomancy, astrology,
chiromancy, and much cabbalistic symbolism, and yet doubted
if the soul outlived the body. He awaited the magical work
full of scepticism. He expected nothing more than an air of
romance, an illusion as of the stage, that might capture the
consenting imagination for an hour. The evoker of spirits and
his beautiful wife received us in a little house, on the edge of
some kind of garden or park belonging to an eccentric rich
man, whose curiosities he arranged and dusted, and he made
his evocation in a long room that had a raised place on the
floor at one end, a kind of dais, but was furnished meagrely
and cheaply. I sat with my acquaintance in the middle of the
room, and the evoker of spirits on the dais, and his wife
between us and him. He held a wooden mace in his hand, and
turning to a tablet of many-coloured squares, with a number
on each of the squares, that stood near him on a chair, he
repeated a form of words. Almost at once my imagination
began to move of itself and to bring before me vivid images
that, though never too vivid to be imagination, as I had
always understood it, had yet a motion of their own, a life I
could not change or shape. I remember seeing a number of
white figures, and wondering whether their mitred heads had
been suggested by the mitred head of the mace, and then, of a
sudden, the image of my acquaintance in the midst of them.
I told what I had seen, and the evoker of spirits cried in a deep
voice, 'Let him be blotted out,' and as he said it the image of

my acquaintance vanished, and the evoker of spirits or his
wife saw a man dressed in black with a curious square cap
standing among the white figures. It was my acquaintance,
the seeress said, as he had been in a past life, the life that had
moulded his present, and that life would now unfold before
us. I too seemed to see the man with a strange vividness. The
story unfolded itself chiefly before the mind's eye of the
seeress, but sometimes I saw what she described before I heard
her description. She thought the man in black was perhaps a
Fleming of the sixteenth century, and I could see him pass
along narrow streets till he came to a narrow door with some
rusty ironwork above it. He went in, and wishing to find out
how far we had one vision among us, I kept silent when I saw
a dead body lying upon the table within the door. The seeress
described him going down a long hall and up into what she
called a pulpit, and beginning to speak. She said, 'He is a
clergyman, I can hear his words. They sound like Low Dutch.'
Then after a little silence, 'No, I am wrong. I can see the
listeners; he is a doctor lecturing among his pupils.' I said,
'Do you see anything near the door?' and she said, 'Yes, I see
a subject for dissection.' Then we saw him go out again into
the narrow streets, I following the story of the seeress, sometimes merely following her words, but sometimes seeing for
myself. My acquaintance saw nothing; I think he was forbidden to see, it being his own life, and I think could not in
any case. His imagination had no will of its own. Presently the
man in black went into a house with two gables facing the
road, and up some stairs into a room where a hump-backed
woman gave him a key; and then along a corridor, and down
some stairs into a large cellar full of retorts and strange vessels
of all kinds. Here he seemed to stay a long while, and one saw
him eating bread that he took down from a shelf. The evoker
of spirits and the seeress began to speculate about the man's

character and habits, and decided, from a visionary impression, that his mind was absorbed in naturalism, but that his imagination had been excited by stories of the marvels wrought by magic in past times, and that he was trying to copy them by naturalistic means. Presently one of them saw him go to a vessel that stood over a slow fire, and take out of the vessel a thing wrapped up in numberless cloths, which he partly unwrapped, showing at length what looked like the image of a man made by somebody who could not model. The evoker of spirits said that the man in black was trying to make flesh by chemical means, and though he had not succeeded, his brooding had drawn so many evil spirits about him that the image was partly alive. He could see it moving a little where it lay upon a table. At that moment I heard something like little squeals, but kept silent, as when I saw the dead body. In a moment more the seeress said, 'I hear little squeals.' Then the evoker of spirits heard them, but said, 'They are not squeals; he is pouring a red liquid out of a retort through a slit in the cloth; the slit is over the mouth of the image and the liquid is gurgling in rather a curious way.' Weeks seemed to pass by hurriedly, and somebody saw the man still busy in his cellar. Then more weeks seemed to pass, and now we saw him lying sick in a room upstairs, and a man in a conical cap standing beside him. We could see the image too. It was in the cellar, but now it could move feebly about the floor. I saw fainter images of the image passing continually from where it crawled to the man in his bed, and I asked the evoker of spirits what they were. He said, 'They are the images of his terror'. Presently the man in the conical cap began to speak, but who heard him I cannot remember. He made the sick man get out of bed and walk, leaning upon him, and in much terror till they came to the cellar. There the man in the conical cap made some symbol over the image, which fell back as if asleep, and putting a knife into the other's hand he said, 'I have taken from it the magical life, but you must take from it the life you gave.' Somebody saw the sick man stoop and sever the head of the image from its body, and then fall as if he had given himself a mortal wound, for he had filled it with his own life. And then the vision changed and fluttered, and he was lying sick again in the room upstairs. He seemed to lie there a long time with the man in the conical cap watching beside him, then, I cannot remember how, the evoker of spirits discovered that though he would in part recover, he would never be well, and that the story had got abroad in the town and shattered his good name. His pupils had left him and men avoided him. He was accursed. He was a magician.

The story was finished, and I looked at my acquaintance. He was white and awestruck. He said, as nearly as I can remember, 'All my life I have seen myself in dreams making a man by some means like that. When I was a child I was always thinking out contrivances for galvanising a corpse into life.' Presently he said, 'Perhaps my bad health in this life comes from that experiment'. I asked if he had read *Frankenstein*, and he answered that he had. He was the only one of us who had, and he had taken no part in the vision.

III

Then I asked to have some past life of mine revealed, and a new evocation was made before the tablet full of little squares. I cannot remember so well who saw this or that detail, for now I was interested in little but the vision itself. I had come to a conclusion about the method. I knew that the vision may be in part common to several people.

A man in chain armour passed through a castle door, and the seeress noticed with surprise the bareness and rudeness of castle rooms. There was nothing of the magnificence or the

pageantry she had expected. The man came to a large hall
and to a little chapel opening out of it, where a ceremony was
taking place. There were six girls dressed in white, who took
from the altar some yellow object — I thought it was gold,
for though, like my acquaintance, I was told not to see, I
could not help seeing. Somebody else thought that it was
yellow flowers, and I think the girls, though I cannot remember clearly, laid it between the man's hands. He went out
for a time, and as he passed through the great hall one of us,
I forget who, noticed that he passed over two gravestones.
Then the vision became broken, but presently he stood in a
monk's habit among men-at-arms in the middle of a village
reading from a parchment. He was calling villagers about
him, and presently he and they and the men-at-arms took
ship for some long voyage. The vision became broken again,
and when we could see clearly they had come to what seemed
the Holy Land. They had begun some kind of sacred labour
among palm-trees. The common men among them stood
idle, but the gentlemen carried large stones, bringing them
from certain directions, from the cardinal points, I think, with
a ceremonious formality. The evoker of spirits said they must
be making some Masonic house. His mind, like the minds of
so many students of these hidden things, was always running
on Masonry and discovering it in strange places.

We broke the vision that we might have supper, breaking
it with some form of words which I forget. When supper had
ended the seeress cried out that while we had been eating
they had been building, and that they had built not a Masonic
house but a great stone cross. And now they had all gone
away but the man who had been in chain armour and two
monks we had not noticed before. He was standing against the
cross, his feet upon two stone rests a little above the ground,
and his arms spread out. He seemed to stand there all day,

but when night came he went to a little cell, that was beside two other cells. I think they were like the cells I have seen in the Aran Islands, but I cannot be certain. Many days seemed to pass, and all day every day he stood upon the cross, and we never saw anybody there but him and the two monks. Many years seemed to pass, making the vision flutter like a drift of leaves before our eyes, and he grew old and white-haired, and we saw the two monks, old and white-haired, holding him upon the cross. I asked the evoker of spirits why the man stood there, and before he had time to answer I saw two people, a man and a woman, rising like a dream within a dream before the eyes of the man upon the cross. The evoker of spirits saw them too, and said that one of them held up his arms and they were without hands. I thought of the two gravestones the man in chain mail had passed over in the great hall when he came out of the chapel, and asked the evoker of spirits if the knight was undergoing a penance for violence, and while I was asking him, and he was saying that it might be so but he did not know, the vision, having completed its circle, vanished.

It had not, so far as I could see, the personal significance of the other vision, but it was certainly strange and beautiful, though I alone seemed to see its beauty. Who was it that made the story, if it were but a story? I did not, and the seeress did not, and the evoker of spirits did not and could not. It arose in three minds, for I cannot remember my acquaintance taking any part, and it rose without confusion, and without labour, except the labour of keeping the mind's eye awake, and more swiftly than any pen could have written it out. It may be, as Blake said of one of his poems, that the author was in eternity. In coming years I was to see and hear of many such visions, and though I was not to be convinced, though half convinced once or twice, that they were old lives, in an ordinary sense of the word life, I was to learn that they have almost always some quite definite relation to dominant moods and moulding events in this life. They are, perhaps, in most cases, though the vision I have but just described was not, it seems, among the cases, symbolical histories of these moods and events, or rather symbolical shadows of the impulses that have made them, messages as it were out of the ancestral being of the questioner.

At the time these two visions meant little more to me, if I can remember my feeling at the time, than a proof of the supremacy of imagination, of the power of many minds to become one, overpowering one another by spoken words and by unspoken thought till they have become a single, intense, unhesitating energy. One mind was doubtless the master, I thought, but all the minds gave a little, creating or revealing for a moment what I must call a supernatural artist.

*   *   *

VI

I once saw a young Irishwoman, fresh from a convent school, cast into a profound trance, though not by a method known to any hypnotist. In her waking state she thought the apple of Eve was the kind of apple you can buy at the greengrocer's, but in her trance she saw the Tree of Life with eversighing souls moving in its branches instead of sap, and among its leaves all the fowls of the air, and on its highest bough one white fowl wearing a crown. When I went home I took from the shelf a translation of *The Book of Concealed Mystery*,[1] an old Jewish book, and cutting the pages came upon this

[1] Translated by Mathers in *The Kabbalah Unveiled*.

passage, which I cannot think I had ever read: 'The Tree, .
is the Tree of the Knowledge of Good and Evil ... in its
branches the birds lodge and build their nests, the souls and
the angels have their place.'

I once saw a young Church of Ireland man, a bank-clerk
in the West of Ireland, thrown in a like trance. I have no
doubt that he, too, was quite certain that the apple of Eve
was a greengrocer's apple, and yet he saw the tree and heard
the souls sighing through its branches, and saw apples with
human faces, and laying his ear to an apple heard a sound as of
fighting hosts within. Presently he strayed from the tree and
came to the edge of Eden, and there he found himself not by
the wilderness he had learned of at the Sunday-school, but
upon the summit of a great mountain, of a mountain 'two
miles high'. The whole summit, in contradiction to all that
would have seemed probable to his waking mind, was a great
walled garden. Some years afterwards I found a mediaeval
diagram, which pictured Eden as a walled garden upon a high
mountain.

Where did these intricate symbols come from? Neither I
nor the one or two people present nor the seers had ever seen,
I am convinced, the description in *The Book of Concealed
Mystery*, or the mediaeval diagram. Remember that the
images appeared in a moment perfect in all their complexity.
If one can imagine that the seers or that I myself or another
had indeed read of these images and forgotten it, that the
supernatural artist's knowledge of what was in our buried
memories accounted for these visions, there are numberless
other visions to account for. One cannot go on believing in
improbable knowledge for ever. For instance, I find in my
diary that on December 27, 1897, a seer, to whom I had given
a certain old Irish symbol, saw Brigid, the goddess, holding
out 'a glittering and wriggling serpent', and yet I feel certain

that neither I nor he knew anything of her association with the serpent until *Carmina Gaedelica* was published a few months ago. And an old Irishwoman who can neither read nor write has described to me a woman dressed like Dian, with helmet, and short skirt and sandals, and what seemed to be buskins. Why, too, among all the countless stories of visions that I have gathered in Ireland, or that a friend has gathered for me, are there none that mix the dress of different periods? The seers when they are but speaking from tradition will mix everything together, and speak of Finn mac Cumhal going to the Assizes at Cork. Almost every one who has ever busied himself with such matters has come, in trance or dream, upon some new and strange symbol or event, which he has afterwards found in some work he had never read or heard of. Examples like this are as yet too little classified, too little analysed, to convince the stranger, but some of them are proof enough for those they have happened to, proof that there is a memory of Nature that reveals events and symbols of distant centuries. Mystics of many countries and many centuries have spoken of this memory; and the honest men and charlatans, who keep the magical traditions which will some day be studied as a part of folk-lore, base most that is of importance in their claims upon this memory. I have read of it in *Paracelsus* and in some Indian book that describes the people of past days as still living within it, 'thinking the thought and doing the deed'. And I have found it in the 'Prophetic Books' of William Blake, who calls its images 'the bright sculptures of Los's Hall'; and says that all events, 'all love stories', renew themselves from those images. It is perhaps well that so few believe in it, for if many did many would go out of parliaments and universities and libraries and run into the wilderness to so waste the body, and to so hush the unquiet mind that, still living, they might pass the doors the dead pass daily; for who among the wise would trouble himself with making laws or in writing history or in weighing the earth if the things of eternity seemed ready to hand?

VII

I find in my diary of magical events for 1899 that I awoke at 3 a.m. out of a nightmare, and imagined one symbol to prevent its recurrence, and imagined another, a simple geometrical form, which calls up dreams of luxuriant vegetable life, that I might have pleasant dreams. I imagined it faintly, being very sleepy, and went to sleep. I had confused dreams which seemed to have no relation with the symbol. I awoke about eight, having for the time forgotten both nightmare and symbol. Presently I dozed off again and began half to dream and half to see, as one does between sleep and waking, enormous flowers and grapes. I awoke and recognised that what I had dreamed or seen was the kind of thing appropriate to the symbol before I remembered having used it. I find another record, though made some time after the event, of having imagined over the head of a person, who was a little of a seer, a combined symbol of elemental air and elemental water. This person, who did not know what symbol I was using, saw a pigeon flying with a lobster in his bill. I find that on December 13, 1898, I used a certain star-shaped symbol with a seeress, getting her to look at it intently before she began seeing. She saw a rough stone house, and in the middle of the house the skull of a horse. I find that I had used the same symbol a few days before with a seer, and that he had seen a rough stone house, and in the middle of the house something under a cloth marked with the Hammer of Thor. He had lifted the cloth and discovered a skeleton of gold with teeth of diamonds, and eyes of some unknown dim precious stones. I had made a note to this last vision, pointing out that

we had been using a Solar symbol a little earlier. Solar
symbols often call up visions of gold and precious stones.
I do not give these examples to prove my arguments, but to
illustrate them. I know that my examples will awaken in all
who have not met the like, or who are not on other grounds
inclined towards my arguments, a most natural incredulity.
It was long before I myself would admit an inherent power in
symbols, for it long seemed to me that one could account for
everything by the power of one imagination over another, or
by telepathy, as the Society for Psychical Research would say.
The symbol seemed powerful, I thought, merely because we
thought it powerful, and we would do just as well without it.
In those days I used symbols made with some ingenuity instead
of merely imagining them. I used to give them to the person
I was experimenting with, and tell him to hold them to his
forehead without looking at them; and sometimes I made a
mistake. I learned from these mistakes that if I did not myself
imagine the symbol, in which case he would have a mixed
vision, it was the symbol I gave by mistake that[1] produced the
vision. Then I met with a seer who could say to me, 'I have
a vision of a square pond, but I can see your thought, and you
expect me to see an oblong pond', or, 'The symbol you are
imagining has made me see a woman holding a crystal, but
it was a moonlight sea I should have seen'. I discovered that
the symbol hardly ever failed to call up its typical scene, its
typical event, its typical person, but that I could practically
never call up, no matter how vividly I imagined it, the particular scene, the particular event, the particular person I had

[1] I forgot that my 'subconsciousness' would know clairvoyantly what
symbol I had really given and would respond to the associations of that
symbol. I am, however, certain that the main symbols (symbolic roots,
as it were) draw upon associations which are beyond the reach of the
individual 'subconsciousness'.   1924

in my own mind, and that when I could, the two visions rose side by side.

I cannot now think symbols less than the greatest of all powers whether they are used consciously by the masters of magic, or half unconsciously by their successors, the poet, the musician and the artist. At first I tried to distinguish between symbols and symbols, between what I called inherent symbols and arbitrary symbols, but the distinction has come to mean little or nothing. Whether their power has arisen out of themselves, or whether it has an arbitrary origin, matters little, for they act, as I believe, because the Great Memory associates them with certain events and moods and persons. Whatever the passions of man have gathered about, becomes a symbol in the Great Memory, and in the hands of him who has the secret it is a worker of wonders, a caller-up of angels or of devils. The symbols are of all kinds, for everything in heaven or earth has its association, momentous or trivial, in the Great Memory, and one never knows what forgotten events may have plunged it, like the toadstool and the ragweed, into the great passions. Knowledgeable men and women in Ireland sometimes distinguish between the simples that work cures by some medical property in the herb, and those that do their work by magic. Such magical simples as the husk of the flax, water out of the fork of an elm-tree, do their work, as I think, by awaking in the depths of the mind where it mingles with the Great Mind, and is enlarged by the Great Memory, some curative energy, some hypnotic command. They are not what we call faith cures, for they have been much used and successfully, the traditions of all lands affirm, over children and over animals, and to me they seem the only medicine that could have been committed safely to ancient hands. To pluck the wrong leaf would have been to go uncured, but, if one had eaten it, one might have been poisoned.

VIII

I have now described that belief in magic which has set me all but unwilling among those lean and fierce minds who are at war with their time, who cannot accept the days as they pass, simply and gladly; and I look at what I have written with some alarm, for I have told more of the ancient secret than many among my fellow-students think it right to tell. I have come to believe so many strange things because of experience, that I see little reason to doubt the truth of many things that are beyond my experience; and it may be that there are beings who watch over that ancient secret, as all tradition affirms, and resent, and perhaps avenge, too fluent speech. They say in the Aran Islands that if you speak over-much of the things of Faery your tongue becomes like a stone, and it seems to me, though doubtless naturalistic reason would call it auto-suggestion or the like, that I have often felt my tongue become just so heavy and clumsy. More than once, too, as I wrote this very essay I have become uneasy, and have torn up some paragraph, not for any literary reason, but because some incident or some symbol that would perhaps have meant nothing to the reader, seemed, I know not why, to belong to hidden things. Yet I must write or be of no account to any cause, good or evil; I must commit what merchandise of wisdom I have to this ship of written speech, and after all, I have many a time watched it put out to sea with not less alarm when all the speech was rhyme. We who write, we who bear witness, must often hear our hearts cry out against us, complaining because of their hidden things, and I know not but he who speaks of wisdom may some-times, in the change that is coming upon the world, have to fear the anger of the people of Faery, whose country is the heart of the world — 'The Land of the Living Heart'. Who can keep always to the little pathway between speech and silence, where one meets none but discreet revelations? And surely, at whatever risk, we must cry out that imagination is always seeking to remake the world according to the impulses and the patterns in that Great Mind, and that Great Memory? Can there be anything so important as to cry out that what we call romance, poetry, intellectual beauty, is the only signal that the supreme Enchanter, or some one in His councils, is speaking of what has been, and shall be again, in the consummation of time?

1901

such severe or decorative forms of hills and trees and houses as would not overwhelm, as our naturalistic scenery does, the idealistic art of the poet, and all at a little price. Naturalistic scene-painting is not an art, but a trade, because it is, at best, an attempt to copy the more obvious effects of Nature by the methods of the ordinary landscape-painter, and by his methods made coarse and summary. It is but flashy landscape-painting and lowers the taste it appeals to, for the taste it appeals to has been formed by a more delicate art. Decorative scene-painting would be, on the other hand, as inseparable from the movements as from the robes of the players and from the falling of the light; and being in itself a grave and quiet thing it would mingle with the tones of the voices and with the sentiment of the play, without overwhelming them under an alien interest. It would be a new and legitimate art appealing to a taste formed by itself and copying but itself. Mr. Gordon Craig used scenery of this kind at the Purcell Society performance the other day, and despite some marring of his effects by the half-round shape of the theatre, it was the first beautiful scenery our stage has seen. He created an ideal country where everything was possible, even speaking in verse, or speaking to music, or the expression of the whole of life in a dance, and I would like to see Stratford-on-Avon decorate its Shakespeare with like scenery. As we cannot, it seems, go back to the platform and the curtain, and the argument for doing so is not without weight, we can only get rid of the sense of unreality, which most of us feel when we listen to the conventional speech of Shakespeare, by making scenery as conventional. Time after time his people use at some moment of deep emotion an elaborate or deliberate metaphor, or do some improbable thing which breaks an emotion of reality we have imposed upon him by an art that is not his, nor in the spirit of his. It also is an essential part of his method to give slight or obscure motives of many actions that our attention may dwell on what is of chief importance, and we set these cloudy actions among solid-looking houses, and what we hope are solid-looking trees, and illusion comes to an end, slain by our desire to increase it. In his art, as in all the older art of the world, there was much make-believe, and our scenery, too, should remember the time when, as my nurse used to tell me, herons built their nests in old men's beards! Mr. Benson did not venture to play the scene in *Richard III* where the ghosts walk as Shakespeare wrote it, but had his scenery been as simple as Mr. Gordon Craig's purple back-cloth that made Dido and Aeneas seem wandering on the edge of eternity, he would have found nothing absurd in pitching the tents of Richard and Richmond side by side. Goethe has said, 'Art is art, because it is not nature!'

III

In *La Peau de chagrin* Balzac spends many pages in describing a coquette, who seems the image of heartlessness, and then invents an improbable incident that her chief victim may discover how beautifully she can sing. Nobody had ever heard her sing, and yet in her singing, and in her chatter with her maid, Balzac tells us, was her true self. He would have us understand that behind the momentary self, which acts and lives in the world, and is subject to the judgment of the world, there is that which cannot be called before any mortal judgment seat, even though a great poet, or novelist, or philosopher be sitting upon it. Great literature has always been written in a like spirit, and is, indeed, the Forgiveness of Sin, and when we find it becoming the Accusation of Sin, as in George Eliot, who plucks her Tito in pieces with as much assurance as if he had been clockwork, literature has begun to change into something else. George Eliot had a fierceness hardly to be found but in a woman turned argumentative, but the habit of mind her fierceness gave its life to was characteristic of her century, and is the habit of mind of the Shakespearian critics. They and she grew up in a century of utilitarianism, when nothing about a man seemed important except his utility to the State, and nothing so useful to the State as the actions whose effect can be weighed by reason. The deeds of Coriolanus, Hamlet, Timon, Richard III had no obvious use, were, indeed, no more than the expression of their personalities, and so it was thought Shakespeare was accusing them, and telling us to be careful lest we deserve the like accusations. It did not occur to the critics that you cannot know a man from his actions because you cannot watch him in every kind of circumstance, and that men are made useless to the State as often by abundance as by emptiness, and that a man's business may at times be revelation, and not reformation. Fortinbras was, it is likely enough, a better king than Hamlet would have been, Aufidius was a more reasonable man than Coriolanus, Henry V was a better man-at-arms than Richard II, but, after all, were not those others who changed nothing for the better and many things for the worse greater in the Divine Hierarchies? Blake has said that 'the roaring of lions, the howling of wolves, the raging of the stormy sea, and the destructive sword are portions of Eternity, too great for the eye of man', but Blake belonged by right to the ages of Faith, and thought the State of less moment than the Divine Hierarchies. Because reason can only discover completely the use of those obvious actions which everybody admires, and because every character was to be judged by efficiency in action, Shakespearian criticism became a vulgar worshipper of success. I have turned over many books in the library at Stratford-on-Avon, and I have found in nearly all an antithesis, which grew in clearness and violence as the century grew older, between two types, whose representatives were Richard II, 'sentimental', 'weak', 'selfish', 'insincere', and Henry V, 'Shakespeare's only hero'. These books took the same delight in abasing Richard II that schoolboys do in persecuting some boy of fine temperament, who has weak muscles and a distaste for school games. And they had the admiration for Henry V that schoolboys have for the sailor or soldier hero of a romance in some boys' paper. I cannot claim any minute knowledge of these books, but I think that these emotions began among the German critics, who perhaps saw something French and Latin in Richard II, and I know that Professor Dowden, whose book I once read carefully, first made these emotions eloquent and plausible. He lived in Ireland, where everything has failed, and he meditated frequently upon the perfection of character which had, he thought, made England successful, for, as we say, 'cows beyond the water have long horns'. He forgot that England, as Gordon has said, was made by her adventurers, by her people of wildness and imagination and eccentricity; and thought that Henry V, who only seemed to be these things because he had some commonplace vices, was not only the typical Anglo-Saxon, but the model Shakespeare held up before England; and he even thought it worth while pointing out that Shakespeare himself was making a large fortune while he was writing about Henry's victories. In Professor Dowden's successors this apotheosis went further; and it reached its height at a moment of imperialistic enthusiasm, of ever-deepening conviction that the commonplace shall inherit the earth, when somebody of reputation, whose name I cannot remember, wrote that Shakespeare admired this one character alone out of all his characters. The Accusation of Sin produced its necessary fruit, hatred of all that was abundant, extravagant, exuberant, of all that sets a sail for shipwreck, and flattery of the commonplace emotions and conventional ideals of the mob, the chief Paymaster of accusation.

IV

I cannot believe that Shakespeare looked on his Richard II with any but sympathetic eyes, understanding indeed how ill-fitted he was to be king, at a certain moment of history, but understanding that he was lovable and full of capricious fancy, 'a wild creature' as Pater has called him. The man on whom Shakespeare modelled him had been full of French elegances as he knew from Holinshed, and had given life a new luxury, a new splendour, and been 'too friendly' to his friends, 'too favourable' to his enemies. And certainly Shakespeare had these things in his head when he made his king fail, a little because he lacked some qualities that were doubtless common among his scullions, but more because he had certain qualities that are uncommon in all ages. To suppose that Shakespeare preferred the men who deposed his king is to suppose that Shakespeare judged men with the eyes of a Municipal Councillor weighing the merits of a Town Clerk; and that had he been by when Verlaine cried out from his bed, 'Sir, you have been made by the stroke of a pen, but I have been made by the breath of God', he would have thought the Hospital Superintendent the better man. He saw indeed, as I think, in Richard II the defeat that awaits all, whether they be artist or saint, who find themselves where men ask of them a rough energy and have nothing to give but some contemplative virtue, whether lyrical fantasy, or sweetness of temper, or dreamy dignity, or love of God, or love of His creatures. He saw that such a man through sheer bewilderment and impatience can become as unjust or as violent as any common man, any Bolingbroke or Prince John, and yet remain 'that sweet lovely rose'. The courtly and saintly ideals of the Middle Ages were fading, and the practical ideals of the modern age had begun to threaten the unuseful dome of the sky; Merry England was fading, and yet it was not so faded that the poets could not watch the procession of the world with that untroubled sympathy for men as they are, as apart from all they do and seem, which is the substance of tragic irony.

Shakespeare cared little for the State, the source of all our judgments, apart from its shows and splendours, its turmoils and battles, its flamings-out of the uncivilised heart. He did indeed think it wrong to overturn a king, and thereby to swamp peace in civil war, and the historical plays from *Henry IV* to *Richard III*, that monstrous birth and last sign of the wrath of Heaven, are a fulfilment of the prophecy of the Bishop of Carlisle, who was 'raised up by God' to make it; but he had no nice sense of utilities, no ready balance to measure deeds, like that fine instrument, with all the latest improvements, Gervinus and Professor Dowden handle so skilfully. He meditated as Solomon, not as Bentham meditated, upon blind ambitions, untoward accidents, and capricious passions, and the world was almost as empty in his eyes as it must be in the eyes of God.

> Tired with all these, for restful death I cry; –
>   As, to behold desert a beggar born,
> And needy nothing trimm'd in jollity,
>   And purest faith unhappily forsworn,
> And gilded honour shamefully misplaced,
>   And maiden virtue rudely strumpeted,
> And right perfection wrongfully disgraced,
>   And strength by limping sway disabled,

And art made tongue-tied by authority,
    And folly, doctor-like, controlling skill,
And simple truth miscall'd simplicity,
    And captive good attending captain ill:
Tired with all these, from these would I be gone,
Save that, to die, I leave my love alone.

V

The Greeks, a certain scholar has told me, considered that
myths are the activities of the Daimons, and that the Daimons
shape our characters and our lives. I have often had the fancy
that there is some one myth for every man, which, if we but
knew it, would make us understand all he did and thought.
Shakespeare's myth, it may be, describes a wise man who was
blind from very wisdom, and an empty man who thrust him
from his place, and saw all that could be seen from very
emptiness. It is in the story of Hamlet, who saw too great
issues everywhere to play the trivial game of life, and of
Fortinbras, who came from fighting battles about 'a little
patch of ground' so poor that one of his captains would not
give 'six ducats' to 'farm it', and who was yet acclaimed by
Hamlet and by all as the only befitting king. And it is in the
story of Richard II, that unripened Hamlet, and of Henry V,
that ripened Fortinbras. To pose character against character
was an element in Shakespeare's art, and scarcely a play is
lacking in characters that are the complement of one another,
and so, having made the vessel of porcelain, Richard II, he
had to make the vessel of clay, Henry V. He makes him the
reverse of all that Richard was. He has the gross vices, the
coarse nerves, of one who is to rule among violent people,
and he is so little 'too friendly' to his friends that he bundles
them out of doors when their time is over. He is as remorse-

less and undistinguished as some natural force, and the finest
thing in his play is the way his old companions fall out of it
broken-hearted or on their way to the gallows; and instead
of that lyricism which rose out of Richard's mind like the jet
of a fountain to fall again where it had risen, instead of that
fantasy too enfolded in its own sincerity to make any thought
the hour had need of, Shakespeare has given him a resounding
rhetoric that moves men as a leading article does to-day. His
purposes are so intelligible to everybody that everybody talks
of him as if he succeeded, although he fails in the end, as all
men great and little fail in Shakespeare. His conquests abroad
are made nothing by a woman turned warrior. That boy he
and Katharine were to 'compound', 'half French, half English', 'that' was to 'go to Constantinople and take the Turk
by the beard', turns out a saint and loses all his father had built
up at home and his own life.

Shakespeare watched Henry V not indeed as he watched
the greater souls in the visionary procession, but cheerfully,
as one watches some handsome spirited horse, and he spoke
his tale, as he spoke all tales, with tragic irony.

VI

The six plays, that are but one play, have, when played one
after another, something extravagant and superhuman, something almost mythological. These nobles with their indifference to death and their immense energy seem at times no
nearer the common stature of men than do the gods and the
heroes of Greek plays. Had there been no Renaissance and no
Italian influence to bring in the stories of other lands, English
history would, it may be, have become as important to the
English imagination as the Greek myths to the Greek imagination; and many plays by many poets would have woven it

into a single story whose contours, vast as those of Greek myth, would have made living men and women seem like swallows building their nests under the architrave of some Temple of the Giants. English literature, because it would have grown out of itself, might have had the simplicity and unity of Greek literature, for I can never get out of my head that no man, even though he be Shakespeare, can write perfectly when his web is woven of threads that have been spun in many lands. And yet, could those foreign tales have come in if the great famine, the sinking down of popular imagination, the dying out of traditional fantasy, the ebbing out of the energy of race, had not made them necessary? The metaphors and language of Euphuism, compounded of the natural history and mythology of the classics, were doubtless a necessity also that something might be poured into the emptiness. Yet how they injured the simplicity and unity of the speech! Shakespeare wrote at a time when solitary great men were gathering to themselves the fire that had once flowed hither and thither among all men, when individualism in work and thought and emotion was breaking up the old rhythms of life, when the common people, sustained no longer by the myths of Christianity and of still older faiths, were sinking into the earth.

The people of Stratford-on-Avon have remembered little about him, and invented no legend to his glory. They have remembered a drinking-bout of his, and invented some bad verses for him, and that is about all. Had he been some hard-drinking, hard-living, hard-riding, loud-blaspheming squire they would have enlarged his fame by a legend of his dealings with the Devil; but in his day the glory of a poet, like that of all other imaginative powers, had ceased, or almost ceased, outside a narrow class. The poor Gaelic rhymer leaves a nobler memory among his neighbours, who will talk of angels standing like flames about his death-bed, and of voices speaking out of bramble-bushes that he may have the wisdom of the world. The Puritanism that drove the theatres into Surrey was but part of an inexplicable movement that was trampling out the minds of all but some few thousands born to cultivated ease.

May 1901

EDMUND SPENSER

*   *   *

III

When Spenser was buried in Westminster Abbey many poets read verses in his praise, and then threw their verses and the pens that had written them into his tomb. Like him they belonged, for all the moral zeal that was gathering like a London fog, to that indolent, demonstrative Merry England that was about to pass away. Men still wept when they were moved, still dressed themselves in joyous colours, and spoke with many gestures. Thoughts and qualities sometimes come to their perfect expression when they are about to pass away, and Merry England was dying in plays, and in poems, and in strange adventurous men. If one of those poets who threw his copy of verses into the earth that was about to close over his master were to come alive again, he would find some shadow of the life he knew, though not the art he knew, among young men in Paris, and would think that his true country. If he came to England he would find nothing there but the triumph of the Puritan and the merchant — those enemies he had feared and hated — and he would weep perhaps, in that womanish way of his, to think that so much greatness had been, not, as he had hoped, the dawn, but the sunset of a people. He had lived in the last days of what we may call the Anglo-French nation, the old feudal nation that had been established when the Norman and the Angevin made French the language of court and market. In the time of Chaucer

English poets still wrote much in French, and even English labourers lilted French songs over their work; and I cannot read any Elizabethan poem or romance without feeling the pressure of habits of emotion, and of an order of life, which were conscious, for all their Latin gaiety, of a quarrel to the death with that new Anglo-Saxon nation that was arising amid Puritan sermons and Marprelate pamphlets. This nation had driven out the language of its conquerors, and now it was to overthrow their beautiful haughty imagination and their manners, full of abandon and wilfulness, and to set in their stead earnestness and logic and the timidity and reserve of a counting-house. It had been coming for a long while, for it had made the Lollards; and when Anglo-French Chaucer was at Westminster, its poet, Langland, sang the office at Saint Paul's. Shakespeare, with his delight in great persons, with his indifference to the State, with his scorn of the crowd, with his feudal passion, was of the old nation, and Spenser, though a joyless earnestness had cast shadows upon him, and darkened his intellect wholly at times, was of the old nation too. His *Faerie Queene* was written in Merry England, but when Bunyan wrote in prison the other great English allegory, Modern England had been born. Bunyan's men would do right that they might come some day to the Delectable Mountains, and not at all that they might live happily in a world whose beauty was but an entanglement about their feet. Religion had denied the sacredness of an earth that commerce was about to corrupt and ravish, but when Spenser lived the earth had still its sheltering sacredness. His religion, where the paganism that is natural to proud and happy people had been strengthened by the Platonism of the Renaissance, cherished the beauty of the soul and the beauty of the body with, as it seemed, an equal affection. He would have had men live well, not merely that they might win eternal happiness, but that they might live splendidly among men and be celebrated in many songs. How could one live well if one had not the joy of the Creator and of the Giver of gifts? He says in his *Hymne in Honour of Beautie* that a beautiful soul, unless for some stubbornness in the ground, makes for itself a beautiful body, and he even denies that beautiful persons ever lived who had not souls as beautiful. They may have been tempted until they seemed evil, but that was the fault of others. And in his *Hymne of Heavenly Beautie* he sets a woman little known to theology, one that he names Wisdom or Beauty, above Seraphim and Cherubim and in the very bosom of God, and in the *Faerie Queene* it is pagan Venus and her lover Adonis who create the forms of all living things and send them out into the world, calling them back again to the gardens of Adonis at their lives' end to rest there, as it seems, two thousand years between life and life. He began in English poetry, despite a temperament that delighted in sensuous beauty alone with perfect delight, that worship of Intellectual Beauty which Shelley carried to a greater subtlety and applied to the whole of life.

The qualities, to each of whom he had planned to give a Knight, he had borrowed from Aristotle and partly Christianised, but not to the forgetting of their heathen birth. The chief of the Knights, who would have combined in himself qualities of all the others, had Spenser lived to finish the *Faerie Queene*, was King Arthur, the representative of an ancient quality, Magnificence. Born at the moment of change, Spenser had indeed many Puritan thoughts. It has been recorded that he cut his hair short and half regretted his hymns to Love and Beauty. But he has himself told us that the many-headed beast overthrown and bound by Calidore, Knight of Courtesy, was Puritanism itself. Puritanism, its zeal and its narrowness, and the angry suspicion that it had in common with all movements of the ill-educated, seemed no other to him than a slanderer of all fine things. One doubts, indeed, if he could have persuaded himself that there could be any virtue at all without courtesy, perhaps without something of pageant and eloquence. He was, I think, by nature altogether a man of that old Catholic feudal nation, but, like Sidney, he wanted to justify himself to his new masters. He wrote of knights and ladies, wild creatures imagined by the aristocratic poets of the twelfth century, and perhaps chiefly by English poets who had still the French tongue; but he fastened them with allegorical nails to a big barn-door of common sense, of merely practical virtue. Allegory itself had risen into general importance with the rise of the merchant class in the thirteenth and fourteenth centuries; and it was natural when that class was about for the first time to shape an age in its image, that the last epic poet of the old order should mix its art with his own long-descended, irresponsible, happy art.

IV

Allegory and, to a much greater degree, symbolism are a natural language by which the soul when entranced, or even in ordinary sleep, communes with God and with angels. They can speak of things which cannot be spoken of in any other language, but one will always, I think, feel some sense of unreality when they are used to describe things which can be described as well in ordinary words. Dante used allegory to describe visionary things, and the first maker of *The Romance of the Rose*, for all his lighter spirits, pretends that his adventures came to him in a vision one May morning; while Bunyan, by his preoccupation with Heaven and the soul, gives his simple story a visionary strangeness and intensity: he believes so little in the world that he takes us away from all ordinary standards of probability and makes us believe even in allegory for a while. Spenser, on the other hand, to whom allegory was not, as I think, natural at all, makes us feel again and again that it disappoints and interrupts our preoccupation with the beautiful and sensuous life he has called up before our eyes. It interrupts us most when he copies Langland, and writes in what he believes to be a mood of edification, and the least when he is not quite serious, when he sets before us some procession like a Court pageant made to celebrate a wedding or a crowning. One cannot think that he should have occupied himself with moral and religious questions at all. He should have been content to be, as Emerson thought Shakespeare was, a Master of the Revels to mankind. I am certain that he never gets that visionary air which can alone make allegory real, except when he writes out of a feeling for glory and passion. He had no deep moral or religious life. He has never a line like Dante's 'His Will is our Peace', or like Thomas à Kempis's 'The Holy Spirit has liberated me from a multitude of opinions', or even like Hamlet's objection to the bare bodkin. He had been made a poet by what he had almost learnt to call his sins. If he had not felt it necessary to justify his art to some serious friend, or perhaps even to 'that rugged forehead', he would have written all his life long, one thinks, of the loves of shepherdesses and shepherds, among whom there would have been perhaps the morals of the dovecot. One is persuaded that his morality is official and impersonal—a system of life which it was his duty to support — and it is perhaps a half understanding of this that has made so many generations believe that he was the first Poet Laureate, the first salaried moralist among the poets. His processions of deadly sins, and his houses, where the very cornices are arbitrary images of virtue, are an unconscious hypocrisy, an undelighted obedience to the 'rugged forehead', for all the while he is thinking of

nothing but lovers whose bodies are quivering with the
memory or the hope of long embraces. When they are not
together, he will indeed embroider emblems and images
much as those great ladies of the courts of love embroidered
them in their castles; and when these are imagined out of a
thirst for magnificence and not thought out in a mood of
edification, they are beautiful enough; but they are always
tapestries for corridors that lead to lovers' meetings or for the
walls of marriage chambers. He was not passionate, for the
passionate feed their flame in wanderings and absences, when
the whole being of the beloved, every little charm of body
and of soul, is always present to the mind, filling it with
heroical subtleties of desire. He is a poet of the delighted
senses, and his song becomes most beautiful when he writes
of those islands of Phaedria and Acrasia, which angered 'that
rugged forehead', as it seems, but gave to Keats his *Belle
Dame sans merci* and his 'perilous seas in faery lands forlorn',
and to William Morris his 'Water of the Wondrous Isles'.

V

The dramatists lived in a disorderly world, reproached by
many, persecuted even, but following their imagination
wherever it led them. Their imagination, driven hither and
thither by beauty and sympathy, put on something of the
nature of eternity. Their subject was always the soul, the
whimsical, self-awakening, self-exciting, self-appeasing soul.
They celebrated its heroical, passionate will going by its own
path to immortal and invisible things. Spenser, on the other
hand, except among those smooth pastoral scenes and lovely
effeminate islands that have made him a great poet, tried to
be of his time, or rather of the time that was all but at hand.
Like Sidney, whose charm, it may be, led many into slavery,
he persuaded himself that we enjoy Virgil because of the

virtues of Aeneas, and so planned out his immense poem that it would set before the imagination of citizens, in whom there would soon be no great energy, innumerable blameless Aeneases. He had learned to put the State, which desires all the abundance for itself, in the place of the Church, and he found it possible to be moved by expedient emotions, merely because they were expedient, and to think serviceable thoughts with no self-contempt. He loved his Queen a little because she was the protectress of poets and an image of that old Anglo-French nation that lay a-dying, but a great deal because she was the image of the State which had taken possession of his conscience. She was over sixty years old, ugly and, historians will have it, selfish, but in his poetry she is 'fair Cynthia', 'a crown of lilies', 'the image of the heavens', 'without mortal blemish', and has 'an angelic face', where 'the red rose' has 'meddled with the white'; 'Phoebus thrusts out his golden head' but to look upon her, and blushes to find himself outshone. She is 'a fourth Grace', 'a queen of love', 'a sacred saint', and 'above all her sex that ever yet has been'. In the midst of his praise of his own sweetheart he stops to remember that Elizabeth is more beautiful, and an old man in *Daphnaïda*, although he has been brought to death's door by the death of a beautiful daughter, remembers that though his daughter 'seemed of angels' race', she was yet but the primrose to the rose beside Elizabeth. Spenser had learned to look to the State not only as the rewarder of virtue but as the maker of right and wrong, and had begun to love and hate as it bid him. The thoughts that we find for ourselves are timid and a little secret, but those modern thoughts that we share with large numbers are confident and very insolent. We have little else to-day, and when we read our newspaper and take up its cry, above all, its cry of hatred, we will not think very carefully, for we hear the marching feet. When Spenser wrote of Ireland he wrote as an official, and out of thoughts and emotions that had been organised by the State. He was the first of many Englishmen to see nothing but what he was desired to see. Could he have gone there as a poet merely, he might have found among its poets more wonderful imaginations than even those islands of Phaedria and Acrasia. He would have found among wandering story-tellers, not indeed his own power of rich, sustained description, for that belongs to lettered ease, but certainly all the kingdom of Faery, still unfaded, of which his own poetry was often but a troubled image. He would have found men doing by swift strokes of the imagination much that he was doing with painful intellect, with that imaginative reason that soon was to drive out imagination altogether and for a long time. He would have met with, at his own door, story-tellers among whom the perfection of Greek art was indeed as unknown as his own power of sustained description, but who, none the less, imagined or remembered beautiful incidents and strange, pathetic outcrying that made them of Homer's lineage. Flaubert says somewhere: 'There are things in Hugo, as in Rabelais, that I could have mended, things badly built, but then what thrusts of power beyond the reach of conscious art!' Is not all history but the coming of that conscious art which first makes articulate and then destroys the old wild energy? Spenser, the first poet struck with remorse, the first poet who gave his heart to the State, saw nothing but disorder, where the mouths that have spoken all the fables of the poets had not yet become silent. All about him were shepherds and shepherdesses still living the life that made Theocritus and Virgil think of shepherd and poet as the one thing; but though he dreamed of Virgil's shepherds he wrote a book to advise, among many like things, the harrying of all that followed flocks upon the hills, and of all the 'wandering companies that keep the wood'. His *View of the Present State of Ireland* commends indeed the beauty of the hills and woods where they did their shepherding, in that powerful and subtle language of his which I sometimes think more full of youthful energy than even the language of the great playwrights. He is 'sure it is yet a most beautiful and sweet country as any is under heaven', and that all would prosper but for those agitators, those 'wandering companies that keep the wood', and he would rid it of them by a certain expeditious way. There should be four great garrisons. 'And those fowre garrisons issuing foorthe, at such convenient times as they shall have intelligence or espiall upon the enemye, will so drive him from one side to another, and tennis him amongst them, that he shall finde nowhere safe to keepe his creete, or hide himselfe, but flying from the fire shall fall into the water, and out of one daunger into another, that in short space his creete, which is his moste sustenaunce, shall be wasted in preying, or killed in driving, or starved for wante of pasture in the woodes, and he himselfe brought soe lowe, that he shall have no harte nor abilitye to indure his wretchednesse, the which will surely come to passe in very short space; for one winters well following of him will soe plucke him on his knees that he will never be able to stand up agayne.'

He could commend this expeditious way from personal knowledge, and could assure the Queen that the people of the country would soon 'consume themselves and devoure one another. The proofs whereof I saw sufficiently en-sampled in these late warres in Mounster; for notwithstanding that the same was a most rich and plentifull countrey, full of corne and cattell, that you would have thought they would have bene able to stand long, yet ere one yeare and a halfe they were brought to such wretchednesse, as that any stonye harte

would have rued the same. Out of every corner of the woodes
and glynnes they came creeping forth upon theyr hands, for
theyr legges could not beare them; they looked like anatomyes
of death, they spake like ghostes crying out of theyr graves;
they did eate of the dead carrions, happy were they if they
could finde them, yea, and one another soone after, insoemuch
as the very carcasses they spared not to scrape out of theyr
graves; and if they found a plot of watercresses or shamrokes,
there they flocked as to a feast for the time, yet not able long
to continue therewithall; that in short space there were none
allmost left, and a most populous and plentifull countrey
suddaynely made voyde of man or beast; yet sure in all that
warre, there perished not many by the sword, but all by the
extremitye of famine.'

VI

In a few years the Four Masters were to write the history
of that time, and they were to record the goodness or the
badness of Irishman and Englishman with entire impartiality.
They had seen friends and relatives persecuted, but they would
write of that man's poisoning and this man's charities and of
the fall of great houses, and hardly with any other emotion
than a thought of the pitiableness of all life. Friend and enemy
would be for them a part of the spectacle of the world. They
remembered indeed those Anglo-French invaders who
conquered for the sake of their own strong hand, and when
they had conquered became a part of the life about them,
singing its songs, when they grew weary of their own Iseult
and Guinevere. But famines and exterminations had not
made them understand, as I think, that new invaders were
among them, who fought for an alien State, for an alien
religion. Such ideas were difficult to them, for they belonged
to the old individual, poetical life, and spoke a language even

in which it was all but impossible to think an abstract thought. They understood Spain, possibly, which persecuted in the interests of religion, but I doubt if anybody in Ireland could have understood as yet that the Anglo-Saxon nation was beginning to persecute in the service of ideas it believed to be the foundation of the State. I doubt if anybody in Ireland saw that with certainty, till the Great Demagogue had come and turned the old house of the noble into 'the house of the Poor, the lonely house, the accursed house of Cromwell'. He came, another Cairbry Cat-Head, with that great rabble who had overthrown the pageantry of Church and Court, but who turned towards him faces full of the sadness and docility of their long servitude, and the old individual, poetical life went down, as it seems, for ever. He had studied Spenser's book and approved of it, as we know, finding, doubtless, his own head there, for Spenser, a king of the old race, carried a mirror which showed kings yet to come though but kings of the mob. Those Bohemian poets of the theatres were wiser, for the States that touched them nearly were the States where Helen and Dido had sorrowed, and so their mirrors showed none but beautiful heroical heads. They wandered in the places that pale passion loves, and were happy, as one thinks, and troubled little about those marching and hoarse-throated thoughts that the State has in its pay. They knew that those marchers, with the dust of so many roads upon them, are very robust and have great and well-paid generals to write expedient despatches in sound prose; and they could hear Mother Earth singing among her corn-fields:

> Weep not, my wanton! smile upon my knee;
> When thou art old there's grief enough for thee.

VII

There are moments when one can read neither Milton nor
Spenser, moments when one recollects nothing but that their
flesh had partly been changed to stone, but there are other
moments when one recollects nothing but those habits of
emotion that made the lesser poet especially a man of an
older, more imaginative time. One remembers that he
delighted in smooth pastoral places, because men could be
busy there or gather together there, after their work, that he
could love handiwork and the hum of voices. One remembers
that he could still rejoice in the trees, not because they were
images of loneliness and meditation, but because of their
serviceableness. He could praise 'the builder oake', 'the aspine,
good for staves', 'the cypresse funerall', 'the eugh, obedient
to the bender's will', 'the birch for shaftes', 'the sallow for
the mill', 'the mirrhe sweete bleeding in the bitter wound',
'the fruitful olive', and 'the carver holme'. He was of a time
before undelighted labour had made the business of men a
desecration. He carries one's memory back to Virgil's and
Chaucer's praise of trees, and to the sweet-sounding song
made by the old Irish poet in their praise.

I got up from reading the *Faerie Queene* the other day and
wandered into another room. It was in a friend's house, and I
came of a sudden to the ancient poetry and to our poetry
side by side — an engraving of Claude's *Mill* hung under an
engraving of Turner's *Temple of Jupiter*. Those dancing
countrypeople, those cowherds, resting after the day's work,
and that quiet millrace made one think of Merry England
with its glad Latin heart, of a time when men in every land
found poetry and imagination in one another's company and
in the day's labour. Those stately goddesses, moving in slow
procession towards that marble architrave among mysterious

trees, belong to Shelley's thought, and to the religion of the wilderness – the only religion possible to poetry to-day. Certainly Colin Clout, the companionable shepherd, and Calidore, the courtly man-at-arms, are gone, and Alastor is wandering from lonely river to river finding happiness in nothing but in that Star where Spenser too had imagined the fountain of perfect things. This new beauty, in losing so much, has indeed found a new loftiness, a something of religious exaltation that the old had not. It may be that those goddesses, moving with a majesty like a procession of the stars, mean something to the soul of man that those kindly women of the old poets did not mean, for all the fullness of their breasts and the joyous gravity of their eyes. Has not the wilderness been at all times a place of prophecy?

VIII

Our poetry, though it has been a deliberate bringing back of the Latin joy and the Latin love of beauty, has had to put off the old marching rhythms, that once could give delight to more than expedient hearts, in separating itself from a life where servile hands have become powerful. It has ceased to have any burden for marching shoulders, since it learned ecstasy from Smart in his mad cell, and from Blake, who made joyous little songs out of almost unintelligible visions, and from Keats, who sang of a beauty so wholly preoccupied with itself that its contemplation is a kind of lingering trance. The poet, if he would not carry burdens that are not his and obey the orders of servile lips, must sit apart in contemplative indolence playing with fragile things.

If one chooses at hazard a Spenserian stanza out of Shelley and compares it with any stanza by Spenser, one sees the change, though it would be still more clear if one had chosen a lyrical passage. I will take a stanza out of *Laon and Cythna*, for that is story-telling and runs nearer to Spenser than the meditative *Adonais*:

> The meteor to its far morass returned:
> The beating of our veins one interval
> Made still; and then I felt the blood that burned
> Within her frame, mingle with mine, and fall
> Around my heart like fire; and over all
> A mist was spread, the sickness of a deep
> And speechless swoon of joy, as might befall
> Two disunited spirits when they leap
> In union from this earth's obscure and fading sleep.

The rhythm is varied and troubled, and the lines, which are in Spenser like bars of gold thrown ringing one upon another, are broken capriciously. Nor is the meaning the less an inspiration of indolent Muses, for it wanders hither and thither at the beckoning of fancy. It is now busy with a meteor and now with throbbing blood that is fire, and with a mist that is a swoon and a sleep that is life. It is bound together by the vaguest suggestion, while Spenser's verse is always rushing on to some preordained thought. A 'popular poet' can still indeed write poetry of the will, just as factory girls wear the fashion of hat or dress the moneyed classes wore a year ago, but 'popular poetry' does not belong to the living imagination of the world. Old writers gave men four temperaments, and they gave the sanguineous temperament to men of active life, and it is precisely the sanguineous temperament that is fading out of poetry and most obviously out of what is most subtle and living in poetry — its pulse and breath, its rhythm. Because poetry belongs to that element in every race which is most strong, and therefore most individual, the poet is not stirred to imaginative activity by a life which is surrendering its freedom to ever new elaboration, organisation, mechanism. He has no longer a poetical will, and must be content to write out of those parts of himself which are too delicate and fiery for any deadening exercise. Every generation has more and more loosened the rhythm, more and more broken up and disorganised, for the sake of subtlety of detail, those great rhythms which move, as it were, in masses of sound. Poetry has become more spiritual, for the soul is of all things the most delicately organised, but it has lost in weight and measure and in its power of telling long stories and of dealing with great and complicated events. *Laon and Cythna*, though I think it rises sometimes into loftier air than the *Faerie Queene* and *Endymion*, though its shepherds and wandering divinities have a stranger and more intense beauty than Spenser's, has need of too watchful and minute attention for such lengthy poems. In William Morris, indeed, one finds a music smooth and unexacting like that of the old story-tellers, but not their energetic pleasure, their rhythmical wills. One too often misses in his *Earthly Paradise* the minute ecstasy of modern song without finding that old happy-go-lucky tune that had kept the story marching.

Spenser's contemporaries, writing lyrics or plays full of lyrical moments, write a verse more delicately organised than his and crowd more meaning into a phrase than he, but they could not have kept one's attention through so long a poem. A friend who has a fine ear told me the other day that she had read all Spenser with delight and yet could remember only four lines. When she repeated them they were from the poem by Matthew Roydon, which is bound up with Spenser because it is a commendation of Sir Philip Sidney:

> A sweet, attractive kind of grace,
> A full assurance given by looks,
> Continual comfort in a face,
> The lineaments of Gospel books.

Yet if one were to put even these lines beside a fine modern song one would notice that they had a stronger and rougher energy, a featherweight more, if eye and ear were fine enough to notice it, of the active will, of the happiness that comes out of life itself.

*   *   *

October 1902

THE HAPPIEST OF THE POETS

★ ★ ★

IV

When I was a child I often heard my elders talking of an old turreted house where an old great-uncle of mine lived, and of its gardens and its long pond where there was an island with tame eagles; and one day somebody read me some verses and said they made him think of that old house where he had been very happy. The verses ran in my head for years and became to me the best description of happiness in the world, and I am not certain that I know a better even now. They were those first dozen verses of *Golden Wings* that begin:

> Midways of a walled garden,
>   In the happy poplar land,
>   Did an ancient castle stand,
> With an old knight for a warden.
>
> Many scarlet bricks there were
>   In its walls, and old grey stone;
>   Over which red apples shone
> At the right time of the year.
>
> On the bricks the green moss grew,
>   Yellow lichen on the stone,
>   Over which red apples shone;
> Little war that castle knew.

When William Morris describes a house of any kind, and makes his description poetical, it is always, I think, some house that he would have liked to have lived in, and I remember him saying about the time when he was writing of that great house of the Wolfings, 'I decorate modern houses for people, but the house that would please me would be some great room where one talked to one's friends in one corner and ate in another and slept in another and worked in another.' Indeed all he writes seems to me like the make-believe of a child who is remaking the world, not always in the same way, but always after its own heart; and so, unlike all other modern writers, he makes his poetry out of unending pictures of happiness that is often what a child might imagine, and always a happiness that sets mind and body at ease. Now it is a picture of some great room full of merriment, now of the wine-press, now of the golden threshing-floor, now of an old mill among apple-trees, now of cool water after the heat of the sun, now of some well-sheltered, well-tilled place among woods or mountains, where men and women live happily, knowing of nothing that is too far off or too great for the affections. He has but one story to tell us, how some man or woman lost and found again the happiness that is always half of the body; and even when they are wandering from it, leaves must fall over them, and flowers make fragrances about them, and warm winds fan them, and birds sing to them, for being of Habundia's kin they must not forget the shadow of her Green Tree even for a moment, and the waters of her Well must be always wet upon their sandals. His poetry often wearies us as the unbroken green of July wearies us, for there is something in us, some bitterness because of the Fall, it may be, that takes a little from the sweetness of Eve's apple after the first mouthful; but he who did all things gladly and easily, who never knew the curse of labour, found it always as sweet as it was in Eve's mouth. All kinds of associations have gathered about the pleasant things of the world and half taken the pleasure out of them for the greater number of men, but he saw them as when they came from the Divine Hand. I often see him in my mind as I saw him once at Hammersmith holding up a glass of claret towards the light and saying, 'Why do people say it is prosaic to get inspiration out of wine? Is it not the sunlight and the sap in the leaves? Are not grapes made by the sunlight and the sap?'

V

In one of his little Socialist pamphlets he tells how he sat under an elm-tree and watched the starlings and thought of an old horse and an old labourer that had passed him by, and of the men and women he had seen in towns; and he wondered how all these had come to be as they were. He saw that the starlings were beautiful and merry, and that men and the old horse they had subdued to their service were ugly and miserable, and yet the starlings, he thought, were of one kind whether there or in the South of England, and the ugly men and women were of one kind with those whose nobility and beauty had moved the ancient sculptors and poets to imagine the gods and the heroes after the images of men. Then, he began, he tells us, to meditate how this great difference might be ended and a new life, which would permit men to have beauty in common among them as the starlings have, be built on the wrecks of the old life. In other words, his mind was illuminated from within and lifted into prophecy in the full right sense of the word, and he saw the natural things he was alone gifted to see in their perfect form; and having that faith which is alone worth having, for it includes all others, a sure knowledge established in the constitution of his mind that perfect things are final things, he announced that all he had seen would come to pass. I do not think he troubled to understand books of economics, and Mr. Mackail says, I think, that they vexed him and wearied him. He found it enough to hold up, as it were, life as it is to-day beside his visions, and to show how faded its colours were and how sapless it was. And if we had not enough artistic feeling, enough feeling for the perfect, that is, to admit the authority of the vision; or enough faith to understand that all that is imperfect passes away, he would not, as I think, have argued with us in a serious spirit. Though I think that he never used the kinds of words I use in writing of him, though I think he would even have disliked a word like faith with its theological associations, I am certain that he understood thoroughly, as all artists understand a little, that the important things, the things we must believe in or perish, are beyond argument. We can no more reason about them than can the pigeon, come but lately from the egg, about the hawk whose shadow makes it cower among the grass. His vision is true because it is poetical, because we are a little happier when we are looking at it; and he knew as Shelley knew, by an act of faith, that the economists should take their measurements not from life as it is, but from the vision of men like him, from the vision of the world made perfect that is buried under all minds. The early Christians were of the kin of the Wilderness and of the Dry Tree, and they saw an unearthly Paradise, but he was of the kin of the Well and of the Green Tree and he saw an Earthly Paradise.

He obeyed his vision when he tried to make first his own house, for he was in this matter also like a child playing with the world, and then houses of other people, places where one could live happily; and he obeyed it when he wrote essays about the nature of happy work, and when he spoke at street-corners about the coming changes.

He knew clearly what he was doing towards the end, for he lived at a time when poets and artists have begun again to

THE GALWAY PLAINS

LADY GREGORY has just given me her beautiful *Poets and Dreamers*, and it has brought to mind a day two or three years ago when I stood on the side of Slieve Echtge, looking out over Galway. The Burren Hills were to my left, and though I forget whether I could see the cairn over Bald Conan of the Fianna, I could certainly see many places there that are in poems and stories. In front of me, over many miles of level Galway plains, I saw a low blue hill flooded with evening light. I asked a countryman who was with me what hill that was, and he told me it was Cruachmaa of the Sidhe. I had often heard of Cruachmaa of the Sidhe even as far north as Sligo, for the countrypeople have told me a great many stories of the great host of the Sidhe who live there, still fighting and holding festivals.

I asked the old countryman about it, and he told me of strange women who had come from it, and who would come into a house having the appearance of countrywomen, but would know all that happened in that house; and how they would always pay back with increase, though not by their own hands, whatever was given to them. And he had heard, too, of people who had been carried away into the hill, and how one man went to look for his wife there, and dug into the hill and all but got his wife again, but at the very moment she was coming out to him, the pick he was digging with struck her upon the head and killed her. I asked him if he had himself seen any of its enchantments, and he said, 'Sometimes when I look over to the hill, I see a mist lying on the top of it, that goes away after a while'.

A great part of the poems and stories in Lady Gregory's book were made or gathered between Burren and Cruachmaa. It was here that Raftery, the wandering country poet of ninety years ago, praised and blamed, chanting fine verses, and playing badly on his fiddle. It is here the ballads of meeting and parting have been sung, and some whose lamentations for defeat are still remembered may have passed through this plain flying from the battle of Aughrim.

'I will go up on the mountain alone; and I will come hither from it again. It is there I saw the camp of the Gael, the poor troop thinned, not keeping with one another; Och Ochone!' And here, if one can believe many devout people whose stories are in the book, Christ has walked upon the roads, bringing the needy to some warm fireside, and sending one of His saints to anoint the dying.

I do not think these country imaginations have changed much for centuries, for they are still busy with those two themes of the ancient Irish poets, the sternness of battle and the sadness of parting and death. The emotion that in other countries has made many love-songs has here been given, in a long wooing, to danger, that ghostly bride. It is not a difference in the substance of things that the lamentations that were sung after battles are now sung for men who have died upon the gallows.

The emotion has become not less, but more noble, by the change, for the man who goes to death with the thought —

> It is with the people I was,
> It is not with the law I was,

has behind him generations of poetry and poetical life.

The poets of to-day speak with the voice of the unknown priest who wrote, some two hundred years ago, that *Sorrowful Lament for Ireland* Lady Gregory has put into passionate and rhythmical prose:

I do not know of anything under the sky
That is friendly or favourable to the Gael,
But only the sea that our need brings us to,
Or the wind that blows to the harbour
The ship that is bearing us away from Ireland;
And there is reason that these are reconciled with us,
For we increase the sea with our tears,
And the wandering wind with our sighs.

There is still in truth upon these great level plains a people, a community bound together by imaginative possessions, by stories and poems which have grown out of its own life, and by a past of great passions which can still waken the heart to imaginative action. One could still, if one had the genius, and had been born to Irish, write for these people plays and poems like those of Greece. Does not the greatest poetry always require a people to listen to it? England or any other country which takes its tunes from the great cities and gets its taste from schools and not from old custom may have a mob, but it cannot have a people. In England there are a few groups of men and women who have good taste, whether in cookery or in books; and the great multitudes but copy them or their copiers. The poet must always prefer the community where the perfected minds express the people, to a community that is vainly seeking to copy the perfected minds. To have even perfectly the thoughts that can be weighed, the knowledge that can be got from books, the precision that can be learned at school, to belong to any aristocracy, is to be a little pool that will soon dry up. A people alone are a great river; and that is why I am persuaded that where a people has died, a nation is about to die.

1903

FIRST PRINCIPLES

Two Irish writers had a controversy a month ago, and they accused one another of being unable to think, with entire sincerity, though it was obvious to uncommitted minds that neither had any lack of vigorous thought. But they had a different meaning when they spoke of thought, for the one, though in actual life he is the most practical man I know, meant thought as Pascal, as Montaigne, as Shakespeare, or as, let us say, Emerson, understood it — a reverie about the adventures of the soul, or of the personality, or some obstinate questioning of the riddle. Many who have to work hard always make time for this reverie, but it comes more easily to the leisured, and in this it is like a broken heart, which is, a Dublin newspaper assured us lately, impossible to a busy man. The other writer had in mind, when he spoke of thought, the shaping energy that keeps us busy, and the obstinate questionings he had most respect for were, how to change the method of government, how to change the language, how to revive our manufactures, and whether it is the Protestant or the Catholic that scowls at the other with the darker scowl. Ireland is so poor, so mis-governed, that a great portion of the imagination of the land must give itself to a very passionate consideration of questions like these, and yet it is precisely these loud questions that drive away the reveries that incline the imagination to the lasting work of literature and give, together with religion, sweetness, and nobility, and dignity to life. We should desire no more from these propagandist thinkers than that they carry out their work, as far as possible, without making it more difficult for those fitted by nature or by circumstance for another kind of thought to do their work also; and certainly it is not well that Martha chide at Mary, for they have the one Master over them.

When one all but despairs, as one does at times, of Ireland welcoming a National literature in this generation, it is because we do not leave ourselves enough of time, or of quiet, to be interested in men and women. A writer in *The Leader*, who is unknown to me, elaborates this argument in an article full of beauty and dignity. He is speaking of our injustice to one another, and he says that we are driven into injustice 'not wantonly but inevitably, and at call of the exacting qualities of the great things. Until this latter dawning, the genius of Ireland has been too preoccupied really to concern itself about men and women; in its drama they play a subordinate part, born tragic comedians though all the sons and daughters of the land are. A nation is the heroic theme we follow, a mourning, wasted land its moving spirit; the impersonal assumes personality for us.' When I wrote my *Countess Cathleen*, I thought, of course, chiefly of the actual picture that was forming before me, but there was a secondary meaning that came into my mind continually. 'It is the soul of one that loves Ireland', I thought, 'plunging into unrest, seeming to lose itself, to bargain itself away to the very wickedness of the world, and to surrender what is eternal for what is temporary', and I know that this meaning seemed natural to others, for that great orator, J. F. Taylor, who was not likely to have searched very deeply into any work of mine, for he cared little for mine, or, indeed, any modern work, turned the play into such a parable in one of his speeches.

There is no use being angry with necessary conditions, or failing to see that a man who is busy with some reform that can only be carried out in a flame of energetic feeling, will not only be indifferent to what seems to us the finer kind of thinking, but will support himself by generalisations that seem untrue to the man of letters. A little play, *The Rising of the Moon*, which is in the present number of *Samhain*, and is among those we are to produce during the winter, has, for instance, roused the suspicions of a very resolute leader of the people, who has a keen eye for rats behind the arras. A Fenian ballad-singer partly converts a policeman, and is it not unwise under any circumstances to show a policeman in so favourable a light? It is well known that many of the younger policemen were Fenians; but it is necessary that the Dublin crowds should be kept of so high a heart that they will fight the police at any moment. Are not morals greater than literature? Others have objected to Mr. Synge's *Shadow of the Glen* because Irish women, being more chaste than those of England and Scotland, are a valuable part of our National argument. Mr. Synge should not, it is said by some, have chosen an exception for the subject of his play, for who knows but the English may misunderstand him? Some even deny that such a thing could happen at all, while others that know the country better, or remember the statistics, say that it could, but should never, have been staged. All these arguments, by their methods, even more than by what they have tried to prove, misunderstand how literature does its work. Men of letters have sometimes said that the characters of a romance or of a play must be typical. They mean that the character must be typical of something which exists in all men because the writer has found it in his own mind. It is one of the most inexplicable things about human nature that a writer, with a strange temperament, an Edgar Allan Poe, let us say, made what he is by conditions that never existed before, can create personages and lyric emotions which startle us by being at once bizarre and an image of our own secret thoughts. Are we not face to face with the microcosm, mirroring everything in universal Nature? It is no more necessary for the characters created by a romance-writer, or a dramatist, to have existed before, than for his own personality to have done so; characters and personality alike, as is perhaps true in the instance of Poe, may draw half their life not from the solid earth but from some dreamy drug. This is true even of historical drama, for it was Goethe, the founder of the historical drama of Germany, who said, 'We do the people of history the honour of naming after them the creations of our own minds'. All that a dramatic writer need do is to persuade us, during the two hours' traffic of the stage, that the events of his play did really happen. He must know enough of the life of his country, or of history, to create this illusion, but no matter how much he knows, he will fail if his audience is not ready to give up something of the dead letter. If his mind is full of energy he will not be satisfied with little knowledge, but he will be far more likely to alter incidents and characters, wilfully even as it may seem, than to become a literal historian. It was one of the complaints against Shakespeare, in his own day, that he made Sir John Falstaff out of a praiseworthy old Lollard preacher. One day, as he sat over Holinshed's *History of England*, he persuaded himself that Richard II, with his French culture, 'his too great friendliness to his friends', his beauty of mind, and his fall before dry, repelling Bolingbroke, would be a good image for an accustomed mood of fanciful, impracticable lyricism in his own mind. The historical Richard has passed away for ever and the Richard of the play lives more intensely, it seems, than did ever living man. Yet Richard II, as Shakespeare made him, could never have been born before the Renaissance, before the Italian influence, or even one hour before the innumerable streams that flowed in upon Shakespeare's mind, the innumerable experiences we can never know, brought Shakespeare to the making of him. He is typical not because he ever existed, but because he has made us know of something in our own minds we had never known of had he never been imagined.

Our propagandists have twisted this theory of the men of letters into its direct contrary, and when they say that a writer should make typical characters they mean personifications of averages, of statistics, or even personified opinions, or men and women so faintly imagined that there is nothing about them to separate them from the crowd, as it appears to our hasty eyes. We must feel that we could engage a hundred others to wear the same livery as easily as we could engage a coachman. We must never forget that we are engaging them to be the ideal young peasant, or the true patriot, or the happy Irish wife, or the policeman of our prejudices, or to express some other of those invaluable generalisations without which our practical movements would lose their energy. Who is there that likes a coachman to be too full of human nature, when he has his livery on? No one man is like another, but one coachman should be as like another as possible, though he may assert himself a little when he meets the gardener. The patriots would impose on us heroes and heroines, like those young couples in the Gaelic plays, who might all change brides or bridegrooms in the dance and never find out the difference. The personifications need not be true even, if they are about our enemy, for it might be more difficult to fight out our necessary fight if we remembered his virtue at wrong moments; and might not Teigue and Bocach, that are light in the head, go over to his party?

Ireland is indeed poor, is indeed hunted by misfortune, and

has indeed to give up much that makes life desirable and lovely, but is she so very poor that she can afford no better literature than this? Perhaps so, but if it is a Spirit from beyond the world that decides when a nation shall awake into imaginative energy, and no philosopher has ever found what brings the moment, it cannot be for us to judge. It may be coming upon us now, for it is certain that we have more writers who are thinking, as men of letters understand thought, than we have had for a century, and he who wilfully makes their work harder may be setting himself against the purpose of that Spirit.

I would not be trying to form an Irish National Theatre if I did not believe that there existed in Ireland, whether in the minds of a few people or of a great number I do not know, an energy of thought about life itself, a vivid sensitiveness as to the reality of things, powerful enough to overcome all those phantoms of the night. Everything calls up its contrary, unreality calls up reality, and, besides, life here has been sufficiently perilous to make men think. I do not think it a national prejudice that makes me believe we are harder, a more masterful race than the comfortable English of our time, and that this comes from an essential nearness to reality of those few scattered people who have the right to call themselves the Irish race. It is only in the exceptions, in the few minds where the flame has burnt, as it were, pure, that one can see the permanent character of a race. If one remembers the men who have dominated Ireland for the last hundred and fifty years, one understands that it is strength of personality, the individualising quality in a man, that stirs Irish imagination most deeply in the end. There is scarcely a man who has led the Irish people, at any time, who may not give some day to a great writer precisely that symbol he may require for the expression of himself. The critical mind of

Ireland is far more subjugated than the critical mind of England by the phantoms and misapprehensions of politics and social necessity, but the life of Ireland has rejected them more resolutely. Indeed, it is in life itself in England that one finds the dominion of what is not human life.

We have no longer in any country a literature as great as the literature of the old world, and that is because the newspapers, all kinds of second-rate books, the preoccupation of men with all kinds of practical changes, have driven the living imagination out of the world. I have read hardly any books this summer but Cervantes and Boccaccio and some Greek plays. I have felt that these men, divided from one another by so many hundreds of years, had the same mind. It is we who are different; and then the thought would come to me, that has come to me so often before, that they lived in times when the imagination turned to life itself for excitement. The world was not changing quickly about them. There was nothing to draw their imagination from the ripening of the fields, from the birth and death of their children, from the destiny of their souls, from all that is the unchanging substance of literature. They had not to deal with the world in such great masses that it could only be represented to their minds by figures and by abstract generalisations. Everything that their minds ran on came on them vivid with the colour of the senses, and when they wrote it was out of their own rich experience, and they found their symbols of expression in things that they had known all their life long. Their very words were more vigorous than ours, for their phrases came from a common mint, from the market, or the tavern, or from the great poets of a still older time. It is the change that followed the Renaissance, and was completed by newspaper government and the scientific movement, that has brought upon us all these phrases and generalisations, made by minds that would grasp what they have never seen. Yesterday I went out to see the reddening apples in the garden, and they faded from my imagination sooner than they would have from the imagination of that old poet who made the songs of the seasons for the Fianna, or out of Chaucer's, that celebrated so many trees. Theories, opinions, these opinions among the rest, flowed in upon me and blotted them away. Even our greatest poets see the world with preoccupied minds. Great as Shelley is, those theories about the coming changes of the world, which he has built up with so much elaborate passion, hurry him from life continually. There is a phrase in some old Cabbalistic writer about man falling into his own circumference, and every generation we get further away from life itself, and come more and more under the influence which Blake had in his mind when he said, 'Kings and Parliament seem to me something other than human life'. We lose our freedom more and more as we get away from ourselves, and not merely because our minds are overthrown by abstract phrases and generalisations, reflections in a mirror that seem living, but because we have turned the table of values upside-down, and believe that the root of reality is not in the centre but somewhere in that whirling circumference. How can we create like the ancients, while innumerable considerations of external probability or social utility destroy the seeming irresponsible creative power that is life itself? Who to-day could set Richmond's and Richard's tents side by side on the battlefield, or make Don Quixote, mad as he was, mistake a windmill for a giant in broad daylight? And when I think of free-spoken Falstaff I know of no audience but the tinkers of the roadside that could encourage the artist to an equal comedy. The old writers were content if their inventions had but an emotional and moral consistency, and created out of themselves a fantastic, energetic, extravagant art. A civilisation is very like a man or a woman, for it comes in but a few years into its beauty, and its strength, and then, while many years go by, it gathers and makes order about it, the strength and beauty going out of it the while, until in the end it lies there with its limbs straightened out and a clean linen cloth folded upon it. That may well be, and yet we need not follow among the mourners, for, it may be, before they are at the tomb, a messenger will run out of the hills and touch the pale lips with a red ember, and wake the limbs to the disorder and the tumult that is life. Though he does not come, even so we will keep from among the mourners and hold some cheerful conversation among ourselves; for has not Virgil, a know-ledgeable man and a wizard, foretold that other Argonauts shall row between cliff and cliff, and other fair-haired Achaeans sack another Troy?

Every argument carries us backwards to some religious conception, and in the end the creative energy of men depends upon their believing that they have, within themselves, some-thing immortal and imperishable, and that all else is but as an image in a looking-glass. So long as that belief is not a formal thing, a man will create out of a joyful energy, seeking little for any external test of an impulse that may be sacred, and looking for no foundation outside life itself. If Ireland could escape from those phantoms of hers she might create, as did the old writers; for she has a faith that is as theirs, and keeps alive in the Gaelic traditions — and this has always seemed to me the chief intellectual value of Gaelic — a portion of the old imaginative life. When Dr. Hyde or Father Peter O'Leary is the writer, one's imagination goes straight to the century of Cervantes, and, having gone so far, one thinks at every moment that they will discover his energy. It is precisely because of this reason that one is indignant with those who would substitute for the ideas of the folk-life the rhetoric of the newspapers, who would muddy what had begun to seem a fountain of life with the feet of the mob. Is it impossible to revive Irish and yet to leave the finer intellects a sufficient mastery over the more gross, to prevent it from becoming, it may be, the language of a nation, and yet losing all that has made it worthy of a revival, all that has made it a new energy in the mind?

Before the modern movement, and while it was but new, the ordinary man, whether he could read and write or not, was ready to welcome great literature. When Ariosto found himself among the brigands, they repeated to him his own verses, and the audience in the Elizabethan theatres must have been all but as clever as an Athenian audience. But to-day we come to understand great literature by a long preparation, or by some accident of nature, for we only begin to understand life when our minds have been purified of temporary interests by study.

But if literature has no external test, how are we to know that it is indeed literature? The only test that Nature gives, to show when we obey her, is that she gives us happiness, and when we are no longer obedient she brings us to pain sooner or later. Is it not the same with the artist? The sign that she makes to him is that happiness we call delight in beauty. He can only convey this in its highest form after he has purified his mind with the great writers of the world; but their example can never be more than a preparation. If his art does not seem, when it comes, to be the creation of a new personality, in a few years it will not seem to be alive at all. If he is a dramatist his characters must have a like newness. If they could have existed before his day, or have been imagined before his day, we may be certain that the spirit of life is not in them in its fullness. This is because art, in its highest moments, is not a deliberate creation, but the creation of intense feeling, of pure life; and every feeling is the child of all past ages and would be different if even a moment had been left out. Indeed, is it not that delight in beauty which tells the artist that he has imagined what may never die, itself but a delight in the permanent yet ever-changing form of life, in her very limbs and lineaments? When life has given it, has she given anything but herself? Has she any other reward, even for the saints? If one flies to the wilderness, is not that clear light that falls about the soul when all irrelevant things have been taken away, but life that has been about one always, enjoyed in all its fullness at length? It is as though she had put her arms about one, crying, 'My beloved, you have given up everything for me'. If a man spend all his days in good works till there is no emotion in his heart that is not full of virtue, is not the reward he prays for eternal life? The artist, too, has prayers and a cloister, and if he do not turn away from temporary things, from the zeal of the reformer and the passion of revolution, that jealous mistress will give him but a scornful glance.

What attracts me to drama is that it is, in the most obvious way, what all the arts are upon a last analysis. A farce and a tragedy are alike in this, that they are a moment of intense life. An action is taken out of all other actions; it is reduced to its simplest form, or at any rate to as simple a form as it can be brought to without our losing the sense of its place in the world. The characters that are involved in it are freed from everything that is not a part of that action; and whether it is, as in the less important kinds of drama, a mere bodily activity, a hairbreadth escape or the like, or as it is in the more important kinds, an activity of the souls of the characters, it is an energy, an eddy of life purified from everything but itself. The dramatist must picture life in action, with an unpreoccupied mind, as the musician pictures it in sound and the sculptor in form.

But if this be true, has art nothing to do with moral judgments? Surely it has, and its judgments are those from which there is no appeal. The character whose fortune we have been called in to see, or the personality of the writer, must keep our sympathy, and whether it be farce or tragedy, we must laugh and weep with him and call down blessings on his head. This character who delights us may commit murder like Macbeth, or fly the battle for his sweetheart as did Antony, or betray his country like Coriolanus, and yet we will rejoice in every happiness that comes to him and sorrow at his death as if it were our own. It is no use telling us that the murderer and the betrayer do not deserve our sympathy. We thought so yesterday, and we still know what crime is, but everything has been changed of a sudden; we are caught up into another code, we are in the presence of a higher court. Complain of us if you will, but it will be useless, for before the curtain falls, a thousand ages, grown conscious in our sympathies, will have cried *Absolvo te*. Blame if you will the codes, the philosophies, the experiences of all past ages that have made us what we are, as the soil under our feet has been made out of unknown vegetations: quarrel with the acorns of Eden if you will, but what has that to do with us? We understand the verdict and not the law; and yet there is some law, some code, some judgment. If the poet's hand had slipped, if Antony had railed at Cleopatra in the monument, if Coriolanus had abated that high pride of his in the presence of death, we might have gone away muttering the Ten Commandments. Yet maybe

we are wrong to speak of judgment, for we have but contemplated life, and what more is there to say when she that is
all virtue, the gift and the giver, the fountain whither all flows
again, has given all herself? If the subject of drama or any
other art were a man himself, an eddy of momentary breath,
we might desire the contemplation of perfect characters; but
the subject of all art is passion, and a passion can only be
contemplated when separated by itself, purified of all but
itself, and aroused into a perfect intensity by opposition with
some other passion, or it may be with the law, that is the
expression of the whole whether of Church or Nation or
external nature. Had Coriolanus not been a law-breaker,
neither he nor we had ever discovered, it may be, that noble
pride of his, and if we had not seen Cleopatra through the
eyes of so many lovers, would we have known that soul of
hers to be all flame, and wept at the quenching of it? If we
were not certain of law we would not feel the struggle, the
drama, but the subject of art is not law, which is a kind of
death, but the praise of life, and it has no commandments that
are not positive.

But if literature does not draw its substance from history, or
anything about us in the world, what is a National literature?
Our friends have already told us, writers for the Theatre in
Abbey Street, that we have no right to the name, some
because we do not write in Irish, and others because we do not
plead the National cause in our plays, as if we were writers
for the newspapers. I have not asked my fellow-workers what
they mean by the words National literature, but though I
have no great love for definitions, I would define it in some
such way as this: It is the work of writers who are moulded
by influences that are moulding their country, and who write
out of so deep a life that they are accepted there in the end.

It leaves a good deal unsettled — was Rossetti an Englishman, or Swift an Irishman? — but it covers more kinds of National literature than any other I can think of. If you say a National literature must be in the language of the country, there are many difficulties. Should it be written in the language that your country does speak or the language that it ought to speak? Was Milton an Englishman when he wrote in Latin or Italian, and had we no part in Columbanus when he wrote in Latin the beautiful sermon comparing life to a highway and to a smoke? And then there is Beckford, who is in every history of English literature, and yet his one memorable book, a story of Persia, was written in French.

Our theatre is of no great size, for though we know that if we write well we shall find acceptance among our country-men in the end, we would think our emotions were on the surface if we found a ready welcome. Edgar Allan Poe and Walt Whitman are National writers of America, although the one had his first true acceptance in France and the other in England and Ireland. When I was a boy, six persons, who, alone out of the whole world, it may be, believed Walt Whitman a great writer, sent him a message of admiration, and of those names four were English and two Irish, my father's and Prof. Dowden's. It is only in our own day that America has begun to prefer him to Lowell, who is not a poet at all.

I mean by deep life that men must put into their writing the emotions and experiences that have been most important to themselves. If they say, 'I will write of Irish countrypeople and make them charming and picturesque like those dear peasants my great-grandmother used to put in the foreground of her water-colour paintings', then they had better be satisfied with the word 'provincial'. If one condescends to one's material, if it is only what a popular novelist would call local colour, it is certain that one's real soul is somewhere else. Mr. Synge, upon the other hand, who is able to express his own finest emotions in those curious ironical plays of his, where, for all that, by the illusion of admirable art, every one seems to be thinking and feeling as only countrymen could think and feel, is truly a National writer, as Burns was when he wrote finely and as Burns was not when he wrote *Highland Mary* and *The Cotter's Saturday Night*.

A writer is not less National because he shows the influence of other countries and of the great writers of the world. No nation, since the beginning of history, has ever drawn all its life out of itself. Even The Well of English Undefiled, the Father of English Poetry himself, borrowed his metres, and much of his way of looking at the world, from French writers, and it is possible that the influence of Italy was more powerful among the Elizabethan poets than any literary influence out of England herself. Many years ago, when I was contending with Sir Charles Gavan Duffy over what seemed to me a too narrow definition of Irish interests, Professor York Powell either said or wrote to me that the creative power of England was always at its greatest when her receptive power was greatest. If Ireland is about to produce a literature that is important to her, it must be the result of the influences that flow in upon the mind of an educated Irishman to-day, and, in a greater degree, of what came into the world with himself. Gaelic can hardly fail to do a portion of the work, but one cannot say whether it may not be some French or German writer who will do most to make him an articulate man. If he really achieve the miracle, if he really make all that he has seen and felt and known a portion of his own intense nature, if he puts it all into the fire of his energy, he need not fear being a stranger among his own people in the end. There never have been men more unlike an Englishman's idea of himself than Keats and Shelley, while Campbell, whose emotion came out of a shallow well, was very like that idea. We call certain minds creative because they are among the moulders of their nation and are not made upon its mould, and they resemble one another in this only — they have never been foreknown or fulfilled an expectation.

It is sometimes necessary to follow in practical matters some definition which one knows to have but a passing use. We, for instance, have always confined ourselves to plays upon Irish subjects, as if no others could be National literature. Our Theatre inherits this limitation from previous movements, which found it necessary and fruitful. Goldsmith and Sheridan and Burke had become so much a part of English life, were so greatly moulded by the movements that were moulding England, that, despite certain Irish elements that clung about them, we could not think of them as more important to us than any English writer of equal rank. Men told us that we should keep our hold of them, as it were, for they were a part of our glory; but we did not consider our glory very important. We had no desire to turn braggarts, and we did suspect the motives of our advisers. Perhaps they had reasons, which were not altogether literary, for thinking it might be well if Irish men of letters, in our day also, would turn their faces to England. But what moved me always the most, and I had something to do with forcing this limitation upon our organisations, is that a new language of expression would help to awaken a new attitude in writers themselves, and that if our organisations were satisfied to interpret a writer to his own countrymen merely because he was of Irish birth, the organisations would become a kind of trade union for the helping of Irishmen to catch the ear of London publishers and managers, and for upholding writers who had been beaten by abler Englishmen. Let a man turn his face to us, accepting the commercial disadvantages that would bring upon him, and talk of what is near to our hearts, Irish Kings and Irish Legends and Irish Countrymen, and we would find it a joy to interpret him. Our one philosophical critic, Mr. John Eglinton, thinks we were very arbitrary, and yet I would not have us enlarge our practice. England and France, almost alone among nations, have great works of literature which have taken their subjects from foreign lands, and even in France and England this is more true in appearance than reality. Shakespeare observed his Roman crowds in London, and saw, one doubts not, somewhere in his own Stratford, the old man that gave Cleopatra the asp. Somebody I have been reading lately finds the Court of Louis XIV in *Phèdre* and *Andromaque*. Even in France and England almost the whole prose fiction professes to describe the life of the country, often of the districts where its writers have lived, for, unlike a poem, a novel requires so much minute observation of the surface of life that a novelist who cares for the illusion of reality will keep to familiar things. A writer will indeed take what is most creative out of himself, not from observation, but experience, yet he must master a definite language, a definite symbolism of incident and scene. Flaubert explains the comparative failure of his *Salammbô* by saying, 'One cannot frequent her'. He could create her soul, as it were, but he could not tell with certainty how it would express itself before Carthage fell to ruins. In the small nations which have to struggle for their national life, one finds that almost every creator, whether poet or novelist, sets all his stories in his own country. I do not recollect that Björnson ever wrote of any land but Norway, and Ibsen, though he lived in exile for many years, driven out by his countrymen, as he believed, carried the little seaboard towns of Norway everywhere in his imagination. So far as we can be certain of anything, we may be certain that Ireland with her long National struggle, her old literature, her unbounded folk-imagination, will, in so far as her literature is National at all, be more like Norway than England or France.

If literature is but praise of life, if our writers are not to plead the National cause, nor insist upon the Ten Commandments, nor upon the glory of their country, what part remains for it, in the common life of the country? It will influence the life of the country immeasurably more, though seemingly less, than have our propagandist poems and stories. It will leave to others the defence of all that can be codified for ready understanding, of whatever is the especial business of sermons, and of leading articles; but it will bring all the ways of men before that ancient tribunal of our sympathies. It will measure all things by the measure not of things visible but of things invisible. In a country like Ireland, where personifications have taken the place of life, men have more hate than love, for the unhuman is nearly the same as the inhuman, but literature, which is a part of that charity that is the forgiveness of sins, will make us understand men no matter how little they conform to our expectations. We will be more interested in heroic men than in heroic actions, and will have a little distrust for everything that can be called good or bad in itself with a very confident heart. Could we understand it so well, we will say, if it were not something other than human life? We will have a scale of virtues, and value most highly those that approach the indefinable. Men will be born among us of whom it is possible to say, not 'What a philanthropist', 'What a patriot', 'How practical a man', but, as we say of the men of the Renaissance, 'What a nature', 'How much abundant life'. Even at the beginning we will value qualities more than actions, for these may be habit or accident; and should we say to a friend, 'You have advertised for an English cook', or 'I hear that you have no clerks who are not of your own faith', or 'You have voted an address to the King', we will add to our complaint, 'You have been unpatriotic and I am ashamed of you, but if you cease from doing any of these things because you have been terrorised out of them, you will cease to be my friend'. We will not forget how to be stern, but we will remember always that the highest life unites, as in one fire, the greatest passion and the greatest courtesy.

A feeling for the form of life, for the graciousness of life, for the dignity of life, for the moving limbs of life, for the nobleness of life, for all that cannot be written in codes, has always been greatest among the gifts of literature to mankind. Indeed, the Muses being women, all literature is but their love-cries to the manhood of the world. It is now one and now another that cries, but the words are the same: 'Love of my heart, what matter to me that you have been quarrelsome in your cups, and have slain many, and have given your love here and there? It was because of the whiteness of your flesh and the mastery in your hands that I gave you my love, when all life came to me in your coming.' And then in a low voice that none may overhear — 'Alas! I am greatly afraid that the more they cry against you the more I love you'.

There are two kinds of poetry, and they are commingled in all the greatest works. When the tide of life sinks low there are pictures, as in the *Ode on a Grecian Urn* and in Virgil at the plucking of the Golden Bough. The pictures make us sorrowful. We share the poet's separation from what he describes. It is life in the mirror, and our desire for it is as the desire of the lost souls for God; but when Lucifer stands among his friends, when Villon sings his dead ladies to so gallant a rhythm, when Timon makes his epitaph, we feel no sorrow, for life herself has made one of her eternal gestures, has called up into our hearts her energy that is eternal delight. In Ireland, where the tide of life is rising, we turn, not to picture-making, but to the imagination of personality — to drama, gesture.

1904

DISCOVERIES

*　　*　　*

THE PLAY OF MODERN MANNERS

Of all artistic forms that have had a large share of the world's attention, the worst is the play about modern educated people. Except where it is superficial or deliberately argumentative it fills one's soul with a sense of commonness as with dust. It has one mortal ailment. It cannot become impassioned, that is to say, vital, without making somebody gushing and sentimental. Educated and well-bred people do not wear their hearts upon their sleeves, and they have no artistic and charming language except light persiflage and no powerful language at all, and when they are deeply moved they look silently into the fireplace. Again and again I have watched some play of this sort with growing curiosity through the opening scene. The minor people argue, chaff one another, hint sometimes at some deeper stream of life just as we do in our houses, and I am content. But all the time I have been wondering why the chief character, the man who is to bear the burden of fate, is gushing, sentimental and quite without ideas. Then the great scene comes and I understand that he cannot be well-bred or self-possessed or intellectual, for if he were he would draw a chair to the fire and there would be no duologue at the end of the third act. Ibsen understood the difficulty and made all his characters a little provincial that they might not put each other out of countenance, and made a leading-article sort of poetry — phrases about vine-leaves and harps in the air — it was possible to believe them using in their moments of excitement, and if the play needed more than that, they could always do something stupid. They could go out and hoist a flag as they do at the end of *Little Eyolf*. One only understands that this manner, deliberately adopted, one doubts not, had gone into his soul and filled it with dust, when one has noticed that he could no longer create a man of genius. The happiest writers are those that, knowing this form of play to be slight and passing, keep to the surface, never showing anything but the arguments and the persiflage of daily observation, or now and then, instead of the expression of passion, a stage picture, a man holding a woman's hand or sitting with his head in his hands in dim light by the red glow of a fire. It was certainly an understanding of the slightness of the form, of its incapacity for the expression of the deeper sorts of passion, that made the French invent the play with a thesis, for where there is a thesis people can grow hot in argument, almost the only kind of passion that displays itself in our daily life. The novel of contemporary educated life is upon the other hand a permanent form because, having the power of psychological description, it can follow the thought of a man who is looking into the grate.

HAS THE DRAMA OF CONTEMPORARY LIFE A ROOT OF ITS OWN?

In watching a play about modern educated people, with its meagre language and its action crushed into the narrow limits of possibility, I have found myself constantly saying: 'Maybe it has its power to move, slight as that is, from being able to suggest fundamental contrasts and passions which

romantic and poetical literature have shown to be beautiful.'
A man facing his enemies alone in a quarrel over the purity
of the water in a Norwegian Spa and using no language but
that of the newspapers can call up into our minds, let us say,
the passion of Coriolanus. The lovers and fighters of old
imaginative literature are more vivid experiences in the soul
than anything but one's own ruling passion that is itself riddled
by their thought as by lightning, and even two dumb figures
on the roads can call up all that glory. Put the man who has no
knowledge of literature before a play of this kind and he will
say, as he has said in some form or other in every age at the
first shock of naturalism, 'Why should I leave my home
to hear but the words I have used there when talking of the
rates?' And he will prefer to it any play where there is visible
beauty or mirth, where life is exciting, at high tide as it were.
It is not his fault that he will prefer in all likelihood a worse
play although its kind may be greater, for we have been
following the lure of science for generations and have forgotten him and his. I come always back to this thought.
There is something of an old wives' tale in fine literature.
The makers of it are like an old peasant telling stories of the
great famine or the hangings of '98 or from his own memories.
He has felt something in the depth of his mind and he wants
to make it as visible and powerful to our senses as possible.
He will use the most extravagant words or illustrations if they
suit his purpose. Or he will invent a wild parable, and the
more his mind is on fire or the more creative it is, the less
will he look at the outer world or value it for its own sake.
It gives him metaphors and examples, and that is all. He is
even a little scornful of it, for it seems to him while the fit is on
that the fire has gone out of it and left it but white ashes. I
cannot explain it, but I am certain that every high thing was
invented in this way, between sleeping and waking, as it

were, and that peering and peeping persons are but hawkers of stolen goods. How else could their noses have grown so ravenous or their eyes so sharp?

WHY THE BLIND MAN IN ANCIENT TIMES WAS MADE A POET

A description in the *Iliad* or the *Odyssey*, unlike one in the *Aeneid* or in most modern writers, is the swift and natural observation of a man as he is shaped by life. It is a refinement of the primary hungers and has the least possible of what is merely scholarly or exceptional. It is, above all, never too observant, too professional, and when the book is closed we have had our energies enriched, for we have been in the mid-current. We have never seen anything Odysseus could not have seen while his thought was of the Cyclops, or Achilles when Briseis moved him to desire. In the art of the greatest periods there is something careless and sudden in all habitual moods, though not in their expression, because these moods are a conflagration of all the energies of active life. In primitive times the blind man became a poet, as he became a fiddler in our villages, because he had to be driven out of activities all his nature cried for, before he could be contented with the praise of life. And often it is Villon or Verlaine, with impediments plain to all, who sings of life with the ancient simplicity. Poets of coming days, when once more it will be possible to write as in the great epochs, will recognise that their sacrifice shall be to refuse what blindness and evil name, or imprisonment at the outsetting, denied to men who missed thereby the sting of a deliberate refusal. The poets of the ages of silver need no refusal of life, the dome of many-coloured glass is already shattered while they live. They look at life deliberately and as if from beyond life, and the greatest of them need suffer nothing but the sadness that the saints have known. This is their aim, and their temptation is not a passionate activity, but the approval of their fellows, which comes to them in full abundance only when they delight in the general thoughts that hold together a cultivated middle-class, where irresponsibilities of position and poverty are lacking; the things that are more excellent among educated men who have political preoccupations, Augustus Caesar's affability, all that impersonal fecundity which muddies the intellectual passions. Ben Jonson says in *The Poetaster* that even the best of men without Promethean fire is but a hollow statue, and a studious man will commonly forget after some forty winters that of a certainty Promethean fire will burn somebody's fingers. It may happen that poets will be made more often by their sins than by their virtues, for general praise is unlucky, as the villages know, and not merely as I imagine — for I am superstitious about these things — because the praise of all but an equal enslaves and adds a pound to the ball at the ankle with every compliment.

All energy that comes from the whole man is as irregular as the lightning, for the communicable and forecastable and discoverable is a part only, a hungry chicken under the breast of the pelican, and the test of poetry is not in reason but in a delight not different from the delight that comes to a man at the first coming of love into the heart. I knew an old man who had spent his whole life cutting hazel and privet from the paths, and in some seventy years he had observed little but had many imaginations. He had never seen like a naturalist, never seen things as they are, for his habitual mood had been that of a man stirred in his affairs; and Shakespeare, Tintoretto, though the times were running out when Tintoretto painted, nearly all the great men of the Renaissance, looked at the world with eyes like his. Their minds were never quiescent, never, as it were, in a mood for scientific observations, always in exaltation, never — to use known words — founded upon an elimination of the personal factor; and their attention and the attention of those they worked for dwelt constantly with what is present to the mind in exaltation. I am too modern fully to enjoy Tintoretto's *Origin of the Milky Way*, I cannot fix my thoughts upon that glowing and palpitating flesh intently enough to forget, as I can the make-believe of a faery-tale, that heavy drapery hanging from a cloud, though I find my pleasure in *King Lear* heightened by the make-believe that comes upon it all when the Fool says, 'This prophecy Merlin shall make, for I live before his time'; — and I always find it quite natural, so little does logic in the mere circumstance matter in the finest art, that Richard's and Richmond's tents should be side by side. I saw with delight *The Knight of the Burning Pestle* when Mr. Carr revived it, and found it none the worse because the apprentice acted a whole play upon the spur of the moment and without committing a line to heart. When *The Silent Woman* rammed a century of laughter into the two hours' traffic, I found with amazement that almost every journalist had put logic on the seat where our Lady Imagination should pronounce that unjust and favouring sentence her woman's heart is ever plotting, and had felt bound to cherish none but reasonable sympathies and to resent the baiting of that grotesque old man. I have been looking over a book of engravings made in the eighteenth century from those wall-pictures of Herculaneum and Pompeii that were, it seems, the work of journeymen copying from finer paintings, for the composition is always too good for the execution. I find in great numbers an indifference to obvious logic, to all that the eye sees at common moments. Perseus shows Andromeda the death she lived by in a pool, and though the lovers are carefully drawn the reflection is shown reversed that the forms it reflects may be seen the right side up and our eyes be the more content. There is hardly an old master who has not made known to us in some like way how little he cares for what every fool can see and every knave can praise. The men who imagined the arts were not less superstitious in religion, understanding the spiritual relations, but not the mechanical, and finding nothing that need strain the throat in those gnats the floods of Noah and Deucalion.

CONCERNING SAINTS AND ARTISTS

I took the Indian hemp with certain followers of Saint-Martin on the ground floor of a house in the Latin Quarter. I had never taken it before, and was instructed by a boisterous young poet, whose English was no better than my French. He gave me a little pellet, if I am not forgetting, an hour before dinner, and another after we had dined together at some restaurant. As we were going through the streets to the meeting-place of the Martinists, I felt suddenly that a cloud I was looking at floated in an immense space, and for an instant my being rushed out, as it seemed, into that space with ecstasy. I was myself again immediately, but the poet was wholly above himself, and presently he pointed to one of the street-lamps now brightening in the fading twilight, and cried at the top of his voice, 'Why do you look at me with your great eye?' There were perhaps a dozen people already much excited when we arrived; and after I had drunk some cups of coffee and eaten a pellet or two more, I grew very anxious to dance, but did not, as I could not remember any steps. I sat down and closed my eyes; but no, I had no visions, nothing but a sensation of some dark shadow which seemed to be telling me that some day I would go into a trance and so out of my body for a while, but not yet. I opened my eyes and looked at some red ornament on the mantelpiece, and at once the room was full of harmonies of red, but when a blue china figure caught my eye the harmonies became blue upon the instant. I was puzzled, for the reds were all there, nothing had changed, but they were no longer important or harmonious; and why had the blues so unimportant but a moment ago become exciting and delightful? Thereupon it struck me that I was seeing like a painter, and that in the course of the evening every one there would change through every kind of artistic perception.

After a while a Martinist ran towards me with a piece of paper on which he had drawn a circle with a dot in it, and pointing at it with his finger he cried out, 'God, God!' Some immeasurable mystery had been revealed, and his eyes shone; and at some time or other a lean and shabby man, with rather a distinguished face, showed me his horoscope and pointed with an ecstasy of melancholy at its evil aspects. The boisterous poet, who was an old eater of the Indian hemp, had told me that it took one three months growing used to it, three months more enjoying it, and three months being cured of it. These men were in their second period; but I never forgot myself, never really rose above myself for more than a moment, and was even able to feel the absurdity of that gaiety, a Herr Nordau among the men of genius, but one that was abashed at his own sobriety. The sky outside was beginning to grey when there came a knocking at the window-shutters. Somebody opened the window, and a woman and two young girls in evening dress, who were not a little bewildered to find so many people, were helped down into the room. She and her husband's two sisters had been at a

students' ball unknown to her husband, who was asleep over-
head, and had thought to have crept home unobserved, but
for a confederate at the window. All those talking or dancing
men laughed in a dreamy way; and she, understanding that
there was no judgment in the laughter of men that had no
thought but of the spectacle of the world, blushed, laughed,
and darted through the room and so upstairs. Alas that the
hangman's rope should be own brother to that Indian happiness that keeps alone, were it not for some stray cactus, mother
of as many dreams, immemorial impartiality.

THE SUBJECT-MATTER OF DRAMA

I read this sentence a few days ago, or one like it, in an
obituary of Ibsen: 'Let nobody again go back to the old ballad
material of Shakespeare, to murders, and ghosts, for what
interests us on the stage is modern experience and the discussion of our interests'; and in another part of the article
Ibsen was blamed because he had written of suicides and in
other ways made use of 'the morbid terror of death'. Dramatic literature has for a long time been left to the criticism of
journalists, and all these, the old stupid ones and the new clever
ones, have tried to impress upon it their absorption in the life
of the moment, their delight in obvious originality and in
obvious logic, their shrinking from the ancient and insoluble.
The writer I have quoted is much more than a journalist,
but he has lived their hurried life, and instinctively turns to
them for judgment. He is not thinking of the great poets and
painters, of the cloud of witnesses, who are there that we may
become, through our understanding of their minds, spectators
of the ages, but of this age. Drama is a means of expression,
not a special subject-matter, and the dramatist is as free to
choose where he has a mind to, as the poet of *Endymion*, or

as the painter of Mary Magdalene at the door of Simon the Pharisee. So far from the discussion of our interests and the immediate circumstance of our life being the most moving to the imagination, it is what is old and far off that stirs us the most deeply.

There is a sentence in *The Marriage of Heaven and Hell* that is meaningless until we understand Blake's system of corespondences. 'The best wine is the oldest, the best water the newest.' Water is experience, immediate sensation, and wine is emotion, and it is with the intellect, as distinguished from imagination, that we enlarge the bounds of experience and separate it from all but itself, from illusion, from memory, and create among other things science and good journalism. Emotion, on the other hand, grows intoxicating and delightful after it has been enriched with the memory of old emotions, with all the uncounted flavours of old experience; and it is necessarily some antiquity of thought, emotions that have been deepened by the experiences of many men of genius, that distinguishes the cultivated man. The subject-matter of his meditation and invention is old, and he will disdain a too conscious originality in the arts as in those matters of daily life where, is it not Balzac who says, 'we are all conservatives'? He is above all things well-bred, and whether he write or paint will not desire a technique that denies or obtrudes his long and noble descent.

*   *   *

1906

POETRY AND TRADITION

*   *   *

II

Him who trembles before the flame and the flood,
And the winds that blow through the starry ways,
Let the starry winds and the flame and the flood
Cover over and hide, for he has no part
With the proud, majestical multitude.

Three types of men have made all beautiful things, Aristo-
cracies have made beautiful manners, because their place in
the world puts them above the fear of life, and the countrymen
have made beautiful stories and beliefs, because they have
nothing to lose and so do not fear, and the artists have made
all the rest, because Providence has filled them with reckless-
ness. All these look backward to a long tradition, for, being
without fear, they have held to whatever pleased them. The
others, being always anxious, have come to possess little that
is good in itself, and are always changing from thing to thing,
for whatever they do or have must be a means to something
else, and they have so little belief that anything can be an end
in itself that they cannot understand you if you say, 'All the
most valuable things are useless'. They prefer the stalk to the
flower, and believe that painting and poetry exist that there
may be instruction, and love that there may be children, and
theatres that busy men may rest, and holidays that busy men
may go on being busy. At all times they fear and even hate
the things that have worth in themselves, for that worth may

suddenly, as it were a fire, consume their Book of Life, where the world is represented by ciphers and symbols; and before all else, they fear irreverent joy and unserviceable sorrow. It seems to them that those who have been freed by position, by poverty, or by the traditions of art, have something terrible about them, a light that is unendurable to eyesight. They complain much of that commandment that we can do almost what we will, if we do it gaily, and think that freedom is but a trifling with the world.

If we would find a company of our own way of thinking, we must go backward to turreted walls, to Courts, to high rocky places, to little walled towns, to jesters like that jester of Charles V who made mirth out of his own death; to the Duke Guidobaldo in his sickness, or Duke Frederick in his strength, to all those who understood that life is not lived, if not lived for contemplation or excitement.

Certainly we could not delight in that so courtly thing, the poetry of light love, if it were sad; for only when we are gay over a thing, and can play with it, do we show ourselves its master, and have minds clear enough for strength. The raging fire and the destructive sword are portions of eternity, too great for the eye of man, wrote Blake, and it is only before such things, before a love like that of Tristan and Iseult, before noble or ennobled death, that the free mind permits itself aught but brief sorrow. That we may be free from all the rest, sullen anger, solemn virtue, calculating anxiety, gloomy suspicion, prevaricating hope, we should be reborn in gaiety. Because there is submission in a pure sorrow, we should sorrow alone over what is greater than ourselves, nor too soon admit that greatness, but all that is less than we are should stir us to some joy, for pure joy masters and impregnates; and so to world end, strength shall laugh and wisdom mourn.

III

In life courtesy and self-possession, and in the arts style, are the sensible impressions of the free mind, for both arise out of a deliberate shaping of all things, and from never being swept away, whatever the emotion, into confusion or dullness. The Japanese have numbered with heroic things courtesy at all times whatsoever, and though a writer, who has to withdraw so much of his thought out of his life that he may learn his craft, may find many his betters in daily courtesy, he should never be without style, which is but high breeding in words and in argument. He is indeed the creator of the standards of manners in their subtlety, for he alone can know the ancient records and be like some mystic courtier who has stolen the keys from the girdle of Time, and can wander where it please him amid the splendours of ancient Courts.

Sometimes, it may be, he is permitted the licence of cap and bell, or even the madman's bunch of straws, but he never forgets or leaves at home the seal and the signature. He has at all times the freedom of the well-bred, and being bred to the tact of words can take what theme he pleases, unlike the linen-drapers, who are rightly compelled to be very strict in their conversation. Who should be free if he were not? for none other has a continual deliberate self-delighting happiness — style, 'the only thing that is immortal in literature', as Sainte-Beuve has said, a still unexpended energy, after all that the argument or the story needs, a still unbroken pleasure after the immediate end has been accomplished — and builds this up into a most personal and wilful fire, transfiguring words and sounds and events. It is the playing of strength when the day's work is done, a secret between a craftsman and his craft, and is so inseparate in his nature that he has it most of all amid overwhelming emotion, and in the face of death. Shakespeare's persons, when the last darkness has gathered about them, speak out of an ecstasy that is one-half the self-surrender of sorrow, and one-half the last playing and mockery of the victorious sword before the defeated world.

It is in the arrangement of events as in the words, and in that touch of extravagance, of irony, of surprise, which is set there after the desire of logic has been satisfied and all that is merely necessary established, and that leaves one, not in the circling necessity, but caught up into the freedom of self-delight; it is, as it were, the foam upon the cup, the long pheasant's feather on the horse's head, the spread peacock over the pasty. If it be very conscious, very deliberate, as it may be in comedy, for comedy is more personal than tragedy, we call it fantasy, perhaps even mischievous fantasy, recognising how disturbing it is to all that drag a ball at the ankle. This joy, because it must be always making and mastering, remains in the hands and in the tongue of the artist, but with his eyes he enters upon a submissive, sorrowful contemplation of the great irremediable things, and he is known from other men by making all he handles like himself, and yet by the unlikeness to himself of all that comes before him in a pure contemplation. It may have been his enemy or his love or his cause that set him dreaming, and certainly the phoenix can but open her young wings in a flaming nest; but all hate and hope vanishes in the dream, and if his mistress brag of the song or his enemy fear it, it is not that either has its praise or blame, but that the twigs of the holy nest are not easily set afire. The verses may make his mistress famous as Helen or give a victory to his cause, not because he has been either's servant, but because men delight to honour and to remember all that have served contemplation. It had been easier to fight, to die even, for Charles's house with Marvell's poem in the memory, but there is no zeal of service that had not been an

ANIMA HOMINIS

I

WHEN I come home after meeting men who are strange to me, and sometimes even after talking to women, I go over all I have said in gloom and disappointment. Perhaps I have overstated everything from a desire to vex or startle, from hostility that is but fear; or all my natural thoughts have been drowned by an undisciplined sympathy. My fellow-diners have hardly seemed of mixed humanity, and how should I keep my head among images of good and evil, crude allegories?

But when I shut my door and light the candle, I invite a marmorean Muse, an art where no thought or emotion has come to mind because another man has thought or felt something different, for now there must be no reaction, action only, and the world must move my heart but to the heart's discovery of itself, and I begin to dream of eyelids that do not quiver before the bayonet: all my thoughts have ease and joy, I am all virtue and confidence. When I come to put in rhyme what I have found, it will be a hard toil, but for a moment I believe I have found myself and not my anti-self. It is only the shrinking from toil, perhaps, that convinces me that I have been no more myself than is the cat the medicinal grass it is eating in the garden.

How could I have mistaken for myself an heroic condition that from early boyhood has made me superstitious? That which comes as complete, as minutely organised, as are those elaborate, brightly lighted buildings and sceneries appearing in a moment, as I lie between sleeping and waking, must come from above me and beyond me. At times I remember that place in Dante where he sees in his chamber the 'Lord of Terrible Aspect', and how, seeming 'to rejoice inwardly that it was a marvel to see, speaking, he said many things among the which I could understand but few, and of these this: ego dominus tuus'; or should the conditions come, not, as it were, in a gesture — as the image of a man — but in some fine landscape, it is of Boehme, maybe, that I think, and of that country where we 'eternally solace ourselves in the excellent beautiful flourishing of all manner of flowers and forms, both trees and plants, and all kinds of fruit'.

II

When I consider the minds of my friends, among artists and emotional writers, I discover a like contrast. I have sometimes told one close friend that her only fault is a habit of harsh judgment with those who have not her sympathy, and she has written comedies where the wickedest people seem but bold children. She does not know why she has created that world where no one is ever judged, a high celebration of indulgence, but to me it seems that her ideal of beauty is the compensating dream of nature wearied out by over-much judgment. I know a famous actress who, in private life, is like the captain of some buccaneer ship holding his crew to good behaviour at the mouth of a blunderbuss, and upon the stage she excels in the representation of women who stir to pity and to desire because they need our protection, and is most adorable as one of those young queens imagined by Maeterlinck who have so little will, so little self, that they are like shadows sighing at the edge of the world. When I last saw her in her own house she lived in a torrent of words and movements, she could not listen, and all about her upon the walls were women drawn by Burne-Jones in his latest period. She had invited me in the hope that I would defend those women, who were always listening, and are as necessary to her as a contemplative Buddha to a Japanese Samurai, against a French critic who would persuade her to take into her heart in their stead a Post-Impressionist picture of a fat, flushed woman lying naked upon a Turkey carpet.

There are indeed certain men whose art is less an opposing virtue than a compensation for some accident of health or circumstance. During the riots over the first production of *The Playboy of the Western World*, Synge was confused, without clear thought, and was soon ill — indeed the strain of that week may perhaps have hastened his death — and he was, as is usual with gentle and silent men, scrupulously accurate in all his statements. In his art he made, to delight his ear and his mind's eye, voluble daredevils who 'go romancing through a romping lifetime...to the dawning of the Judgment Day'. At other moments this man, condemned to the life of a monk by bad health, takes an amused pleasure in 'great queens ... making themselves matches from the start to the end'. Indeed, in all his imagination he delights in fine physical life, in life when the moon pulls up the tide. The last act of *Deirdre of the Sorrows*, where his art is at its noblest, was written upon his death-bed. He was not sure of any world to come, he was leaving his betrothed and his unwritten play — 'O, what a waste of time,' he said to me; he hated to die, and in the last speeches of Deirdre and in the middle act he accepted death and dismissed life with a gracious gesture. He gave to Deirdre the emotion that seemed to him most desirable, most difficult, most fitting, and maybe saw in those delighted seven years, now dwindling from her, the fulfilment of his own life.

III

When I think of any great poetical writer of the past (a realist is a historian and obscures the cleavage by the record of his eyes), I comprehend, if I know the lineaments of his life, that the work is the man's flight from his entire horoscope, his blind struggle in the network of the stars. William Morris, a happy, busy, most irascible man, described dim colour and pensive emotion, following, beyond any man of his time, an indolent Muse; while Savage Landor topped us all in calm nobility when the pen was in his hand, as in the daily violence of his passion when he had laid it down. He had in his *Imaginary Conversations* reminded us, as it were, that the Venus de Milo is a stone, and yet he wrote when the copies did not come from the printer as soon as he expected: 'I have . . . had the resolution to tear in pieces all my sketches and projects and to forswear all future undertakings. I have tried to sleep away my time and pass two-thirds of the twenty-four hours in bed. I may speak of myself as a dead man.' I imagine Keats to have been born with that thirst for luxury common to many at the outsetting of the Romantic Movement, and not able, like wealthy Beckford, to slake it with beautiful and strange objects. It drove him to imaginary delights; ignorant, poor, and in poor health, and not perfectly well-bred, he knew himself driven from tangible luxury; meeting Shelley, he was resentful and suspicious because he, as Leigh Hunt recalls, 'being a little too sensitive on the score of his origin, felt inclined to see in every man of birth his natural enemy'.

IV

Some thirty years ago I read a prose allegory by Simeon Solomon, long out of print and unprocurable, and remember or seem to remember a sentence, 'a hollow image of fulfilled desire'. All happy art seems to me that hollow image, but when its lineaments express also the poverty or the exasperation that set its maker to the work, we call it tragic art. Keats but gave us his dream of luxury; but while reading Dante we never long escape the conflict, partly because the verses are at moments a mirror of his history, and yet more because that history is so clear and simple that it has the quality of art. I am no Dante scholar, and I but read him in Shadwell or in Dante Rossetti, but I am always persuaded that he celebrated the most pure lady poet ever sung and the Divine Justice, not merely because death took that lady and Florence banished her singer, but because he had to struggle in his own heart with his unjust anger and his lust; while, unlike those of the great poets who are at peace with the world and at war with themselves, he fought a double war. 'Always,' says Boccaccio, 'both in youth and maturity he found room among his virtues for lechery'; or as Matthew Arnold preferred to change the phrase, 'his conduct was exceeding irregular'. Guido Cavalcanti, as Rossetti translates him, finds 'too much baseness' in his friend:

> And still thy speech of me, heartfelt and kind,
> Hath made me treasure up thy poetry;
> But now I dare not, for thy abject life,
> Make manifest that I approve thy rhymes.

And when Dante meets Beatrice in Eden, does she not reproach him because, when she had taken her presence away, he followed, in spite of warning dreams, false images, and now, to save him in his own despite, she has 'visited . . . the Portals of the Dead', and chosen Virgil for his courier? While Gino da Pistoia complains that in his *Commedia* his 'lovely heresies . . . beat the right down and let the wrong go free':

Therefore his vain decrees, wherein he lied,
Must be like empty nutshells flung aside;
Yet through the rash false witness set to grow,
French and Italian vengeance on such pride
May fall like Antony on Cicero.

Dante himself sings to Giovanni Guirino 'at the approach of death':

The King, by whose rich grave his servants be
With plenty beyond measure set to dwell,
Ordains that I my bitter wrath dispel,
And lift mine eyes to the great Consistory.

V

We make out of the quarrel with others, rhetoric, but of the quarrel with ourselves, poetry. Unlike the rhetoricians, who get a confident voice from remembering the crowd they have won or may win, we sing amid our uncertainty; and, smitten even in the presence of the most high beauty by the knowledge of our solitude, our rhythm shudders. I think, too, that no fine poet, no matter how disordered his life, has ever, even in his mere life, had pleasure for his end. Johnson and Dowson, friends of my youth, were dissipated men, the one a drunkard, the other a drunkard and mad about women, and yet they had the gravity of men who had found life out and were awakening from the dream; and both, one in life and art and one in art and less in life, had a continual preoccupation with religion. Nor has any poet I have read of or heard of or met with been a sentimentalist. The other self, the anti-self or the antithetical self, as one may choose to name it, comes but to those who are no longer deceived, whose passion is reality. The sentimentalists are practical men who believe in money, in position, in a marriage bell, and whose understanding of happiness is to be so busy whether at work or at play that all is forgotten but the momentary aim. They find their pleasure in a cup that is filled from Lethe's wharf, and for the awakening, for the vision, for the revelation of reality, tradition offers us a different word — ecstasy. An old artist wrote to me of his wanderings by the quays of New York, and how he found there a woman nursing a sick child, and drew her story from her. She spoke, too, of other children who had died: a long tragic story. 'I wanted to paint her,' he wrote; 'if I denied myself any of the pain I could not believe in my own ecstasy.' We must not make a false faith by hiding from our thoughts the causes of doubt, for faith is the highest achievement of the human intellect, the only gift man can make to God, and therefore it must be offered in sincerity. Neither must we create, by hiding ugliness, a false beauty as our offering to the world. He only can create the greatest imaginable beauty who has endured all imaginable pangs, for only when we have seen and foreseen what we dread shall we be rewarded by that dazzling, unforeseen, wing-footed wanderer. We could not find him if he were not in some sense of our being, and yet of our being but as water with fire, a noise with silence. He is of all things not impossible the most difficult, for that only which comes easily can never be a portion of our being; 'soon got, soon gone', as the proverb says. I shall find the dark grow luminous, the void fruitful when I understand I have nothing, that the ringers in the tower have appointed for the hymen of the soul a passing bell.

The last knowledge has often come most quickly to turbulent men, and for a season brought new turbulence. When life puts away her conjuring tricks one by one, those that deceive us longest may well be the wine-cup and the sensual kiss, for our Chambers of Commerce and of Commons have not the divine architecture of the body, nor has their frenzy been ripened by the sun. The poet, because he may not stand within the sacred house but lives amid the whirlwinds that beset its threshold, may find his pardon.

VI

I think the Christian saint and hero, instead of being merely dissatisfied, make deliberate sacrifice. I remember reading once an autobiography of a man who had made a daring journey in disguise to Russian exiles in Siberia, and his telling how, very timid as a child, he schooled himself by wandering at night through dangerous streets. Saint and hero cannot be content to pass at moments to that hollow image and after become their heterogeneous selves, but would always, if they could, re-semble the antithetical self. There is a shadow of type on type, for in all great poetical styles there is saint or hero, but when it is all over Dante can return to his chambering and Shakespeare to his 'pottle-pot'. They sought no impossible perfection but when they handled paper or parchment. So too will saint or hero, because he works in his own flesh and blood and not in paper or parchment, have more deliberate understanding of that other flesh and blood.

Some years ago I began to believe that our culture, with its doctrine of sincerity and self-realisation, made us gentle and passive, and that the Middle Ages and the Renaissance were right to found theirs upon the imitation of Christ or of some classic hero. Saint Francis and Caesar Borgia made themselves overmastering, creative persons by turning from the mirror to meditation upon a mask. When I had this thought I could see nothing else in life. I could not write the play I had planned, for all became allegorical, and though I tore up hundreds of pages in my endeavour to escape from allegory, my imagina-tion became sterile for nearly five years and I only escaped at last when I had mocked in a comedy my own thought. I was always thinking of the element of imitation in style and in life, and of the life beyond heroic imitation. I find in an old diary: 'I think all happiness depends on the energy to assume the mask of some other life, on a re-birth as something not one's self, something created in a moment and perpetually renewed; in playing a game like that of a child where one loses the infinite pain of self-realisation, in a grotesque or solemn painted face put on that one may hide from the terror of judgment. ... Perhaps all the sins and energies of the world are but the world's flight from an infinite blinding beam'; and again at an earlier date: 'If we cannot imagine ourselves as different from what we are, and try to assume that second self, we cannot impose a discipline upon ourselves though we may accept one from others. Active virtue, as distinguished from the passive acceptance of a code, is therefore theatrical, consciously dramatic, the wearing of a mask. ... Wordsworth, great poet though he be, is so often flat and heavy partly because his moral sense, being a discipline he had not created, a mere obedience, has no theatrical element. This increases his popularity with the better kind of journalists and politicians who have written books.'

VII

I thought the hero found hanging upon some oak of Dodona an ancient mask, where perhaps there lingered something of Egypt, and that he changed it to his fancy, touching it a little here and there, gilding the eyebrows or putting a gilt line where the cheek-bone comes; that when at last he looked out of its eyes he knew another's breath came and went within his breath upon the carven lips, and that his eyes were upon the instant fixed upon a visionary world: how else could the god have come to us in the forest? The good, unlearned books

say that He who keeps the distant stars within His fold comes
without intermediary, but Plutarch's precepts and the experience of old women in Soho, ministering their witchcraft to
servant-girls at a shilling apiece, will have it that a strange
living man may win for Daimon[1] an illustrious dead man; but
now I add another thought: the Daimon comes not as like to
like but seeking its own opposite, for man and Daimon feed
the hunger in one another's hearts. Because the ghost is simple,
the man heterogeneous and confused, they are but knit together when the man has found a mask whose lineaments permit the expression of all the man most lacks, and it may be
dreads, and of that only.

The more insatiable in all desire, the more resolute to refuse
deception or an easy victory, the more close will be the bond,
the more violent and definite the antipathy.

VIII

I think that all religious men have believed that there is a
hand not ours in the events of life, and that, as somebody says
in *Wilhelm Meister*, accident is destiny; and I think it was
Heraclitus who said: the Daimon is our destiny. When I think
of life as a struggle with the Daimon who would ever set us
to the hardest work among those not impossible, I understand
why there is a deep enmity between a man and his destiny,
and why a man loves nothing but his destiny. In an Anglo-
Saxon poem a certain man is called, as though to call him
something that summed up all heroism, 'Doom eager'. I am
persuaded that the Daimon delivers and deceives us, and that
he wove that netting from the stars and threw the net from his

[1] I could not distinguish at the time between the permanent Daimon
and the impermanent, who may be 'an illustrious dead man', though I
knew the distinction was there. I shall deal with the matter in *A Vision*.
                                                        February 1924.

shoulder. Then my imagination runs from Daimon to sweet-heart, and I divine an analogy that evades the intellect. I remember that Greek antiquity has bid us look for the principal stars, that govern enemy and sweetheart alike, among those that are about to set, in the Seventh House as the astrologers say; and that it may be 'sexual love', which is 'founded upon spiritual hate', is an image of the warfare of man and Daimon; and I even wonder if there may not be some secret communion, some whispering in the dark between Daimon and sweetheart. I remember how often women when in love grow superstitious, and believe that they can bring their lovers good luck; and I remember an old Irish story of three young men who went seeking for help in battle into the house of the gods at Slieve-na-mon. 'You must first be married,' some god told them, 'because a man's good or evil luck comes to him through a woman.'

I sometimes fence for half an hour at the day's end, and when I close my eyes upon the pillow I see a foil playing before me, the button to my face. We meet always in the deep of the mind, whatever our work, wherever our reverie carries us, that other Will.

IX

The poets finds and makes his mask in disappointment, the hero in defeat. The desire that is satisfied is not a great desire, nor has the shoulder used all its might that an unbreakable gate has never strained. The saint alone is not deceived, neither thrusting with his shoulder nor holding out unsatisfied hands. He would climb without wandering to the antithetical self of the world, the Indian narrowing his thought in meditation or driving it away in contemplation, the Christian copying Christ, the antithetical self of the classic world. For a hero loves the world till it breaks him, and the poet till it has broken faith; but while the world was yet debonair, the saint has turned away, and because he renounced experience itself, he will wear his mask as he finds it. The poet or the hero, no matter upon what bark they found their mask, so teeming their fancy, somewhat change its lineaments, but the saint, whose life is but a round of customary duty, needs nothing the whole world does not need, and day by day he scourges in his body the Roman and Christian conquerors: Alexander and Caesar are famished in his cell. His nativity is neither in disappointment nor in defeat, but in a temptation like that of Christ in the Wilderness, a contemplation in a single instant perpetually renewed of the Kingdoms of the World; all — because all renounced — continually present showing their empty thrones. Edwin Ellis, remembering that Christ also measured the sacrifice, imagined himself in a fine poem as meeting at Golgotha the phantom of 'Christ the Less', the Christ who might have lived a prosperous life without the knowledge of sin, and who now wanders 'companionless, a weary spectre day and night'.

> I saw him go and cried to him,
> 'Eli, thou hast forsaken me.'
> The nails were burning through each limb,
> He fled to find felicity.

And yet is the saint spared — despite his martyr's crown and his vigil of desire — defeat, disappointed love, and the sorrow of parting.

> O Night, that didst lead thus,
> O Night, more lovely than the dawn of light,
> O Night, that broughtest us
> Lover to lover's sight,
> Lover with loved in marriage of delight!

Upon my flowery breast,
Wholly for him, and save himself for none,
There did I give sweet rest
To my beloved one;
The fanning of the cedars breathed thereon.

When the first morning air
Blew from the tower, and waved his locks aside,
His hand, with gentle care,
Did wound me in the side,
And in my body all my senses died.

All things I then forgot,
My cheek on him who for my coming came;
All ceased and I was not,
Leaving my cares and shame
Among the lilies, and forgetting them.[1]

X

It is not permitted to a man who takes up pen or chisel, to seek originality, for passion is his only business, and he cannot but mould or sing after a new fashion because no disaster is like another. He is like those phantom lovers in the Japanese play who, compelled to wander side by side and never mingle, cry: 'We neither wake nor sleep and, passing our nights in a sorrow which is in the end a vision, what are these scenes of spring to us?' If when we have found a mask we fancy that it will not match our mood till we have touched with gold the cheek, we do it furtively, and only where the oaks of Dodona cast their deepest shadow, for could he see our handiwork the Daimon would fling himself out, being our enemy.

[1] Translated by Arthur Symons from 'San Juan de la Cruz'.

XI

Many years ago I saw, between sleeping and waking, a
woman of incredible beauty shooting an arrow into the sky,
and from the moment when I made my first guess at her
meaning I have thought much of the difference between the
winding movement of Nature and the straight line, which is
called in Balzac's *Séraphita* the 'Mark of Man', but is better
described as the mark of saint or sage. I think that we who are
poets and artists, not being permitted to shoot beyond the
tangible, must go from desire to weariness and so to desire
again, and live but for the moment when vision comes to our
weariness like terrible lightning, in the humility of the brutes.
I do not doubt those heaving circles, those winding arcs,
whether in one man's life or in that of an age, are mathematical, and that some in the world, or beyond the world,
have foreknown the event and pricked upon the calendar the
life-span of a Christ, a Buddha, a Napoleon: that every movement, in feeling or in thought, prepares in the dark by its own
increasing clarity and confidence its own executioner. We
seek reality with the slow toil of our weakness and are smitten
from the boundless and the unforeseen. Only when we are
saint or sage, and renounce experience itself, can we, in
imagery of the Christian Cabbala, leave the sudden lightning
and the path of the serpent and become the bowman who aims
his arrow at the centre of the sun.

XII

The doctors of medicine have discovered that certain
dreams of the night, for I do not grant them all, are the day's
unfulfilled desire, and that our terror of desires condemned by
the conscience has distorted and disturbed our dreams. They
have only studied the breaking into dream of elements that

have remained unsatisfied without purifying discouragement. We can satisfy in life a few of our passions and each passion but a little, and our characters indeed but differ because no two men bargain alike. The bargain, the compromise, is always threatened, and when it is broken we become mad or hysterical or are in some way deluded; and so when a starved or banished passion shows in a dream we, before awaking, break the logic that had given it the capacity of action and throw it into chaos again. But the passions, when we know that they cannot find fulfilment, become vision; and a vision, whether we wake or sleep, prolongs its power by rhythm and pattern, the wheel where the world is butterfly. We need no protection, but it does, for if we become interested in ourselves, in our own lives, we pass out of the vision. Whether it is we or the vision that create the pattern, who set the wheel turning, it is hard to say, but certainly we have a hundred ways of keeping it near us: we select our images from past times, we turn from our own age and try to feel Chaucer nearer than the daily paper. It compels us to cover all it cannot incorporate, and would carry us when it comes in sleep to that moment when even sleep closes her eyes and dreams begin to dream; and we are taken up into a clear light and are forgetful even of our own names and actions and yet in perfect possession of ourselves murmur like Faust, 'Stay, moment', and murmur in vain.

XIII

A poet, when he is growing old, will ask himself if he cannot keep his mask and his vision without new bitterness, new disappointment. Could he if he would, knowing how frail his vigour from youth up, copy Landor who lived loving and hating, ridiculous and unconquered, into extreme old age, all lost but the favour of his Muses?

A PEOPLE'S THEATRE[1]

A LETTER TO LADY GREGORY

I

My dear Lady Gregory — Of recent years you have done all that is anxious and laborious in the supervision of the Abbey Theatre and left me free to follow my own thoughts. It is therefore right that I address to you this letter, wherein I shall explain, half for your ears, half for other ears, certain thoughts that have made me believe that the Abbey Theatre can never do all we had hoped. We set out to make a 'People's Theatre', and in that we have succeeded. But I did not know until very lately that there are certain things, dear to both our hearts, which no 'People's Theatre' can accomplish.

II

All exploitation of the life of the wealthy, for the eye and the ear of the poor and half-poor, in plays, in popular novels, in musical comedy, in fashion papers, at the cinema, in *Daily Mirror* photographs, is a travesty of the life of the rich; and if it were not would all but justify some Red Terror; and it impoverishes and vulgarises the imagination, seeming to hold up for envy and to commend a life where all is display and hurry, passion without emotion, emotion without intellect,

---

[1] I took the title from a book by Romain Rolland on some French theatrical experiments. 'A People's Theatre' is not quite the same thing as 'A Popular Theatre'. The essay was published in the *Irish Statesman* in the autumn of 1919.—1923.

and where there is nothing stern and solitary. The plays and novels are the least mischievous, for they still have the old-fashioned romanticism — their threepenny bit, if worn, is silver yet — but they are without intensity and intellect and cannot convey the charm of either as it may exist in those they would represent. All this exploitation is a rankness that has grown up recently among us and has come out of an historical necessity that has made the furniture and the clothes and the brains, of all but the leisured and the lettered, copies and travesties.

Shakespeare set upon the stage kings and queens, great historical or legendary persons about whom there is nothing unreal except the circumstance of their lives which remain vague and summary, because he could only write his best — his mind and the mind of his audience being interested in emotion and intellect at their moment of union and at their greatest intensity — when he wrote of those who controlled the mechanism of life. Had they been controlled by it, intellect and emotion entangled by intricacy and detail could never have mounted to that union which, as Swedenborg said of the marriage of the angels, is a conflagration of the whole being. But since great crowds, changed by popular education with its eye always on some objective task, have begun to find reality in mechanism alone,[1] our popular commercial art has substituted for Lear and Cordelia the real millionaire and the real peeress, and seeks to make them charming by insisting perpetually that they have all that wealth can buy, or rather all that average men and women would buy if they had wealth. Shakespeare's groundlings watched the stage in terrified sympathy, while the British working-man looks perhaps at the

[1] I have read somewhere statistics that showed how popular education has coincided with the lessening of Shakespeare's audience. In every chief town before it began Shakespeare was constantly played.

photographs of these lords and ladies, whom he admires beyond measure, with the pleasant feeling that they will all be
robbed and murdered before he dies.

III

Then, too, that turning into ridicule of peasant and citizen
and all lesser men could but increase our delight when the
great personified spiritual power, but seems unnatural when
the great are but the rich. During an illness lately I read two
popular novels which I had borrowed from the servants. They
were good stories and half consoled me for the sleep I could
not get, but I was a long time before I saw clearly why everybody with less than a thousand a year was a theme of comedy
and everybody with less than five hundred a theme of farce.
Even Rosencrantz and Guildenstern, courtiers and doubtless
great men in their world, could be but foils for Hamlet because Shakespeare had nothing to do with objective truth, but
we who have nothing to do with anything else, in so far as we
are of our epoch, must not allow a greater style to corrupt us.

An artisan or a small shopkeeper feels, I think, when he sees
upon our Abbey stage men of his own trade, that they are
represented as he himself would represent them if he had the
gift of expression. I do not mean that he sees his own life ex-
pounded there without exaggeration, for exaggeration is selection and the more passionate the art the more marked is the
selection, but he does not feel that he has strayed into some
other man's seat. If it is comedy he will laugh at ridiculous
people, people in whose character there is some contortion,
but their station of life will not seem ridiculous. The best
stories I have listened to outside the theatre have been told me
by farmers or sailors when I was a boy, one or two by fellow-
travellers in railway carriages, and most had some quality of
romance, romance of a class and its particular capacity for

adventure; and our theatre is a people's theatre in a sense which no mere educational theatre can be, because its plays are to some extent a part of that popular imagination. It is very seldom that a man or woman bred up among the propertied or professional classes knows any class but his own, and that a class which is much the same all over the world, and already written of by so many dramatists that it is nearly impossible to see its dramatic situations with our own eyes, and those dramatic situations are perhaps exhausted — as Nietzsche thought the whole universe would be some day — and nothing left but to repeat the same combinations over again.

When the Abbey Manager sends us a play for our opinion and it is my turn to read it, if the handwriting of the MS. or of the author's accompanying letter suggests a leisured life I start prejudiced. There will be no fresh observation of character, I think, no sense of dialogue, all will be literary secondhand, at best what Rossetti called the 'soulless self-reflections of man's skill'. On the other hand, until the Abbey plays began themselves to be copied, a handwriting learned in a National School always made me expect dialogue written out by some man who had admired good dialogue before he had seen it upon paper. The construction would probably be bad, for there the student of plays has the better luck, but plays made impossible by rambling and redundance have often contained some character or some dialogue that has stayed in my memory for years. At first there was often vulgarity, and there still is in those comic love scenes which we invariably reject, and there is often propaganda with all its distortion, but these weigh light when set against life seen as if newly created. At first, in face of your mockery, I used to recommend some reading of Ibsen or Galsworthy, but no one has benefited by that reading or by anything but the Abbey audience and our own rejection of all gross propaganda and gross imitation of the comic column in the newspapers. Our dramatists, and I am not speaking of your work or Synge's but of those to whom you and Synge and I gave an opportunity, have been excellent just in so far as they have become all eye and ear, their minds not smoking lamps, as at times they would have wished, but clear mirrors.

Our players, too, have been vivid and exciting because they have copied a life personally known to them, and of recent years, since our Manager has had to select from the ordinary stage-struck young men and women who have seen many players and perhaps no life but that of the professional class, it has been much harder, though players have matured more rapidly, to get the old, exciting, vivid playing. I have never recovered the good opinion of one recent Manager because I urged him to choose instead some young man or woman from some little shop who had never given his or her thoughts to the theatre. 'Put all the names into a hat,' I think I said, 'and pick the first that comes.' One of our early players was exceedingly fine in the old woman in *Riders to the Sea*. 'She has never been to Aran, she knows nothing but Dublin, surely in that part she is not objective, surely she creates from imagination,' I thought; but when I asked her she said, 'I copied from my old grandmother.' Certainly it is this objectivity, this making of all from sympathy, from observation, never from passion, from lonely dreaming; that has made our players, at their best, great comedians, for comedy is passionless.

We have been the first to create a true 'People's Theatre', and we have succeeded because it is not an exploitation of local colour, or of a limited form of drama possessing a temporary novelty, but the first doing of something for which the world is ripe, something that will be done all over the world and done more and more perfectly: the making articulate of all the dumb classes each with its own knowledge of the world, its own dignity, but all objective with the objectivity of the office and the workshop, of the newspaper and the street, of mechanism and of politics.

IV

Yet we did not set out to create this sort of theatre, and its success has been to me a discouragement and a defeat. Dante in that passage in the *Convito* which is, I think, the first passage of poignant autobiography in literary history, for there is nothing in Saint Augustine not formal and abstract beside it, in describing his poverty and his exile counts as his chief misfortune that he has had to show himself to all Italy and so publish his human frailties that men who honoured him unknown honour him no more. Lacking means, he had lacked seclusion, and he explains that men such as he should have but few and intimate friends. His study was unity of being, the subordination of all parts to the whole as in a perfectly proportioned human body — his own definition of beauty — and not, as with those I have described, the unity of things in the world; and like all subjectives he shrank, because of what he was, because of what others were, from contact with many men. Had he written plays he would have written from his own thought and passion, observing little and using little, if at all, the conversation of his time — and whether he wrote in verse or in prose his style would have been distant, musical, metaphorical, moulded by antiquity. We stand on the margin between wilderness and wilderness, that which we observe through our senses and that which we can experience only, and our art is always the description of one or the other. If our art is mainly from experience we have need of learned speech, of agreed symbols, because all those things whose names renew experience have accompanied that experience already many times. A personage in one of Turgenev's novels is reminded by the odour of, I think, heliotrope, of some sweetheart that had worn it, and poetry is any flower that brings a memory of emotion, while an unmemoried flower is prose, and a flower pressed and named and numbered science; but our poetical heliotrope need bring to mind no sweetheart of ours, for it suffices that it crowned the bride of Paris, or Peleus' bride. Neither poetry nor any subjective art can exist but for those who do in some measure share its traditional knowledge, a knowledge learned in leisure and contemplation. Even Burns, except in those popular verses which are as lacking in tradition, as modern, as topical, as Longfellow, was, as Henley said, not the founder but the last of a dynasty.

Once such men could draw the crowd because the circumstance of life changed slowly and there was little to disturb contemplation, and so men repeated old verses and old stories, and learned and simple had come to share in common much allusion and symbol. Where the simple were ignorant they were ready to learn and so became receptive, or perhaps even to pretend knowledge like the clowns in the mediaeval poem that describes the arrival of Chaucer's Pilgrims at Canterbury, who that they may seem gentlemen pretend to know the legends in the stained-glass windows. Shakespeare, more objective than Dante — for, alas, the world must move —, was still predominantly subjective, and he wrote during the latest crisis of history that made possible a theatre of his kind. There were still among the common people many traditional songs and stories, while Court and University, which were much more important to him, had an interest Chaucer never shared in great dramatic persons, in those men and women of Plutarch, who made their death a ritual of passion; for what is passion but the straining of man's being against some obstacle that obstructs its unity?

You and I and Synge, not understanding the clock, set out
to bring again the theatre of Shakespeare or rather perhaps of
Sophocles. I had told you how at Young Ireland Societies and
the like, young men when I was twenty had read papers to
one another about Irish legend and history, and you yourself
soon discovered the Gaelic League, then but a new weak thing,
and taught yourself Irish. At Spiddal or near it an inn-keeper
had sung us Gaelic songs, all new village work that though
not literature had *naïveté* and sincerity. The writers, caring
nothing for cleverness, had tried to express emotion, tragic or
humorous, and great masterpieces, *The Grief of a Girl's Heart*,
for instance, had been written in the same speech and manner
and were still sung. We know that the songs of the Thames
boatmen, to name but these, in the age of Queen Elizabeth had
the same relation to great masterpieces. These Gaelic songs
were as unlike as those to the songs of the music-hall with
their clever ear-catching rhythm, the work of some mind as
objective as that of an inventor or of a newspaper reporter.
We thought we could bring the old folk-life to Dublin,
patriotic feeling to aid us, and with the folk-life all the life of
the heart, understanding heart, according to Dante's definition, as the most interior being; but the modern world is more
powerful than any propaganda or even than any special circumstance, and our success has been that we have made a
Theatre of the head, and persuaded Dublin playgoers to think
about their own trade or profession or class and their life
within it, so long as the stage curtain is up, in relation to Ireland as a whole. For certain hours of an evening they have
objective modern eyes.

v

The objective nature and the subjective are mixed in different proportion as are the shadowed and the bright parts in the

lunar phases. In Dante there was little shadow, in Shakespeare a larger portion, while you and Synge, it may be, resemble the moon when it has just passed its third quarter, for you have constant humour — and humour is of the shadowed part — much observation and a speech founded upon that of real life. You and he will always hold our audience, but both have used so constantly a measure of lunar light, have so elaborated style and emotion, an individual way of seeing, that neither will ever, till a classic and taught in school, find a perfect welcome.

The outcry against *The Playboy* was an outcry against its style, against its way of seeing; and when the audience called Synge 'decadent' — a favourite reproach from the objective everywhere — it was but troubled by the stench of its own burnt cakes. How could they that dreaded solitude love that which solitude had made? And never have I heard any that laugh the loudest at your comedies praise that musical and delicate style that makes them always a fit accompaniment for verse and sets them at times among the world's great comedies. Indeed, the louder they laugh the readier are they to rate them with the hundred ephemeral farces they have laughed at and forgotten. Synge they have at least hated. When you and Synge find such an uneasy footing, what shall I do there who have never observed anything, or listened with an attentive ear, but value all I have seen or heard because of the emotions they call up or because of something they remind me of that exists, as I believe, beyond the world? O yes, I am listened to — am I not a founder of the Theatre? — and here and there scattered solitaries delight in what I have made and return to hear it again; but some young Corkman, all eyes and ears, whose first rambling play we have just pulled together or half together, can do more than that. He will be played by players who have spoken dialogue like his every night for years, and sentences that it had been a bore to read will so delight the whole house that to keep my hands from clapping I shall have to remind myself that I gave my voice for the play's production and must not applaud my own judgment.

VI

I want to create for myself an unpopular theatre and an audience like a secret society where admission is by favour and never to many. Perhaps I shall never create it, for you and I and Synge have had to dig the stone for our statue and I am aghast at the sight of a new quarry, and besides I want so much — an audience of fifty, a room worthy of it (some great dining-room or drawing-room), half a dozen young men and women who can dance and speak verse or play drum and flute and zither, and all the while, instead of a profession, I but offer them 'an accomplishment'. However, there are my *Four Plays for Dancers* as a beginning, some masks by Mr. Dulac, music by Mr. Dulac and by Mr. Rummell. In most towns one can find fifty people for whom one need not build all on observation and sympathy, because they read poetry for their pleasure and understand the traditional language of passion. I desire a mysterious art, always reminding and half-reminding those who understand it of dearly loved things, doing its work by suggestion, not by direct statement, a complexity of rhythm, colour, gesture, not space-pervading like the intellect, but a memory and a prophecy: a mode of drama Shelley and Keats could have used without ceasing to be themselves, and for which even Blake in the mood of *The Book of Thel* might not have been too obscure. Instead of advertisements in the Press I need a hostess, and even the most accomplished hostess must choose with more than usual care, for I have noticed that city-living cultivated people, those whose names would first occur to her, set great value on painting, which is a form of property, and on music, which is a part of the organisation of life, while the lovers of literature, those who read a book many times, are either young men with little means or live far away from big towns.

What alarms me most is how a new art needing so elaborate a technique can make its first experiments before those who, as Molière said of the courtiers of his day, have seen so much. How shall our singers and dancers be welcomed by those who have heard Chaliapin in all his parts and who know all the dances of the Russians? Yet where can I find Mr. Dulac and Mr. Rummel or any to match them, but in London[1] or in Paris, and who but the leisured will welcome an elaborate art or pay for its first experiments? In one thing the luck might be upon our side. A man who loves verse and the visible arts has, in a work such as I imagined, the advantage of the professional player. The professional player becomes the amateur, the other has been preparing all his life, and certainly I shall not soon forget the rehearsal of *At the Hawk's Well*, when Mr. Ezra Pound, who had never acted on any stage, in the absence of our chief player rehearsed for half an hour. Even the forms of subjective acting that were natural to the professional stage have ceased. Where all now is sympathy and observation no Irving can carry himself with intellectual pride, nor any Salvini in half-animal nobility, both wrapped in solitude.

I know that you consider Ireland alone our business, and in that we do not differ, except that I care very little where a play of mine is first played so that it find some natural audience and good players. My rooks may sleep abroad in the fields for a while, but when the winter comes they will remember the

[1] I live in Dublin now, and indolence and hatred of travel will probably compel me to make my experiment there after all.—1923.

way home to the rookery trees. Indeed, I have Ireland especially in mind, for I want to make, or to help some man some day to make, a feeling of exclusiveness, a bond among chosen spirits, a mystery almost for leisured and lettered people. Ireland has suffered more than England from democracy, for since the Wild Geese fled, who might have grown to be leaders in manners and in taste, she has had but political leaders. As a drawing is defined by its outline and taste by its rejections, I too must reject and draw an outline about the thing I seek; and say that I seek, not a theatre but the theatre's anti-self, an art that can appease all within us that becomes uneasy as the curtain falls and the house breaks into applause.

VII

Meanwhile the Popular Theatre should grow always more objective; more and more a reflection of the general mind; more and more a discovery of the simple emotions that make all men kin, clearing itself the while of sentimentality, the wreckage of an obsolete popular culture, seeking always not to feel and to imagine but to understand and to see. Let those who are all personality, who can only feel and imagine, leave it, before their presence become a corruption and turn it from its honesty. The rhetoric of D'Annunzio, the melodrama and spectacle of the later Maeterlinck, are the insincerities of subjectives, who being very able men have learned to hold an audience that is not their natural audience. To be intelligible they are compelled to harden, to externalise and deform. The popular play left to itself may not lack vicissitude and development, for it may pass, though more slowly than the novel which need not carry with it so great a crowd, from the physical objectivity of Fielding and Defoe to the spiritual objectivity of Tolstoi and Dostoievsky, for beyond the whole we reach by unbiassed intellect there is another whole reached by resignation and the denial of self.

VIII

The two great energies of the world that in Shakespeare's day penetrated each other have fallen apart as speech and music fell apart at the Renaissance, and that has brought each to greater freedom, and we have to prepare a stage for the whole wealth of modern lyricism, for an art that is close to pure music, for those energies that would free the arts from imitation, that would ally acting to decoration and to the dance. We are not yet conscious, for as yet we have no philosophy, while the opposite energy is conscious. All visible history, the discoveries of science, the discussions of politics, are with it; but as I read the world, the sudden changes, or rather the sudden revelations of future changes, are not from visible history but from its anti-self. Blake says somewhere in a 'Prophetic Book' that things must complete themselves before they pass away, and every new logical development of the objective energy intensifies in an exact correspondence a counter-energy, or rather adds to an always deepening unanalysable longing. That counter-longing, having no visible past, can only become a conscious energy suddenly, in those moments of revelation which are as a flash of lightning. Are we approaching a supreme moment of self-consciousness, the two halves of the soul separate and face to face? A certain friend of mine has written upon this subject a couple of intricate poems called *The Phases of the Moon* and *The Double Vision* respectively, which are my continual study, and I must refer the reader to these poems for the necessary mathematical calculations. Were it not for that other gyre turning inward in exact measure with the outward whirl of its fellow, we would

fall in a generation or so under some tyranny that would cease
at last to be a tyranny, so perfect our acquiescence.

> Constrained, arraigned, baffled, bent and unbent
> By these wire-jointed jaws and limbs of wood,
> Themselves obedient,
> Knowing not evil and good;
>
> Obedient to some hidden magical breath.
> They do not even feel, so abstract are they,
> So dead beyond our death,
> Triumph that we obey.

[1919]

THE IRISH DRAMATIC MOVEMENT

A LECTURE DELIVERED TO THE ROYAL ACADEMY
OF SWEDEN

YOUR ROYAL HIGHNESS, ladies and gentlemen, I have chosen as my theme the Irish Dramatic Movement, because when I remember the great honour that you have conferred upon me, I cannot forget many known and unknown persons. Perhaps the English committees would never have sent you my name if I had written no plays, no dramatic criticism, if my lyric poetry had not a quality of speech practised upon the stage, perhaps even — though this could be no portion of their deliberate thought — if it were not in some degree the symbol of a movement. I wish to tell the Royal Academy of Sweden of the labours, triumphs and troubles of my fellow-workers.

The modern literature of Ireland, and indeed all that stir of thought which prepared for the Anglo-Irish war, began when Parnell fell from power in 1891. A disillusioned and embittered Ireland turned from parliamentary politics; an event was conceived; and the race began, as I think, to be troubled by that event's long gestation. Dr. Hyde founded the Gaelic League, which was for many years to substitute for political argument a Gaelic grammar, and for political meetings village gatherings, where songs were sung and stories told in the Gaelic language. Meanwhile I had begun a movement in English, in the language in which modern Ireland thinks and does its business; founded certain societies where clerks, working men, men of all classes, could study the Irish poets, novelists and historians who had written in English, and as much of Gaelic literature as had been translated into English. But the great mass of our people, accustomed to interminable political speeches, read little, and so from the very start we felt that we must have a theatre of our own. The theatres of Dublin had nothing about them that we could call our own. They were empty buildings hired by the English travelling companies, and we wanted Irish plays and Irish players. When we thought of these plays we thought of everything that was romantic and poetical, because the nationalism we had called up — the nationalism every generation had called up in moments of discouragement — was romantic and poetical. It was not, however, until I met in 1896 Lady Gregory, a member of an old Galway family, who had spent her life between two Galway houses, the house where she was born, the house into which she married, that such a theatre became possible. All about her lived a peasantry who told stories in a form of English which has much of its syntax from Gaelic, much of its vocabulary from Tudor English, but it was very slowly that we discovered in that speech of theirs our most powerful dramatic instrument, not indeed until she herself began to write. Though my plays were written without dialect and in English blank verse, I think she was attracted to our movement because their subject-matter differed but little from the subject-matter of the country stories. Her own house has been protected by her presence, but the house where she was born was burned down by incendiaries some few months ago, and there has been like disorder over the greater part of Ireland. A trumpery dispute about an acre of land can rouse our people to monstrous savagery, and if in their war with the English auxiliary police they were shown no mercy, they showed none: murder answered murder. Yet their ignorance and violence can remember the noblest beauty. I have in Galway a little old tower, and when I climb to the top of it I can see at no great distance a green field where stood once the thatched cottage of a famous country beauty, the mistress of a small local landed proprietor. I have spoken to old men and women who remembered her, though all are dead now, and they spoke of her as the old men upon the wall of Troy spoke of Helen, nor did man and woman differ in their praise. One old woman of whose youth the neighbours cherished a scandalous tale said of her, 'I tremble all over when I think of her'; and there was another on the neighbouring mountain who said, 'The sun and the moon never shone on anybody so handsome, and her skin was so white that it looked blue, and she had two little blushes on her cheeks'. And there were men that told of the crowds that gathered to look at her upon a fair day, and of a man 'who got his death swimming a river', that he might look at her. It was a song written by the Gaelic poet Raftery that brought her such great fame, and the cottages still sing it, though there are not so many to sing it as when I was young:

> O star of light and O sun in harvest,
> O amber hair, O my share of the world,
> It is Mary Hynes, the calm and easy woman,
> Has beauty in her body and in her mind.

It seemed as if the ancient world lay all about us with its freedom of imagination, its delight in good stories, in man's force and woman's beauty, and that all we had to do was to make the town think as the country felt; yet we soon discovered that the town would only think town thoughts.

In the country you are alone with your own violence, your own ignorance and heaviness, and with the common tragedy of life, and if you have any artistic capacity you desire beautiful emotion; and, certain that the seasons will be the same always, care not how fantastic its expression. In the town, where everybody crowds upon you, it is your neighbour not yourself that you hate, and if you are not to embitter his life and your own life, perhaps even if you are not to murder him in some kind of revolutionary frenzy, somebody must teach reality and justice. You will hate that teacher for a while, calling his books and plays ugly, misdirected, morbid, or something of that kind, but you must agree with him in the end. We were to find ourselves in a quarrel with public opinion that compelled us against our own will and the will of our players to become always more realistic, substituting dialect for verse, common speech for dialect.

I had told Lady Gregory that I saw no likelihood of getting money for a theatre and so must put away that hope, and she promised to find the money among her friends. Her neighbour, Mr. Edward Martyn, paid for our first performances; and our first players came from England; but presently we began our real work with a company of Irish amateurs. Somebody had asked me at a lecture, 'Where will you get your actors?' and I had said, 'I will go into some crowded room, put the name of everybody in it on a different piece of paper, put all those pieces of paper into a hat and draw the first twelve'. I have often wondered at that prophecy, for though it was spoken probably to confound and confuse a questioner it was very nearly fulfilled. Our two best men actors were not indeed chosen by chance, for one was a stage-struck solicitors' clerk and the other a working man who had toured Ireland in a theatrical company managed by a Negro. I doubt if he had learned much in it, for its methods were rough and noisy, the Negro whitening his face when he played a white man, but, so strong is stage convention, blackening it when he played a black man. If a player had to open a letter on the stage I have no doubt that he struck it with the flat of his hand, as I have seen players do in my youth, a gesture that lost its meaning generations ago when blotting-paper was substituted for sand.

We got our women, however, from a little political society which described its object as educating the children of the poor, or, according to its enemies, teaching them a catechism that began with this question, 'What is the origin of evil?' and the answer, 'England'.

And they came to us for patriotic reasons and acted from precisely the same impulse that had made them teach, and yet two of them proved players of genius, Miss Allgood and Miss Maire O'Neill. They were sisters, one all simplicity, her mind shaped by folk-song and folk-story; the other sophisticated, lyrical and subtle. I do not know what their thoughts were as that strange new power awoke within them, but I think they must have suffered from a bad conscience, a feeling that the patriotic impulse had gone, that they had given themselves up to vanity or ambition. Yet I think it was that first misunderstanding of themselves made their peculiar genius possible, for had they come to us with theatrical ambitions they would have imitated some well-known English player and sighed for well-known English plays. Nor would they have found their genius if we had not remained for a long time obscure like the bird within its shell, playing in little halls, generally in some shabby out-of-the-way street. We could experiment and wait, with nothing to fear but political misunderstanding. We had little money and at first needed little, twenty-five pounds given by Lady Gregory and twenty pounds by myself and a few pounds picked up here and there. And our theatrical organisation was preposterous, players and authors all sitting together and settling by vote what play should be performed and who should play it. It took a series of disturbances, weeks of argument during which no performance could be given, before Lady Gregory and John Synge and I were put in control. And our relations with the public were even more disturbed. One play was violently attacked by the patriotic

Press because it described a married peasant woman who had
a lover, and when we published the old Aran folk-tale upon
which it was founded the Press said the tale had reached Aran
from some decadent author of pagan Rome. Presently Lady
Gregory wrote her first comedy. My verse plays were not
long enough to fill an evening and so she wrote a little play on
a country love story in the dialect of her neighbourhood. A
countryman returns from America with a hundred pounds
and discovers his old sweetheart married to a bankrupt
farmer. He plays cards with the farmer, and by cheating
against himself gives him the hundred pounds. The company
refused to perform it because they said to admit an emigrant's
return with a hundred pounds would encourage emigration.
We produced evidence of returned emigrants with much
larger sums, but were told that only made the matter worse.
Then after interminable argument had worn us all out Lady
Gregory agreed to reduce the sum to twenty, and the actors
gave way. That little play was sentimental and conventional,
but her next discovered her genius. She too had desired
to serve, and that genius must have seemed miraculous to
herself. She was in middle life, and had written nothing but
a volume of political memoirs and had no interest in the
theatre.

Nobody reading today her *Seven Short Plays* can understand
why one of them, now an Irish classic, *The Rising of the Moon*,
could not be performed for two years because of political hostility. A policeman discovers an escaped Fenian prisoner and
lets him free, because the prisoner has aroused with some old
songs the half-forgotten patriotism of his youth. The players
would not perform it because they said it was an unpatriotic
act to admit that a policeman was capable of patriotism. One
well-known leader of the mob wrote to me, 'How can the
Dublin mob be expected to fight the police if it looks upon

them as capable of patriotism?' When performed at last the play was received with enthusiasm, but only to get us into new trouble. The chief Unionist Dublin newspaper denounced us for slandering His Majesty's forces, and Dublin Castle denied to us a privilege which we had shared with the other Dublin theatres of buying, for stage purposes, the cast-off clothes of the police. Castle and Press alike knew that the police had frequently let off political prisoners, but 'that only made the matter worse'. Every political party had the same desire to substitute for life, which never does the same thing twice, a bundle of reliable principles and assertions. Nor did religious orthodoxy like us any better than political; my *Countess Cathleen* was denounced by Cardinal Logue as an heretical play, and when I wrote that we would like to perform 'foreign masterpieces' a Nationalist newspaper declared that 'a foreign masterpiece is a very dangerous thing'. The little halls where we performed could hold a couple of hundred people at the utmost and our audience was often not more than twenty or thirty, and we performed but two or three times a month, and during our periods of quarrelling not even that. But there was no lack of leading articles, we were from the first a recognized public danger. Two events brought us victory: a friend gave us a theatre, and we found a strange man of genius, John Synge. After a particularly angry leading article I had come in front of the curtain and appealed to the hundred people of the audience for their support. When I came down from the stage an old friend, Miss Horniman, from whom I had been expecting a contribution of twenty pounds, said, 'I will find you a theatre'. She found and altered for our purpose what is now the Abbey Theatre, Dublin, and gave us a small subsidy for a few years.

I had met John Synge in Paris in 1896. Somebody had said, 'There is an Irishman living on the top floor of your hotel; I will introduce you'. I was very poor, but he was much poorer. He belonged to a very old Irish family and, though a simple courteous man, remembered it and was haughty and lonely. With just enough to keep him from starvation and not always from half-starvation, he had wandered about Europe, travelling third-class or upon foot, playing his fiddle to poor men on the road or in their cottages. He was the man that we needed, because he was the only man I have ever known incapable of a political thought or of a humanitarian purpose. He could walk the roadside all day with some poor man without any desire to do him good or for any reason except that he liked him. He was to do for Ireland, though more by his influence on other dramatists than by his direct influence, what Robert Burns did for Scotland. When Scotland thought herself gloomy and religious, Providence restored her imaginative spontaneity by raising up Robert Burns to commend drink and the Devil. I did not, however, see what was to come when I advised John Synge to go to a wild island off the Galway coast and study its life because that life 'had never been expressed in literature'. He had learned Gaelic at College and I told him that, as I would have told it to any young man who had learned Gaelic and wanted to write. When he found that wild island he became happy for the first time, escaping, as he said, 'from the nullity of the rich and the squalor of the poor'. He had bad health, he could not stand the island hardship long, but he would go to and fro between there and Dublin.

Burns himself could not have more shocked a gathering of Scots clergy than did he our players. Some of the women got about him and begged him to write a play about the rebellion of '98, and pointed out very truthfully that a play on such a patriotic theme would be a great success. He returned at the end of a fortnight with a scenario upon which he had toiled in his laborious way. Two women take refuge in a cave, a Protestant woman and a Catholic, and carry on an interminable argument about the merits of their respective religions. The Catholic woman denounces Henry VIII and Queen Elizabeth, and the Protestant woman the Inquisition and the Pope. They argue in low voices, because one is afraid of being ravished by the rebels and the other by the loyal soldiers. But at last either the Protestant or the Catholic says that she prefers any fate to remaining any longer in such wicked company and climbs out. The play was neither written nor performed, and neither then nor at any later time could I discover whether Synge understood the shock that he was giving. He certainly did not foresee in any way the trouble that his greatest play brought on us all.

When I had landed from a fishing yawl on the middle of the island of Aran, a few months before my first meeting with Synge, a little group of islanders, who had gathered to watch a stranger's arrival, brought me to 'the oldest man upon the island'. He spoke but two sentences, speaking them very slowly: 'If any gentleman has done a crime we'll hide him. There was a gentleman that killed his father, and I had him in my house six months till he got away to America.' It was a play founded on that old man's story Synge brought back with him. A young man arrives at a little public-house and tells the publican's daughter that he has murdered his father. He so tells it that he has all her sympathy, and every time he retells it, with new exaggerations and additions, he wins the sympathy of somebody or other, for it is the countryman's habit to be against the law. The countryman thinks the more terrible the crime, the greater must the provocation have been. The young man himself, under the excitement of his own story, becomes gay, energetic and lucky. He prospers in love, comes in first at the local races, and bankrupts the roulette

tables afterwards. Then the father arrives with his head ban-
daged but very lively, and the people turn upon the impostor.
To win back their esteem he takes up a spade to kill his father
in earnest, but, horrified at the threat of what had sounded so
well in the story, they bind him to hand over to the police.
The father releases him and father and son walk off together,
the son, still buoyed up by his imagination, announcing that
he will be master henceforth. Picturesque, poetical, fantastical,
a masterpiece of style and of music, the supreme work of our
dialect theatre, his *Playboy* roused the populace to fury. We
played it under police protection, seventy police in the theatre
the last night, and five hundred, some newspaper said, keeping
order in the streets outside. It is never played before any Irish
audience for the first time without something or other being
flung at the players. In New York a currant cake and a watch
were flung, the owner of the watch claiming it at the stage
door afterwards. The Dublin audience has, however, long
since accepted the play. It has noticed, I think, that everyone
upon the stage is somehow lovable and companionable, and
that Synge has described, through an exaggerated symbolism,
a reality which he loved precisely because he loved all reality.
So far from being, as they had thought, a politician working
in the interests of England, he was so little a politician that the
world merely amused him and touched his pity. Yet when
Synge died in 1909 opinion had hardly changed, we were
playing to an almost empty theatre and were continually denounced. Our victory was won by those who had learned
from him courage and sincerity but belonged to a different
school. Synge's work, the work of Lady Gregory, my own
Cathleen ni Houlihan and my *Hour-Glass* in its prose form, are
characteristic of our first ambition. They bring the imagination and speech of the country, all that poetical tradition descended from the Middle Ages, to the people of the town.

Those who learned from Synge had often little knowledge of the country and always little interest in its dialect. Their plays are frequently attacks upon obvious abuses, the bribery at the appointment of a dispensary Doctor, the attempts of some local politician to remain friends with all parties. Indeed the young Ministers and party politicians of the Free State have had, I think, some of their education from our plays. Then, too, there are many comedies which are not political satires though they are concerned with the life of the politics-ridden people of the town. Of these Mr. Lennox Robinson's are the best known; his *Whiteheaded Boy* has been played in England and America. Of late it has seemed as if this school were coming to an end, for the old plots are repeated with slight variations and the characterisation grows mechanical. It is too soon yet to say what will come to us from the melodrama and tragedy of the last four years, but if we can pay our players and keep our theatre open something will come. We are burdened with debt, for we have come through war and civil war and audiences grow thin when there is firing in the streets. We have, however, survived so much that I believe in our luck, and think that I have a right to say my lecture ends in the middle or even, perhaps, at the beginning of the story. But certainly I have said enough to make you understand why, when I received from the hands of your King the great honour your Academy has conferred upon me, I felt that a young man's ghost should have stood upon one side of me and at the other a living woman sinking into the infirmity of age. Indeed I have seen little in this last week that would not have been memorable and exciting to Synge and to Lady Gregory, for Sweden has achieved more than we have hoped for our own country. I think most of all, perhaps, of that splendid spectacle of your Court, a family beloved and able that has gathered about it not the rank only but the intellect of its

INTRODUCTION TO FIGHTING THE WAVES

I WROTE *The Only Jealousy of Emer* for performance in a private house or studio, considering it, for reasons which I have explained, unsuited to a public stage. Then somebody put it on a public stage in Holland and Hildo van Krop made his powerful masks. Because the dramatist who can collaborate with a great sculptor is lucky, I rewrote the play not only to fit it for such a stage but to free it from abstraction and confusion. I have retold the story in prose which I have tried to make very simple, and left imaginative suggestion to dancers, singers, musicians. I have left the words of the opening and closing lyrics unchanged, for sung to modern music in the modern way they suggest strange patterns to the ear without obtruding upon it their difficult, irrelevant words. The masks get much of their power from enclosing the whole head; this makes the head out of proportion to the body, and I found some difference of opinion as to whether this was a disadvantage or not in an art so distant from reality; that it was not a disadvantage in the case of the Woman of the Sidhe all were agreed. She was a strange, noble, unforgettable figure.

I do not say that it is always necessary when one writes for a general audience to make the words of the dialogue so simple and so matter-of-fact; but it is necessary where the appeal is mainly to the eye and to the ear through songs and music. *Fighting the Waves* is in itself nothing, a mere occasion for sculptor and dancer, for the exciting dramatic music of George Antheil.

II

'It is that famous man Cuchulain. . . .' In the eighties of the last century Standish O'Grady, his mind full of Homer, re-told the story of Cuchulain that he might bring back an heroic ideal. His work, which founded modern Irish literature, was hasty and ill-constructed, his style marred by imitation of Carlyle; twenty years later Lady Gregory translated the whole body of Irish heroic legend into the dialect of the cottages in those great books *Cuchulain of Muirthemne* and *Gods and Fighting Men*, her eye too upon life. In later years she often quoted the saying of Aristotle: 'To think like a wise man, but express oneself like the common people,' and always her wise man was heroic man. Synge wrote his *Deirdre of the Sorrows* in peasant dialect, but died before he had put the final touches to anything but the last act, the most poignant and noble in Irish drama. I wrote in blank verse, which I tried to bring as close to common speech as the subject permitted, a number of con-nected plays — *Deirdre*, *At the Hawk's Well*, *The Green Helmet*, *On Baile's Strand*, *The Only Jealousy of Emer*. I would have attempted the Battle of the Ford and the Death of Cuchulain, had not the mood of Ireland changed.

III

When Parnell was dragged down, his shattered party gave itself up to nine years' vituperation, and Irish imagination fled the sordid scene. A. E.'s *Homeward Songs by the Way*; Padraic Colum's little songs of peasant life; my own early poems; Lady Gregory's comedies, where, though the dramatic tension is always sufficient, the worst people are no wickeder than children; Synge's *Well of the Saints* and *Playboy of the Western World*, where the worst people are the best company, were as typical of that time as Lady Gregory's translations. Repelled by what had seemed the sole reality, we had turned to romantic dreaming, to the nobility of tradition.

About 1909 the first of the satirists appeared, 'The Cork Realists', we called them, men that had come to maturity amidst spite and bitterness. Instead of turning their backs upon the actual Ireland of their day, they attacked everything that had made it possible, and in Ireland and among the Irish in England made more friends than enemies by their attacks. James Joyce, the son of a small Parnellite organiser, had begun to write, but remained unpublished.

> An age is the reversal of an age;
> When strangers murdered Emmet, Fitzgerald, Tone,
> We lived like men that watch a painted stage.
> What matter for the scene, the scene once gone!
> It had not touched our lives; but popular rage,
> *Hysterica passio*, dragged this quarry down.
> None shared our guilt; nor did we play a part
> Upon a painted stage when we devoured his heart.

But even if there had been no such cause of bitterness, of self-contempt, we could not, considering that every man everywhere is more of his time than of his nation, have long kept the attention of our small public, no, not with the whole support, and that we never had, of the Garrets and Cellars. Only a change in European thought could have made that possible. When Stendhal described a masterpiece as a 'mirror dawdling down a lane', he expressed the mechanical philosophy of the French eighteenth century. Gradually literature conformed to his ideal; Balzac became old-fashioned; romanticism grew theatrical in its strain to hold the public; till, by the end of the nineteenth century, the principal characters in the most famous books were the passive analysts of events, or had been brutalised into the likeness of mechanical objects. But Europe is changing its philosophy. Some four years ago the Russian Government silenced the mechanists because social dialectic is impossible if matter is trundled about by some limited force. Certain typical books — *Ulysses*, Virginia Woolf's *The Waves*, Mr. Ezra Pound's *Draft of XXX Cantos* — suggest a philosophy like that of the *Samkara* school of ancient India, mental and physical objects alike material, a deluge of experience breaking over us and within us, melting limits whether of line or tint; man no hard bright mirror dawdling by the dry sticks of a hedge, but a swimmer, or rather the waves themselves. In this new literature announced with much else by Balzac in *Le Chef-d'œuvre inconnu*, as in that which it superseded, man in himself is nothing.

IV

I once heard Sir William Crookes tell half a dozen people that he had seen a flower carried in broad daylight slowly across the room by what seemed an invisible hand. His chemical research led to the discovery of radiant matter, but the science that shapes opinion has ignored his other research that seems to those who study it the slow preparation for the greatest, perhaps the most dangerous, revolution in thought Europe has seen since the Renaissance, a revolution that may, perhaps, establish the scientific complement of certain philosophies that in all ancient countries sustained heroic art. We may meet again, not the old simple celebration of life tuned to the highest pitch, neither Homer nor the Greek dramatists, something more deliberate than that, more systematised, more external, more self-conscious, as must be at a second coming, Plato's Republic, not the Siege of Troy.

I shall remind the Garrets and Cellars of certain signs, that they may, as a Chinese philosopher has advised, shape things at their beginning, when it is easy, not at the end, when it is difficult. I first name Mr. Sacheverell Sitwell's lovely 'Pastoral'; point out that he has celebrated those Minoan shepherds, those tamers of the wild bulls, their waists enclosed from childhood in wide belts of bronze, that they might attain wasp-like elegance; that he prefers them to the natural easy Sicilian shepherds, preferring as it were cowboys to those that 'watched their flocks by night'; then Dr. Gogarty's praise of 'the Submarine Men trained through a lifetime'; and remind them of their own satisfaction in that praise. Then they might, after considering the demand of the black, brown, green, and blue shirts, 'Power to the most disciplined', ask themselves whether D'Annunzio and his terrible drill at Fiume may not prove as symbolic as Shelley, whose art and life became so completely identified with romantic contemplation that young men in their late teens, when I was at that age, identified him with poetry itself.

Here in Ireland we have come to think of self-sacrifice, when worthy of public honour, as the act of some man at the moment when he is least himself, most completely the crowd. The heroic act, as it descends through tradition, is an act done because a man is himself, because, being himself, he can ask nothing of other men but room amid remembered tragedies; a sacrifice of himself to himself, almost, so little may he bargain, of the moment to the moment. I think of some Elizabethan play where, when mutineers threaten to hang the ship's captain, he replies: 'What has that to do with me?' So lonely is that ancient act, so great the pathos of its joy, that I have never been able to read without tears a passage in *Sigurd the Volsung* describing how the new-born child lay in the bed and looked 'straight on the sun'; how the serving-women washed him, bore him back to his mother, wife of the dead Sigmund; how 'they shrank in their rejoicing before the eyes

of the child.'; 'the best sprung from the best'; how though
'the spring morn smiled . . . the hour seemed awful to them'.

> But Hiordis looked on the Volsung,
>   on her grief and her fond desire.
> And the hope of her heart was quickened,
>   and her heart was a living fire;
> And she said: 'Now one of the earthly
>   on the eyes of my child hath gazed
> Nor shrunk before their glory,
>   nor stayed her love amazed:
> I behold thee as Sigmund beholdeth, —
>   and I was the home of thine heart —
> Woe's me for the day when thou wert not,
>   And the hour when we shall part!'

How could one fail to be moved in the presence of the central mystery of the faith of poets, painters, and athletes? I am
carried forty years back and hear a famous old athlete wind up
a speech to country lads — 'The holy people have above them
the communion of saints; we the communion of the *Tuatha de
Danaan* of Erin.'

Science has driven out the legends, stories, superstitions that
protected the immature and the ignorant with symbol, and
now that the flower has crossed our rooms, science must take
their place and demonstrate as philosophy has in all ages, that
States are justified, not by multiplying or, as it would seem,
comforting those that are inherently miserable, but because
sustained by those for whom the hour seems 'awful', and by
those born out of themselves, the best born of the best.

Since my twentieth year, these thoughts have been in my
mind, and now that I am old I sing them to the Garrets and
the Cellars:

Move upon Newton's town,
The town of Hobbes and of Locke,
Pine, spruce, come down
Cliff, ravine, rock:
What can disturb the corn?
What makes its shudder and bend?
The rose brings her thorn,
The Absolute walks behind.

V

Yet it may be that our science, our modern philosophy,
keep a subconscious knowledge that their raft, roped together
at the end of the seventeenth century, must, if they so much as
glance at that slow-moving flower, part and abandon us to the
storm, or it may be, as Professor Richet suggests at the end of
his long survey of psychical research from the first experiments of Sir William Crookes to the present moment, that all
it can do is, after a steady scrutiny, to prove the poverty of the
human intellect, that we are lost amid alien intellects, near but
incomprehensible, more incomprehensible than the most distant stars. We may, whether it scrutinise or not, lacking its
convenient happy explanations, plunge as Rome did in the
fourth century according to some philosopher of that day into
'a fabulous, formless darkness'.

Should H. G. Wells afflict you,
Put whitewash in a pail;
Paint: 'Science — opium of the suburbs'
On some waste wall.

VI

'First I must cover up his face, I must hide him from the
sea.' I am deeply grateful for a mask with the silver glitter of a

fish, for a dance with an eddy like that of water, for music that suggested, not the vagueness, but the rhythm of the sea. A Dublin journalist showed his scorn for 'the new paganism' by writing: 'Mr. Yeats' play is not really original, for something of the kind doubtless existed in Ancient Babylon,' but a German psycho-analyst has traced the 'mother complex' back to our mother the sea — after all, Babylon was a modern inland city — to the loneliness of the first crab or crayfish that climbed ashore and turned lizard; while Gemistus Plethon not only substituted the sea for Adam and Eve, but, according to a friend learned in the Renaissance, made it symbolise the garden's ground or first original, 'that concrete universal which all philosophy is seeking'.

VII

'Everything he loves must fly,' everything he desires; Emer too must renounce desire, but there is another love, that which is like the man-at-arms in the Anglo-Saxon poem, 'doom eager'. Young, we discover an opposite through our love; old, we discover our love through some opposite neither hate nor despair can destroy, because it is another self, a self that we have fled in vain.

1932

ON D. H. LAWRENCE

[These two extracts are from letters to Olivia Shakespear, 22 and 25 May, 1933.]

... My two sensations at the moment are Hulme's *Speculations* and *Lady Chatterley's Lover*. The first in an essay called *Modern Art* relates such opposites as *The Apes of God* and *Lady Chatterley*. Get somebody to lend you the last if you have not read it. Frank Harris's *Memoirs* are vulgar and immoral — the sexual passages were like holes burnt with a match in a piece of old newspaper; their appeal to physical sensation was hateful; but *Lady Chatterley* is noble. Its description of the sexual act is more detailed than in Harris, the language is sometimes that of cabmen and yet the book is all fire. Those two lovers, the gamekeeper and his employer's wife, each separated from their class by their love, and by fate, are poignant in their loneliness, and the coarse language of the one, accepted by both, becomes a forlorn poetry uniting their solitudes, something ancient, humble and terrible ...

... Of course Lawrence is an emphasis directed against modern abstraction. I find the whole book interesting and not merely the sexual parts. They are something that he sets up as against the abstraction of an age that he thinks dead from the waist downward. Of course happiness is not where he seems to place it. We are happy when for everything inside us there is an equivalent something outside us. I think it was Goethe said this. One should add the converse. It is terrible to desire and not possess, and terrible to possess and not desire. Because of this we long for an age which has the unity which Plato somewhere defined as sorrowing and rejoicing over the same things. How else escape the Bank Holiday crowd?

I have bought a suit of rough blue serge.

Yours,

W. B. Yeats.

Read *Twenty Years a-Growing* or some of it. I once told you that you would be happy if you had twelve children and lived on limpets. There are limpets on the Great Blasket.

INTRODUCTION TO THE OXFORD
BOOK OF MODERN VERSE

III

Then in 1900 everybody got down off his stilts; henceforth
nobody drank absinthe with his black coffee; nobody went
mad; nobody committed suicide; nobody joined the Catholic
church; or if they did I have forgotten.

Victorianism had been defeated, though two writers
dominated the moment who had never heard of that defeat
or did not believe in it; Rudyard Kipling and William Watson. Indian residence and associations had isolated the first,
he was full of opinions, of politics, of impurities — to use our
word — and the word must have been right, for he interests a
critical audience to-day by the grotesque tragedy of 'Danny
Deever', the matter but not the form of old street ballads,
and by songs traditional in matter and form like the 'St.
Helena Lullaby'. The second had reached maturity before the
revolt began, his first book had been published in the early
eighties. 'Wring the neck of rhetoric' Verlaine had said, and
the public soon turned against William Watson, forgetting
that at his best he had not rhetoric but noble eloquence. As I
turn his pages I find verse after verse read long ago and still
unforgettable, this to some journalist who, intoxicated perhaps by William Archer's translations from Ibsen, had
described, it may be, some lyric elaborating or deepening its
own tradition as of 'no importance to the age':

Great Heaven! When these with clamour shrill
  Drift out to Lethe's harbour bar
A verse of Lovelace shall be still
  As vivid as a pulsing star:

this, received from some Miltonic cliff that had it from a
Roman voice:

The august, inhospitable, inhuman night
Glittering magnificently unperturbed.

IV

Conflict bequeathed its bias. Folk-song, unknown to the
Victorians as their attempts to imitate it show, must, because
never declamatory or eloquent, fill the scene. If anybody will
turn these pages attending to poets born in the 'fifties, 'sixties,
and 'seventies, he will find how successful are their folk-
songs and their imitations. In Ireland, where still lives almost
undisturbed the last folk tradition of western Europe, the
songs of Campbell and Colum draw from that tradition their
themes, return to it, and are sung to Irish airs by boys and
girls who have never heard the names of the authors; but the
reaction from rhetoric, from all that was prepense and
artificial, has forced upon these writers now and again, as
upon my own early work, a facile charm, a too soft simplicity. In England came like temptations. *The Shropshire Lad*
is worthy of its fame, but a mile further and all had been
marsh. Thomas Hardy, though his work lacked technical
accomplishment, made the necessary correction through his
mastery of the impersonal objective scene. John Synge
brought back masculinity to Irish verse with his harsh disillusionment, and later, when the folk movement seemed to

support vague political mass excitement, certain poets began
to create passionate masterful personality.

V

We remembered the Gaelic poets of the seventeenth and
early eighteenth centuries wandering, after the flight of the
Catholic nobility, among the boorish and the ignorant,
singing their loneliness and their rage; James Stephens, Frank
O'Connor made them symbols of our pride:

> The periwinkle, and the tough dog-fish
> At eventide have got into my dish!
> The great, where are they now! the great had said —
> This is not seemly, bring to him instead
> That which serves his and serves our dignity —
> And that was done.

> I am O'Rahilly:
> Here in a distant place I hold my tongue,
> Who once said all his say, when he was young!

I showed Lady Gregory a few weeks before her death a book
by Day Lewis. 'I prefer,' she said, 'those poems translated by
Frank O'Connor because they come out of original sin.' A
distinguished Irish poet said a month back — I had read him a
poem by Turner — 'We cannot become philosophic like the
English, our lives are too exciting.' He was not thinking of
such where public life is simple and exciting. We are not
many; Ireland has had few poets of any kind outside Gaelic.
I think England has had more good poets from 1900 to the
present day than during any period of the same length since
the early seventeenth century. There are no predominant
figures, no Browning, no Tennyson, no Swinburne, but more

than I have found room for have written two, three, or half a
dozen lyrics that may be permanent.

During the first years of the century the best known were
celebrators of the country-side or of the life of ships; I think
of Davies and of Masefield; some few wrote in the manner of
the traditional country ballad. Others, descended not from
Homer but from Virgil, wrote what the young communist
scornfully calls 'Belles-lettres': Binyon when at his best, as I
think, of Tristram and Isoult: Sturge Moore of centaurs,
amazons, gazelles copied from a Persian picture: De la Mare
short lyrics that carry us back through *Christabel* or *Kubla
Khan*.

> Through what wild centuries
> Roves back the rose?

The younger of the two ladies who wrote under the name of
'Michael Field' made personal lyrics in the manner of
Walter Savage Landor and the Greek anthology.

None of these were innovators; they preferred to keep all
the past their rival; their fame will increase with time. They
have been joined of late years by Sacheverell Sitwell with his
Canons of Giant Art, written in the recently rediscovered
'sprung verse', his main theme changes of colour, or historical
phase, in Greece, Crete, India. *Agamemnon's Tomb*, however,
describes our horror at the presence and circumstance of
death and rises to great intensity.

VII

Robert Bridges seemed for a time, through his influence
on Laurence Binyon and others less known, the patron saint
of the movement. His influence — practice, not theory — was
never deadening; he gave to lyric poetry a new cadence, a
distinction as deliberate as that of Whistler's painting, an

impulse moulded and checked like that in certain poems of Landor, but different, more in the nerves, less in the blood, more birdlike, less human; words often commonplace made unforgettable by some trick of speeding and slowing,

> A glitter of pleasure
> And a dark tomb,

or by some trick of simplicity, not the impulsive simplicity of youth but that of age, much impulse examined and rejected:

> I heard a linnet courting
>   His lady in the spring!
> His mates were idly sporting,
>   Nor stayed to hear him sing
>   His song of love. —
> I fear my speech distorting
>   His tender love.

Every metaphor, every thought a commonplace, emptiness everywhere, the whole magnificent.

VIII

A modern writer is beset by what Rossetti called 'the soulless self-reflections of man's skill'; the more vivid his nature, the greater his boredom, a boredom no Greek, no Elizabethan, knew in like degree, if at all. He may escape to the classics with the writers I have just described, or with much loss of self-control and coherence force language against its will into a powerful, artificial vividness. Edith Sitwell has a temperament of a strangeness so high-pitched that only through this artifice could it find expression. One cannot think of her in any other age or country. She has transformed

with her metrical virtuosity traditional metres reborn not to
be read but spoken, exaggerated metaphors into mythology,
carrying them from poem to poem, compelling us to go
backward to some first usage for the birth of the myth; if the
storm suggest the bellowing of elephants, some later poem
will display 'The elephant trunks of the sea'. Nature appears
before us in a hashish-eater's dream. This dream is double;
in its first half, through separated metaphor, through mythology, she creates, amid crowds and scenery that suggest the
Russian Ballet and Aubrey Beardsley's final phase, a perpetual
metamorphosis that seems an elegant, artificial childhood; in
the other half, driven by a necessity of contrast, a nightmare
vision like that of Webster, of the emblems of mortality. A
group of writers have often a persistent image. There are
'stars' in poem after poem of certain writers of the 'nineties
as though to symbolize an aspiration towards what is inviolate and fixed; and now in poem after poem by Edith
Sitwell or later writers are 'bones' — 'the anguish of the
skeleton', 'the terrible Gehenna of the bone'; Eliot has:

> No contact possible to flesh
> Allayed the fever of the bone.

and Elinor Wylie, an American whose exquisite work is
slighter than that of her English contemporaries because she
has not their full receptivity to the profound hereditary sadness
of English genius:

> Live like the velvet mole:
> Go burrow underground,
> And there hold intercourse
> With roots of trees and stones,
> With rivers at their source
> And disembodied bones.

Laurence Binyon, Sturge Moore, knew nothing of this image; it seems most persistent among those who, throwing aside tradition, seek something somebody has called 'essential form' in the theme itself. A fairly well-known woman painter in September drew my house, at that season almost hidden in foliage; she reduced the trees to skeletons as though it were mid-winter, in pursuit of 'essential form'. Does not intellectual analysis in one of its moods identify man with that which is most persistent in his body? The poets are haunted once again by the Elizabethan image, but there is a difference. Since Poincaré said 'space is the creation of our ancestors', we have found it more and more difficult to separate ourselves from the dead when we commit them to the grave; the bones are not dead but accursed, accursed because unchanging.

> The small bones built in the womb
> The womb that loathed the bones
> And cast out the soul.

Perhaps in this new, profound poetry, the symbol itself is contradictory, horror of life, horror of death.

IX

Eliot has produced his great effect upon his generation because he has described men and women that get out of bed or into it from mere habit; in describing this life that has lost heart his own art seems grey, cold, dry. He is an Alexander Pope, working without apparent imagination, producing his effects by a rejection of all rhythms and metaphors used by the more popular romantics rather than by the discovery of his own, this rejection giving his work an unexaggerated plainness that has the effect of novelty. He has the rhythmical flatness of *The Essay on Man* — despite Miss Sitwell's advocacy

I see Pope as Blake and Keats saw him — later, in *The Waste Land*, amid much that is moving in symbol and imagery there is much monotony of accent:

> When lovely woman stoops to folly and
> Paces about her room again, alone,
> She smooths her hair with automatic hand,
> And put a record on the gramophone.

I was affected, as I am by these lines, when I saw for the first time a painting by Manet. I longed for the vivid colour and light of Rousseau and Courbet, I could not endure the grey middle-tint — and even to-day Manet gives me an incomplete pleasure; he had left the procession. Nor can I put the Eliot of these poems among those that descend from Shakespeare and the translators of the Bible. I think of him as satirist rather than poet. Once only does that early work speak in the great manner:

> The host with someone indistinct
> Converses at the door apart,
> The nightingales are singing near
> The Convent of the Sacred Heart,
>
> And sang within the bloody wood
> When Agamemnon cried aloud,
> And let their liquid siftings fall
> To stain the stiff dishonoured shroud.

Not until *The Hollow Men* and *Ash-Wednesday*, where he is helped by the short lines, and in the dramatic poems where his remarkable sense of actor, chanter, scene, sweeps him away, is there rhythmical animation. Two or three of my friends attribute the change to an emotional enrichment from religion, but his religion compared to that of John Gray, Francis

Thompson, Lionel Johnson in *The Dark Angel*, lacks all strong
emotion; a New England Protestant by descent, there is little
self-surrender in his personal relation to God and the soul.
Murder in the Cathedral is a powerful stage play because the
actor, the monkish habit, certain repeated words, symbolise
what we know, not what the author knows. Nowhere has
the author explained how Becket and the King differ in aim;
Becket's people have been robbed and persecuted in his
absence; like the King he demands strong government.
Speaking through Becket's mouth Eliot confronts a world
growing always more terrible with a religion like that of some
great statesman, a pity not less poignant because it tempers the
prayer book with the results of mathematical philosophy.

> Peace. And let them be, in their exaltation.
> They speak better than they know, and beyond your
>   understanding,
> They know and do not know, that acting is suffering
> And suffering is action. Neither does the actor suffer
> Nor the patient act. But both are fixed
> In an eternal action, an eternal patience
> To which all must consent that it may be willed
> And which all must suffer that they may will it,
> That the pattern may subsist, for the pattern is the action
> And the suffering, that the wheel may turn and still
> Be forever still.

X

Ezra Pound has made flux his theme; plot, characterisation,
logical discourse, seem to him abstractions unsuitable to a man
of his generation. He is mid-way in an immense poem in *vers
libre* called for the moment *The Cantos*, where the metamorphosis of Dionysus, the descent of Odysseus into Hades,

repeat themselves in various disguises, always in association with some third that is not repeated. Hades may become the hell where whatever modern men he most disapproves of suffer damnation, the metamorphosis petty frauds practised by Jews at Gibraltar. The relation of all the elements to one another, repeated or unrepeated, is to become apparent when the whole is finished. There is no transmission through time, we pass without comment from ancient Greece to modern England, from modern England to medieval China; the symphony, the pattern, is timeless, flux eternal and therefore without movement. Like other readers I discover at present merely exquisite or grotesque fragments. He hopes to give the impression that all is living, that there are no edges, no convexities, nothing to check the flow; but can such a poem have a mathematical structure? Can impressions that are in part visual, in part metrical, be related like the notes of a symphony; has the author been carried beyond reason by a theoretical conception? His belief in his own conception is so great that since the appearance of the first Canto I have tried to suspend judgment.

When I consider his work as a whole I find more style than form; at moments more style, more deliberate nobility and the means to convey it than in any contemporary poet known to me, but it is constantly interrupted, broken, twisted into nothing by its direct opposite, nervous obsession, nightmare, stammering confusion; he is an economist, poet, politician, raging at malignants with inexplicable characters and motives, grotesque figures out of a child's book of beasts. This loss of self-control, common among uneducated revolutionists, is rare — Shelley had it in some degree — among men of Ezra Pound's culture and erudition. Style and its opposite can alternate, but form must be full, sphere-like, single. Even where there is no interruption he is often content, if certain

verses and lines have style, to leave unbridged transitions,
unexplained ejaculations, that make his meaning unintelligible.
He has great influence, more perhaps than any contemporary
except Eliot, is probably the source of that lack of form and
consequent obscurity which is the main defect of Auden, Day
Lewis, and their school, a school which, as will presently be
seen, I greatly admire. Even where the style is sustained
throughout one gets an impression, especially when he is
writing in *vers libre*, that he has not got all the wine into the
bowl, that he is a brilliant improvisator translating at sight
from an unknown Greek masterpiece:

> See, they return; ah, see the tentative
> Movements, and the slow feet,
> The trouble in the pace and the uncertain
> Wavering!
>
> See, they return, one, and by one,
> With fear, as half-awakened;
> As if the snow should hesitate
> And murmur in the wind,
>   and half turn back;
>
> These were the Wing'd-with-awe,
>   Inviolable.
> Gods of the winged shoe!
> With them the silver hounds,
>   sniffing the trace of air!

XI

When my generation denounced scientific humanitarian
pre-occupation, psychological curiosity, rhetoric, we had not
found what ailed Victorian literature. The Elizabethans had all

these things, especially rhetoric. A friend writes 'all bravado went out of English literature when Falstaff turned into Oliver Cromwell, into England's bad conscience'; but he is wrong. Dryden's plays are full of it. The mischief began at the end of the seventeenth century when man became passive before a mechanised nature; that lasted to our own day with the exception of a brief period between Smart's *Song of David* and the death of Byron, wherein imprisoned man beat upon the door. Or I may dismiss all that ancient history and say it began when Stendhal described a masterpiece as a 'mirror dawdling down a lane'. There are only two long poems in Victorian literature that caught public attention; *The Ring and the Book* where great intellect analyses the suffering of one passive soul, weighs the persecutor's guilt, and *The Idylls of the King* where a poetry in itself an exquisite passivity is built about an allegory where a characterless king represents the soul. I read few modern novels, but I think I am right in saying that in every novel that has created an intellectual fashion from Huysmans's *La Cathédrale* to Ernest Hemingway's *Farewell to Arms*, the chief character is a mirror. It has sometimes seemed of late years, though not in the poems I have selected for this book, as if the poet could at any moment write a poem by recording the fortuitous scene or thought, perhaps it might be enough to put into some fashionable rhythm — 'I am sitting in a chair, there are three dead flies on a corner of the ceiling.'

Change has come suddenly, the despair of my friends in the 'nineties part of its preparation. Nature, steel-bound or stone-built in the nineteenth century, became a flux where man drowned or swam; the moment had come for some poet to cry 'the flux is in my own mind'.

XII

It was Turner who raised that cry, to gain upon the instant
a control of plastic material, a power of emotional construction, Pound has always lacked. At his rare best he com-
petes with Eliot in precision, but Eliot's genius is human,
mundane, impeccable, it seems to say 'this man will never
disappoint, never be out of character. He moves among
objects for which he accepts no responsibility, among the
mapped and measured.' Generations must pass before man
recovers control of event and circumstance; mind has recognised its responsibility, that is all; Turner himself seems the
symbol of an incomplete discovery. After clearing up some
metaphysical obscurity he leaves obscure what a moment's
thought would have cleared; author of a suave, sophisticated
comedy he can talk about 'snivelling majorities'; a rich-
natured friendly man he has in his satirical platonic dialogue
The Aesthetes shot upon forbidden ground. The first romantic
poets, Blake, Coleridge, Shelley, dazed by new suddenly
opening vistas, had equal though different inconsistencies.
I think of him as the first poet to read a mathematical equation,
a musical score, a book of verse, with an equal understanding;
he seems to ride in an observation balloon, blue heaven above,
earth beneath an abstract pattern.

We know nothing but abstract patterns, generalisations,
mathematical equations, though such the havoc wrought by
newspaper articles and government statistics, two abstractions
may sit down to lunch. But what about the imagery we call
nature, the sensual scene? Perhaps we are always awake and
asleep at the same time; after all going to bed is but a habit;
is not sleep by the testimony of the poets our common
mother? In *The Seven Days of the Sun*, where there is much
exciting thought, I find:

But to me the landscape is like a sea
The waves of the hills
And the bubbles of bush and flower
And the springtide breaking into white foam!

It is a slow sea,
Mare tranquillum,
And a thousand years of wind
Cannot raise a dwarf billow to the moonlight.

But the bosom of the landscape lifts and falls
With its own leaden tide,
That tide whose sparkles are the lilliputian stars.

It is that slow sea
That sea of adamantine languor,
Sleep!

I recall Pater's description of the Mona Lisa; had the
individual soul of da Vinci's sitter gone down with the pearl
divers or trafficked for strange webs? or did Pater foreshadow
a poetry, a philosophy, where the individual is nothing, the
flux of *The Cantos* of Ezra Pound, objects without contour
as in *Le Chef-d'œuvre Inconnu,* human experience no longer
shut into brief lives, cut off into this place and that place, the
flux of Turner's poetry that within our minds enriches itself,
re-dreams itself, yet only in seeming — for time cannot be
divided? Yet one theme perplexes Turner, whether in
comedy, dialogue, poem. Somewhere in the middle of it all
da Vinci's sitter had private reality like that of the Dark Lady
among the women Shakespeare had imagined, but because
that private soul is always behind our knowledge, though
always hidden it must be the sole source of pain, stupefaction,
evil. A musician, he imagines Heaven as a musical com-

position, a mathematician, as a relation of curves, a poet, as a dark, inhuman sea.

> The sea carves innumerable shells
> Rolling itself into crystalline curves
> The cressets of its faintest sighs
> Flickering into filigreed whorls,
> Its lustre into mother-of-pearl
> Its mystery into fishes' eyes
> Its billowing abundance into whales
> Around and under the Poles.

XIII

In *The Mutations of the Phoenix* Herbert Read discovers that the flux is in the mind, not of it perhaps, but in it. The Phoenix is finite mind rising in a nest of light from the sea or infinite; the discovery of Berkeley in 'Siris' where light is 'perception', of Grosseteste, twelfth-century philosopher, who defines it as 'corporeality, or that of which corporeality is made'.

> All existence
>   past, present and to be
>   is in this sea fringe.
> There is no other temporal scene.
>
> The Phoenix burns spiritually
>   among the fierce stars
>   and in the docile brain's recesses.
> Its ultimate spark
> you cannot trace . . .
>
> Light burns the world in the focus of an eye.

XIV

To Dorothy Wellesley nature is a womb, a darkness; its
surface is sleep, upon sleep we walk, into sleep drive the
plough, and there lie the happy, the wise, the unconceived;

> They lie in the loam
> Laid backward by slice of the plough;
> They sit in the rock;
> In a matrix of amethyst crouches a man . . .

but unlike Turner or Read she need not prove or define, that
was all done before she began to write and think. As though
it were the tale of Mother Hubbard or the results of the last
general election, she accepts what Turner and Read accept,
sings her joy or sorrow in its presence, at times facile and
clumsy, at times magnificent in her masculine rhythm, in the
precision of her style. Eliot and Edith Sitwell have much of
their intensity from a deliberate re-moulding or checking of
past impulse, Turner much of his from a deliberate rejection
of current belief, but here is no criticism at all. A new positive
belief has given to her, as it gave to Shelley, an uncheckable
impulse, and this belief is all the more positive because found,
not sought; like certain characters in William Morris she has
'lucky eyes', her sail is full.

I knew nothing of her until a few months ago I read the
opening passage in *Horses*, delighted by its changes in pace,
abrupt assertion, then a long sweeping line, by its vocabulary
modern and precise;

> Who, in the garden-pony carrying skeps
> Of grass or fallen leaves, his knees gone slack,
> Round belly, hollow back,
> Sees the Mongolian Tarpan of the Steppes?

Or, in the Shire with plaits and feathered feet,
The war-horse like the wind the Tartar knew?
Or, in the Suffolk Punch, spells out anew
The wild grey asses fleet
With stripe from head to tail, and moderate ears?

The swing from Stendhal has passed Turner; the individual
soul, the betrayal of the unconceived at birth, are among her
principal themes, it must go further still; that soul must become its own betrayer, its own deliverer, the one activity, the
mirror turn lamp. Not that the old conception is untrue, new
literature better than old. In the greater nations every phase
has characteristic beauty — has not Nicholas of Cusa said
reality is expressed through contradiction? Yet for me, a man
of my time, through my poetical faculty living its history,
after much meat fish seems the only possible diet. I have
indeed read certain poems by Turner, by Dorothy Wellesley,
with more than all the excitement that came upon me when,
a very young man, I heard somebody read out in a London
tavern the poems of Ernest Dowson's despair — that too living
history.

XV

I have a distaste for certain poems written in the midst of
the great war; they are in all anthologies, but I have substituted
Herbert Read's *End of a War* written long after. The writers
of these poems were invariably officers of exceptional courage
and capacity, one a man constantly selected for dangerous
work, all, I think, had the Military Cross; their letters are
vivid and humorous, they were not without joy — for all
skill is joyful — but felt bound, in the words of the best known,
to plead the suffering of their men. In poems that had for a

time considerable fame, written in the first person, they made that suffering their own. I have rejected these poems for the same reason that made Arnold withdraw his *Empedocles on Etna* from circulation; passive suffering is not a theme for poetry. In all the great tragedies, tragedy is a joy to the man who dies; in Greece the tragic chorus danced. When man has withdrawn into the quicksilver at the back of the mirror no great event becomes luminous in his mind; it is no longer possible to write *The Persians*, *Agincourt*, *Chevy Chase*: some blunderer has driven his car on to the wrong side of the road — that is all.

If war is necessary, or necessary in our time and place, it is best to forget its suffering as we do the discomfort of fever, remembering our comfort at midnight when our temperature fell, or as we forget the worse moments of more painful disease. Florence Farr returning third class from Ireland found herself among Connaught Rangers just returned from the Boer War who described an incident over and over, and always with loud laughter: an unpopular sergeant struck by a shell turned round and round like a dancer wound in his own entrails. That too may be a right way of seeing war, if war is necessary; the way of the Cockney slums, of Patrick Street, of the *Kilmainham Minut*, of *Johnny I hardly knew ye*, of the medieval *Dance of Death*.

XVI

Ten years after the war certain poets combined the modern vocabulary, the accurate record of the relevant facts learnt from Eliot, with the sense of suffering of the war poets, that sense of suffering no longer passive, no longer an obsession of the nerves; philosophy had made it part of all the mind. Edith Sitwell with her Russian Ballet, Turner with his *Mare Tran-*

quillum, Dorothy Wellesley, with her ancient names —
'Heraclitus added fire' — her moths, horses and serpents,
Pound with his descent into Hades, his Chinese classics, are
too romantic to seem modern. Browning, that he might seem
modern, created an ejaculating man-of-the-world good
humour; but Day Lewis, Madge, MacNeice, are modern
through the character of their intellectual passion. We have
been gradually approaching this art through that cult of
sincerity, that refusal to multiply personality which is characteristic of our time. They may seem obscure, confused,
because of their concentrated passion, their interest in associations hitherto untravelled; it is as though their words and
rhythms remained gummed to one another instead of separating and falling into order. I can seldom find more than half
a dozen lyrics that I like, yet in this moment of sympathy I
prefer them to Eliot, to myself — I too have tried to be
modern. They have pulled off the mask, the manner writers
hitherto assumed Shelley in relation to his dream, Byron,
Henley, to their adventure, their action. Here stands not this
or that man but man's naked mind.

Although I have preferred, and shall again, constrained
by a different nationality, a man so many years old, fixed
to some one place, known to friends and enemies, full
of mortal frailty, expressing all things not made mysterious
by nature with impatient clarity, I have read with some
excitement poets I had approached with distaste, delighted
in their pure spiritual objectivity as in something long
foretold.

Much of the war poetry was pacificist, revolutionary; it
was easier to look at suffering if you had somebody to blame
for it, or some remedy in mind. Many of these poets have
called themselves communists, though I find in their work
no trace of the recognized communist philosophy and the

practising communist rejects them. The Russian government in 1930 silenced its Mechanists, put Spinoza on his head and claimed him for grandfather; but the men who created the communism of the masses had Stendhal's mirror for a contemporary, believed that religion, art, philosophy, expressed economic change, that the shell secreted the fish. Perhaps all that the masses accept is obsolete — the Orangeman beats his drum every Twelfth of July — perhaps fringes, wigs, furbelows, hoops, patches, stocks, Wellington boots, start up as armed men; but were a poet sensitive to the best thought of his time to accept that belief, when time is restoring the soul's autonomy, it would be as though he had swallowed a stone and kept it in his bowels. None of these men have accepted it, communism is their *Deus ex Machina*, their Santa Claus, their happy ending, but speaking as a poet I prefer tragedy to tragi-comedy. No matter how great a reformer's energy a still greater is required to face, all activities expended in vain, the unreformed. 'God', said an old country-woman 'smiles alike when regarding the good and condemning the lost.' MacNeice, the anti-communist, expecting some descent of barbarism next turn of the wheel, contemplates the modern world with even greater horror than the communist Day Lewis, although with less lyrical beauty. More often I cannot tell whether the poet is communist or anti-communist. On what side is Madge? Indeed I know of no school where the poets so closely resemble each other. Spender has said that the poetry of belief must supersede that of personality, and it is perhaps a belief shared that has created their intensity, their resemblance; but this belief is not political. If I understand aright this difficult art the contemplation of suffering has compelled them to seek beyond the flux something unchanging, inviolate, that country where no ghost haunts, no beloved lures because it has neither past nor future.

This lunar beauty
Has no history
Is complete and early;
If beauty later
Bear any feature
It had a lover
And is another.

*   *   *

1936

MODERN POETRY: A BROADCAST

THE period from the death of Tennyson until the present moment has, it seems, more good lyric poets than any similar period since the seventeenth century — no great overpowering figures, but many poets who have written some three or four lyrics apiece which may be permanent in our literature. It did not always seem so; even two years ago I should have said the opposite; I should have named three or four poets and said there was nobody else who mattered. Then I gave all my time to the study of that poetry. There was a club of poets — you may know its name, 'The Rhymers' Club' — which first met, I think, a few months before the death of Tennyson and lasted seven or eight years. It met in a Fleet Street tavern called 'The Cheshire Cheese'. Two members of the Club are vivid in my memory: Ernest Dowson, timid, silent, a little melancholy, lax in body, vague in attitude; Lionel Johnson, determined, erect, his few words dogmatic, almost a dwarf but beautifully made, his features cut in ivory. His thought dominated the scene and gave the Club its character. Nothing of importance could be discovered, he would say, science must be confined to the kitchen or the workshop; only philosophy and religion could solve the great secret, and they said all their say years ago; a gentleman was a man who who understood Greek. I was full of crude speculation that made me ashamed. I remember praying that I might get my imagination fixed upon life itself, like the imagination of Chaucer. In those days I was a convinced ascetic, yet I envied Dowson his dissipated life. I thought it must be easy to think like Chaucer when you lived among those morbid, elegant, tragic women suggested by Dowson's poetry, painted and drawn by his friends Conder and Beardsley. You must all know those famous lines that are in so many anthologies:

> Unto us they belong,
>   Us the bitter and gay,
> Wine and woman and song.

When I repeated those beautiful lines it never occurred to me to wonder why the Dowson I knew seemed neither gay nor bitter. A provincial, conscious of clumsiness and lack of self-possession, I still more envied Lionel Johnson, who had met, as I believed, everybody of importance. If one spoke of some famous ecclesiastic or statesman he would say: 'I know him intimately,' and quote some conversation that laid bare that man's soul. He was never a satirist, being too courteous, too just, for that distortion. One felt that these conversations had happened exactly as he said. Years were to pass before I discovered that Dowson's life, except when he came to the Rhymers' or called upon some friend selected for an extreme respectability, was a sordid round of drink and cheap harlots; that Lionel Johnson had never met those famous men, that he never met anybody, because he got up at nightfall, got drunk at a public-house or worked half the night, sat the other half, a glass of whisky at his elbow, staring at the brown corduroy curtains that protected from dust the books that lined his walls, imagining the puppets that were the true companions of his mind. He met Dowson, but then Dowson was nobody and he was convinced that he did Dowson good. He had no interest in women, and on that subject was perhaps eloquent. Some friends of mine saw them one moonlight night returning from the 'Crown' public-house which had just closed, their zig-zagging feet requiring the whole width of Oxford Street, Lionel Johnson talking. My friend stood still eavesdropping; Lionel Johnson was expounding a Father of the Church. Their piety, in Dowson a penitential sadness, in Lionel Johnson more often a noble ecstasy, was, as I think, illuminated and intensified by their contrasting puppet-shows, those elegant, tragic penitents, those great men in their triumph. You may know Lionel Johnson's poem on the statue of King Charles, or that characteristic poem that begins: 'Ah, see the fair chivalry come, the Companions of Christ.' In my present mood, remembering his scholarship, remembering that his religious sense was never divided from his sense of the past, I recall most vividly his 'Church of a Dream':

Sadly the dead leaves rustle in the whistling wind,
Around the weather-worn, grey church, low down the vale:
The Saints in golden vesture shake before the gale;
The glorious windows shake, where still they dwell en-
    shrined;
Old Saints by long-dead, shrivelled hands, long since de-
    signed:
There still, although the world autumnal be, and pale,
Still in their golden vesture the old Saints prevail;
Alone with Christ, desolate else, left by mankind.

Only one ancient priest offers the Sacrifice,
Murmuring holy Latin immemorial:
Swaying with tremulous hands the old censer full of spice,
In grey, sweet incense clouds; blue, sweet clouds mystical:
To him, in place of men, for he is old, suffice
Melancholy remembrances and vesperal.

There were other poets, generally a few years younger, who having escaped that first wave of excitement lived tame and orderly lives. But they, too, were in reaction against everything Victorian.

A church in the style of Inigo Jones opens on to a grass lawn a few hundred yards from the Marble Arch. It was designed by a member of the Rhymers' Club, whose architecture, like his poetry, seemed to exist less for his own sake than to illustrate his genius as a connoisseur. I have sometimes thought that masterpiece, perhaps the smallest church in London, the most appropriate symbol of all that was most characteristic in the art of my friends. Their poems seemed to say: 'You will remember us the longer because we are very small, very unambitious.' Yet my friends were most ambitious men; they wished to express life at its intense moments, those moments that are brief because of their intensity, and at those moments alone. In the Victorian era the most famous poetry was often a passage in a poem of some length, perhaps of great length, a poem full of thoughts that might have been expressed in prose. A short lyric seemed an accident, an interruption amid more serious work. Somebody has quoted Browning as saying that he could have written many lyrics had he thought them worth the trouble. The aim of my friends, my own aim, if it sometimes made us prefer the acorn to the oak, the small to the great, freed us from many things that we thought an impurity. Swinburne, Tennyson, Arnold, Browning, had admitted so much psychology, science, moral fervour. Had not Verlaine said of *In Memoriam*, 'When he should have been broken-hearted he had many reminiscences'? We tried to write like the poets of the Greek Anthology, or like Catullus, or like the Jacobean lyrists, men who wrote while poetry was still pure. We did not look forward or look outward, we left that to the prose writers; we looked back. We thought it was in the very nature of poetry to look back, to resemble those Swedenborgian angels who are described as moving for ever towards the dayspring of their youth. In this we were all, orderly and disorderly alike, in full agreement.

When I think of the Rhymers' Club and grow weary of those luckless men, I think of another circle that was in full agreement. It gathered round Charles Ricketts, one of the greatest connoisseurs of any age, an artist whose woodcuts prolonged the inspiration of Rossetti, whose paintings mirrored the rich colouring of Delacroix. When we studied his art we studied our double. We, too, thought always that style should be proud of its ancestry, of its traditional high breeding, that an ostentatious originality was out of place whether in the arts or in good manners. When the Rhymers' Club was breaking up I read enthusiastic reviews of the first book of Sturge Moore and grew jealous. He did not belong to the Rhymers' Club and I wanted to believe that we had all the good poets; but one evening Charles Ricketts brought me to a riverside house at Richmond and introduced me to Edith Cooper. She put into my unwilling hands Sturge Moore's book and made me read out and discuss certain poems. I surrendered. I took back all I had said against him. I was most moved by his poem called *The Dying Swan*:

> O silver-throated Swan
> Struck, struck! a golden dart
> Clean through thy breast has gone
> Home to thy heart.
> Thrill, thrill, O silver throat!
> O silver trumpet, pour
> Love for defiance back
> On him who smote!
> And brim, brim o'er
> With love; and ruby-dye thy track

Down thy last living reach
Of river, sail the golden light . . .
Enter the sun's heart . . . even teach,
O wondrous-gifted Pain, teach thou
The god to love, let him learn how.

Edith Cooper herself seemed a dry, precise, precious, pious, finicking old maid; with an aunt, a Miss Bradley, she had written under the name of 'Michael Field' tragedies in the Elizabethan manner, which I seem to remember after forty or fifty years as occasionally powerful but spoilt by strained emotion and laboured metaphor; they had already fallen into oblivion, but under the influence of Charles Ricketts she had studied Greek and found a new character, a second youth. She had begun, though I did not know it for many years, a series of little poems, masterpieces of simplicity, which resemble certain of Landor's lyrics, though her voice is not so deep, but high, thin, and sweet.

Thine elder that I am, thou must not cling
To me, nor mournful for my love entreat:
And yet, Alcaeus, as the sudden spring
Is love, yea, and to veiled Demeter sweet.
Sweeter than tone of harp, more gold than gold
Is thy young voice to me; yet, ah, the pain
To learn I am beloved now I am old,
Who, in my youth, loved, as thou must, in vain.

And here is another, which because it hints at so much more than it says, is very moving.

They bring me gifts, they honour me,
Now I am growing old;
And wondering youth crowds round my knee,
As if I had a mystery
And worship to unfold.

To me the tender, blushing bride
Doth come with lips that fail;
I feel her heart beat at my side
And cry: 'Like Ares in his pride,
Hail, noble bridegroom, hail!'

My generation, because it disliked Victorian rhetorical
moral fervour, came to dislike all rhetoric. In France, where
there was a similar movement, a poet had written, 'Take
rhetoric and wring its neck'. People began to imitate old
ballads because an old ballad is never rhetorical. I think of *A
Shropshire Lad*, of certain poems by Hardy, of Kipling's *Saint
Helena Lullaby*, and his *The Looking-Glass*. I will not read
any of that famous poetry but a poem nobody ever heard of.
When I was a young man, York Powell, an Oxford Don, was
renowned for his miraculous learning, but only his few
intimates, perhaps only those much younger than himself,
knew that he was not the dry man he seemed. From the top
of a bus, somewhere between Victoria and Walham Green, he
pointed out to me a pawnshop he had once found very useful;
I was in his rooms at Oxford when he replied to somebody
who had asked him to become Proctor that the older he grew
the less and less difference could he see between right and
wrong. He used to frequent prizefights with my brother, a lad
in his twenties, and it was in a Broadside, a mixture of hand-
coloured prints and poetry published by my brother, and now
long out of print, that I discovered the poem I am now about
to read. It is a translation from the French of Paul Fort.

The pretty maid she died, she died, in love-bed as she lay;
They took her to the church-yard; all at the break of day;
They laid her all alone there: all in her white array;
They laid her all alone there: a-coffin'd in the clay:

And they came back so merrily: all at the dawn of day;
A-singing all so merrily: '*The dog must have his day!*'
The pretty maid is dead, is dead; in love-bed as she lay;
And they are off afield to work: as they do every day.

The poems I have read resemble in certain characteristics all
modern poetry up to the Great War. The centaurs and
amazons of Sturge Moore, the Tristram and Isoult of Binyon's noble poem — there were always some long poems; my
Deirdre, my Cuchulain had been written about for centuries
and our public wished for nothing else. Here and there some
young revolutionist would boast that his eyes were on the
present or the future, or even denounce all poetry back to
Dante, but we were content; we wrote as men had always
written. Then established things were shaken by the Great
War. All civilised men had believed in progress, in a warless
future, in always-increasing wealth, but now influential young
men began to wonder if anything could last or if anything
were worth fighting for. In the third year of the War came
the most revolutionary man in poetry during my lifetime,
though his revolution was stylistic alone — T. S. Eliot published his first book. No romantic word or sound, nothing
reminiscent, nothing in the least like the painting of Ricketts
could be permitted henceforth. Poetry must resemble prose,
and both must accept the vocabulary of their time; nor must
there be any special subject-matter. Tristram and Isoult were
not a more suitable theme than Paddington Railway Station.
The past had deceived us: let us accept the worthless present.

> The morning comes to consciousness
> Of faint stale smells of beer
> From the sawdust-trampled street
> With all its muddy feet that press
> To early coffee-stands. . . .

> One thinks of all the hands
> That are raising dingy shades
> In a thousand furnished rooms.

We older writers disliked this new poetry, but were forced
to admit its satiric intensity. It was in Eliot that certain
revolutionary War poets, young men who felt they had been
dragged away from their studies, from their pleasant life, by
the blundering frenzy of old men, found the greater part of
their style. They were too near their subject-matter to do, as I
think, work of permanent importance, but their social passion,
their sense of tragedy, their modernity, have passed into
young influential poets of to-day: Auden, Spender, MacNeice,
Day Lewis, and others. Some of these poets are Communists,
but even in those who are not, there is an overwhelming social
bitterness. Some speak of the War in which none were old
enough to have served:

> I've heard them lilting at loom and belting,
> Lasses lilting before dawn of day;
> But now they are silent, not gamesome and gallant —
> The flowers of the town are rotting away.

> There was laughing and loving in the lanes at evening;
> Handsome were the boys then, and girls were gay.
> But lost in Flanders by medalled commanders
> The lads of the village are melted away.

This poetry is supported by critics who think it the poetry
of the future — in my youth I heard much of the music of the
future — and attack all not of their school. A poet of an older
school has named them 'the racketeers'. Sometimes they
attack Miss Edith Sitwell, who seems to me an important
poet, shaped as they are by the disillusionment that followed

the Great War. Among her fauns, cats, columbines, clowns, wicked fairies, into that phantasmagoria which reminds me of a ballet called *The Sleeping Beauty*, loved by the last of the Tsars, she interjects a nightmare horror of death and decay. I commend to you *The Hambone and the Heart*, and *The Lament of Edward Blastock*, as among the most tragic poems of our time. Her language is the traditional language of literature, but twisted, torn, complicated, jerked here and there by strained resemblances, unnatural contacts, forced upon it by terror or by some violence beating in her blood, some primitive obsession that civilisation can no longer exorcise. I find her obscure, exasperating, delightful. I think I like her best when she seems a child, terrified and delighted by the story it is inventing. I will read you a little poem she has called *Ass-Face*, but first I must explain its imagery which has taken me a couple of minutes to puzzle out, not because it is obscure, but because image follows image too quickly to be understood at a first hearing. I prefer to think of Ass-Face as a personality invented by some child at a nursery window after dark. The starry heavens are the lighted bars and saloons of public-houses, and the descending light is asses' milk which makes Ass-Face drunk. But this light is thought of the next moment as bright threads floating down in spirals to make a dress for Columbine, and the next moment after that as milk spirting on the sands of the sea — one thinks of the glittering foam — a sea which brays like an ass, and is covered because it is a rough sea by an ass's hide. Along the shore there are trees, and under these trees beavers are building Babel, and these beavers think that the noise Ass-Face makes in his drunkenness is Cain and Abel fighting. Then somehow as the vision ends the starlight has turned into the houses that the beavers are building. But their Babel and their houses are like white lace, and we are told that Ass-Face will spoil them all.

of meditation, came Turner's *Seven Days of the Sun*, Dorothy Wellesley's *Matrix*, Herbert Read's *Mutations of the Phoenix*, T. S. Eliot's *Waste Land*; long philosophical poems; and even now the young Communist poets complicate their short lyrics with difficult metaphysics.

If you are lovers of poetry, and it is for such that I speak, you know *The Waste Land*, but perhaps not the other poems that I have named, though you will certainly know Dorothy Wellesley's poem in praise of horses, and probably Turner's praise of a mountain in Mexico with a romantic name. To three, perhaps to all four of these writers, what we call the solid earth was manufactured by the human mind from unknown raw material. They do not think this because of Kant and Berkeley, who are an old story, but because of something that has got into the air since a famous French mathematician wrote 'Space is a creation of our ancestors'. Eliot's historical and scholarly mind seems to have added this further thought, probably from Nicholas of Cusa: reality is expressed in a series of contradictions, or is that unknowable something that supports the centre of the see-saw.

At the still point of the turning world. Neither flesh nor
    fleshless;
Neither from nor towards; at the still point, there the dance is,
But neither arrest nor movement. And do not call it fixity.
Where past and future are gathered. Neither movement from
    nor towards,
Neither ascent nor decline. Except for the point, the still
    point,
There would be no dance, and there is only the dance.

All are pessimists; Dorothy Wellesley thinks that the 'unconceived', as she calls those that have not yet been melted

into that subjective creation we call the world, are alone
happy. They are a part of the unknown raw material which
the manufacturer has neglected. They have escaped the torture
of the senses, the boredom of that automatic return of the
same sensation Eliot has described. I will read you a passage
from her poem *Matrix*:

> Where, then, are the unborn ones?
> Do they eternally go,
> Cloud-wracks of souls tormented,
> Through ether for ever?
>
> No such ventures theirs, no.
> They crowd in the core of the earth;
> They lie in the loam,
> Laid backward by slice of the plough;
> They sit in the rock:
> In a matrix of amethyst crouches a man,
> Pigmy, a part of the womb,
> Of the stone,
> For ever, for all time, now.
>
> All things there are his own:
> The light on water, the leaves,
> The spray of the wild yellow rose;
> Beautiful as to the born
> Are the stars to the unconceived;
> The twilight, the morn, of their sight,
> Are lovelier than to the born.

Turner, the poet, mathematician, musician, thinks that the
horror of the world is in its beauty. Beautiful forms deceive us,
because if we grasp them, they dissolve into what he calls

'confused sensation'; and destroy us because they drag us under the machinery of nature; if it were possible he would, like a Buddhist, or a connoisseur, kill or suspend desire. He does not see men and women as the puppets of Eliot's poetry, repeating over and over the same trivial movements, but as the reflections of a terrible Olympus. I will read you his poem upon the procession of the mannequins.

I have seen mannequins,
As white and gold as lilies,
Swaying their tall bodies across the burnished floor
Of *Reville* or *Paquin*;
Writhing in colour and line,
Curved tropical flowers
As bright as thunderbolts,
Or hooded in dark furs
The sun's pale splash
In English autumn woods.

And I have watched these soft explosions of life
As astronomers watch the combustion of stars.
The violence of supernatural power
Upon their faces,
White orbits
Of incalculable forces.

And I have had no desire for their bodies
But have felt the whiteness of a lily
Upon my palate;
And the solidity of their slender curves
Like a beautiful mathematical proposition
In my brain.

But in the expression of their faces
Terror.

Cruelty in the eyes, nostrils, and lips —
Pain
thou passion-flower, thou wreath, thou orbit,
thou spiritual rotation,
thou smile upon a pedestal,
Peony of the garden of Paradise!

Many Irish men and women must be listening, and they may wonder why I have said nothing of modern Irish poetry. I have not done so because it moves in a different direction and belongs to a different story. Modern Irish poetry began in the midst of that rediscovery of folk thought I described when quoting York Powell's translation from Paul Fort. The English movement, checked by the realism of Eliot, the social passion of the War poets, gave way to an impersonal philosophical poetry. Because Ireland has a still living folk tradition, her poets cannot get it out of their heads that they themselves, good-tempered or bad-tempered, tall or short, will be remembered by the common people. Instead of turning to impersonal philosophy, they have hardened and deepened their personalities. I could have taken as examples Synge or James Stephens, men I have never ceased to delight in. But I prefer to quote poetry of which you have probably never heard, though it is among the greatest lyric poetry of our time.

Some twelve years ago political enemies came to Senator Gogarty's house while they knew he would be in his bath and so unable to reach his revolver, made him dress, brought him to an empty house on the edge of the Liffey. They told him nothing, but he felt certain he was to be kept as hostage and shot after the inevitable execution of a certain man then in prison. Self-possessed and daring, he escaped, and while swimming the cold December river, vowed two swans to it if it would land him safely. I was present some weeks later when, in the presence of the Head of the State and other notables, the two swans were launched. That story shows the man — scholar, wit, poet, gay adventurer. In one poem, written years afterwards, the man who dedicated the swans dedicates the poems, and the mood has not changed:

> Tall unpopular men,
> Slim proud women who move
> As women walked in the islands when
> Temples were built to Love,
> I sing to you. With you
> Beauty at best can live,
> Beauty that dwells with the rare and few,
> Cold and imperative.
> He who had Caesar's ear
> Sang to the lonely and strong.
> Virgil made an austere
> Venus Muse of his song.

Here is another poem characteristic of those poems which have restored the emotion of heroism to lyric poetry:

> Our friends go with us as we go
>   Down the long path where Beauty wends,
> Where all we love forgathers, so
>   Why should we fear to join our friends?
>
> Who would survive them to outlast
>   His children; to outwear his fame —
> Left when the Triumph has gone past —
>   To win from Age, not Time, a name?

> Then do not shudder at the knife
>   That Death's indifferent hand drives home,
> But with the Strivers leave the Strife,
>   Nor, after Caesar, skulk in Rome.

When I have read you a poem I have tried to read it
rhythmically; I may be a bad reader; or read badly because
I am out of sorts, or self-conscious; but there is no other
method. A poem is an elaboration of the rhythms of common
speech and their association with profound feeling. To read a
poem like prose, that hearers unaccustomed to poetry may
find it easy to understand, is to turn it into bad, florid prose.
If anybody reads or recites poetry as if it were prose from
some public platform, I ask you, speaking for poets, living,
dead, or unborn, to protest in whatever way occurs to your
perhaps youthful minds; if they recite or read by wireless,
I ask you to express your indignation by letter. William
Morris, coming out of a hall where somebody had read or
recited his *Sigurd the Volsung*, said: 'It cost me a lot of damned
hard work to get that thing into verse.'

1936

A GENERAL INTRODUCTION FOR MY WORK[1]

I. THE FIRST PRINCIPLE

A POET writes always of his personal life, in his finest work out of its tragedy, whatever it be, remorse, lost love, or mere loneliness; he never speaks directly as to someone at the breakfast table, there is always a phantasmagoria. Dante and Milton had mythologies, Shakespeare the characters of English history or of traditional romance; even when the poet seems most himself, when he is Raleigh and gives potentates the lie, or Shelley 'a nerve o'er which do creep the else unfelt oppressions of this earth', or Byron when 'the soul wears out the breast' as 'the sword outwears its sheath', he is never the bundle of accident and incoherence that sits down to breakfast; he has been reborn as an idea, something intended, complete. A novelist might describe his accidence, his incoherence, he must not; he is more type than man, more passion than type. He is Lear, Romeo, Oedipus, Tiresias; he has stepped out of a play, and even the woman he loves is Rosalind, Cleopatra, never The Dark Lady. He is part of his own phantasmagoria and we adore him because nature has grown intelligible, and by so doing a part of our creative power. 'When mind is lost in the light of the Self', says the Prashna Upanishad, 'it dreams no more; still in the body it is lost in happiness.' 'A wise man seeks in Self', says the Chandogya Upanishad, 'those that are alive and those that are dead

[1] Written for a complete edition of Yeats's works which was never produced.

255

and gets what the world cannot give.' The world knows
nothing because it has made nothing, we know everything
because we have made everything.

II. SUBJECT-MATTER

It was through the old Fenian leader John O'Leary I found
my theme. His long imprisonment, his longer banishment, his
magnificent head, his scholarship, his pride, his integrity, all
that aristocratic dream nourished amid little shops and little
farms, had drawn around him a group of young men; I was
but eighteen or nineteen and had already, under the influence
of *The Faerie Queene* and *The Sad Shepherd*, written a pastoral
play, and under that of Shelley's *Prometheus Unbound* two
plays, one staged somewhere in the Caucasus, the other in a
crater of the moon; and I knew myself to be vague and
incoherent. He gave me the poems of Thomas Davis, said
they were not good poetry but had changed his life when a
young man, spoke of other poets associated with Davis and
The Nation newspaper, probably lent me their books. I saw
even more clearly than O'Leary that they were not good
poetry. I read nothing but romantic literature; hated that dry
eighteenth-century rhetoric; but they had one quality I
admired and admire: they were not separated individual men;
they spoke or tried to speak out of a people to a people; behind
them stretched the generations. I knew, though but now and
then as young men know things, that I must turn from that
modern literature Jonathan Swift compared to the web a
spider draws out of its bowels; I hated and still hate with an
ever growing hatred the literature of the point of view. I
wanted, if my ignorance permitted, to get back to Homer, to
those that fed at his table. I wanted to cry as all men cried,
to laugh as all men laughed, and the Young Ireland poets
when not writing mere politics had the same want, but they

did not know that the common and its befitting language is the research of a lifetime and when found may lack popular recognition. Then somebody, not O'Leary, told me of Standish O'Grady and his interpretation of Irish legends. O'Leary had sent me to O'Curry, but his unarranged and uninterpreted history defeated my boyish indolence.

A generation before *The Nation* newspaper was founded the Royal Irish Academy had begun the study of ancient Irish literature. That study was as much a gift from the Protestant aristocracy which had created the Parliament as *The Nation* and its school, though Davis and Mitchel were Protestants; was a gift from the Catholic middle classes who were to create the Irish Free State. The Academy persuaded the English Government to finance an ordnance survey on a large scale; scholars, including that great scholar O'Donovan, were sent from village to village recording names and their legends. Perhaps it was the last moment when such work could be well done, the memory of the people was still intact, the collectors themselves had perhaps heard or seen the banshee; the Royal Irish Academy and its public with equal enthusiasm welcomed Pagan and Christian; thought the Round Towers a commemoration of Persian fire-worship. There was little orthodoxy to take alarm; the Catholics were crushed and cowed; an honoured great-uncle of mine — his portrait by some forgotten master hangs upon my bedroom wall — a Church of Ireland rector, would upon occasion boast that you could not ask a question he could not answer with a perfectly appropriate blasphemy or indecency. When several counties had been surveyed but nothing published, the Government, afraid of rousing dangerous patriotic emotion, withdrew support; large manuscript volumes remain containing much picturesque correspondence between scholars.

When modern Irish literature began, O'Grady's influence

predominated. He could delight us with an extravagance we were too critical to share; a day will come, he said, when Slieve-na-mon will be more famous than Olympus; yet he was no Nationalist as we understood the word, but in rebellion, as he was fond of explaining, against the House of Commons, not against the King. His cousin, that great scholar Hayes O'Grady, would not join our non-political Irish Literary Society because he considered it a Fenian body, but boasted that although he had lived in England for forty years he had never made an English friend. He worked at the British Museum compiling their Gaelic catalogue and translating our heroic tales in an eighteenth-century frenzy; his heroine 'fractured her heart', his hero 'ascended to the apex of the eminence' and there 'vibrated his javelin', and afterwards took ship upon 'colossal ocean's superficies'. Both O'Gradys considered themselves as representing the old Irish land-owning aristocracy; both probably, Standish O'Grady certainly, thought that England, because decadent and democratic, had betrayed their order. It was another member of that order, Lady Gregory, who was to do for the heroic legends in *Gods and Fighting Men* and in *Cuchulain of Muirthemne* what Lady Charlotte Guest's *Mabinogion* had done with less beauty and style for those of Wales. Standish O'Grady had much modern sentiment, his style, like that of John Mitchel forty years before, shaped by Carlyle; she formed her style upon the Anglo-Irish dialect of her neighbourhood, an old vivid speech with a partly Tudor vocabulary, a syntax partly moulded by men who still thought in Gaelic.

I had heard in Sligo cottages or from pilots at Rosses Point endless stories of apparitions, whether of the recent dead or of the people of history and legend, of that Queen Maeve whose reputed cairn stands on the mountain over the bay.

Then at the British Museum I read stories Irish writers of the 'forties and 'fifties had written of such apparitions, but they enraged me more than pleased because they turned the country visions into a joke. But when I went from cottage to cottage with Lady Gregory and watched her hand recording that great collection she has called *Visions and Beliefs* I escaped disfiguring humour.

Behind all Irish history hangs a great tapestry, even Christianity had to accept it and be itself pictured there. Nobody looking at its dim folds can say where Christianity begins and Druidism ends; 'There is one perfect among the birds, one perfect among the fish, and one among men that is perfect.' I can only explain by that suggestion of recent scholars — Professor Burkitt of Cambridge commended it to my attention — that St. Patrick came to Ireland not in the fifth century but towards the end of the second. The great controversies had not begun; Easter was still the first full moon after the Equinox. Upon that day the world had been created, the Ark rested upon Ararat, Moses led the Israelites out of Egypt; the umbilical cord which united Christianity to the ancient world had not yet been cut, Christ was still the half-brother of Dionysus. A man just tonsured by the Druids could learn from the nearest Christian neighbour to sign himself with the Cross without sense of incongruity, nor would his children acquire that sense. The organised clans weakened Church organisation, they could accept the monk but not the bishop.

A modern man, *The Golden Bough* and *Human Personality* in his head, finds much that is congenial in St. Patrick's Creed as recorded in his Confessions, and nothing to reject except the word 'soon' in the statement that Christ will soon judge the quick and the dead. He can repeat it, believe it even, without a thought of the historic Christ, or ancient Judea, or of anything subject to historical conjecture and shifting evidence;

I repeat it and think of 'the Self' in the Upanishads. Into this tradition, oral and written, went in later years fragments of Neo-Platonism, cabbalistic words — I have heard the words 'tetragrammaton agla' in Doneraile — the floating debris of mediaeval thought, but nothing that did not please the solitary mind. Even the religious equivalent for Baroque and Rococo could not come to us as thought, perhaps because Gaelic is incapable of abstraction. It came as cruelty. That tapestry filled the scene at the birth of modern Irish literature, it is there in the Synge of *The Well of the Saints*, in James Stephens, and in Lady Gregory throughout, in all of George Russell that did not come from the Upanishads, and in all but my later poetry.

Sometimes I am told in commendation, if the newspaper is Irish, in condemnation if English, that my movement perished under the firing squads of 1916; sometimes that those firing squads made our realistic movement possible. If that statement is true, and it is only so in part, for romance was everywhere receding, it is because in the imagination of Pearse and his fellow soldiers the Sacrifice of the Mass had found the Red Branch in the tapestry; they went out to die calling upon Cuchulain:

> Fall, Hercules, from Heaven in tempests hurled
> To cleanse the beastly stable of this world.

In one sense the poets of 1916 were not of what the newspapers call my school. The Gaelic League, made timid by a modern popularisation of Catholicism sprung from the aspidistra and not from the root of Jesse, dreaded intellectual daring and stuck to dictionary and grammar. Pearse and MacDonagh and others among the executed men would have done, or attempted, in Gaelic what we did or attempted in English.

Our mythology, our legends, differ from those of other European countries because down to the end of the seventeenth century they had the attention, perhaps the unquestioned belief, of peasant and noble alike; Homer belongs to sedentary men, even to-day our ancient queens, our mediaeval soldiers and lovers, can make a pedlar shudder. I can put my own thought, despair perhaps from the study of present circumstance in the light of ancient philosophy, into the mouth of rambling poets of the seventeenth century, or even of some imagined ballad singer of to-day, and the deeper my thought the more credible, the more peasant-like, are ballad singer and rambling poet. Some modern poets contend that jazz and music-hall songs are the folk art of our time, that we should mould our art upon them; we Irish poets, modern men also, reject every folk art that does not go back to Olympus. Give me time and a little youth and I will prove that even 'Johnny, I hardly knew ye' goes back.

Mr. Arnold Toynbee in an annex to the second volume of *The Study of History* describes the birth and decay of what he calls the Far Western Christian culture; it lost at the Synod of Whitby its chance of mastering Europe, suffered final ecclesiastical defeat in the twelfth century with 'the thoroughgoing incorporation of the Irish Christendom into the Roman Church. In the political and literary spheres' it lasted unbroken till the seventeenth century. He then insists that if 'Jewish Zionism and Irish Nationalism succeed in achieving their aims, then Jewry and Irishry will each fit into its own tiny niche . . . among sixty or seventy national communities', find life somewhat easier, but cease to be 'the relic of an independent society . . . the romance of Ancient Ireland has at last come to an end . . . Modern Ireland has made up her mind, in our generation, to find her level as a willing inmate in our workaday Western world.'

If Irish literature goes on as my generation planned it, it may do something to keep the 'Irishry.' living, nor will the work of the realists hinder, nor the figures they imagine, nor those described in memoirs of the revolution. These last especially, like certain great political predecessors, Parnell, Swift, Lord Edward, have stepped back into the tapestry. It may be indeed that certain characteristics of the 'Irishry' must grow in importance. When Lady Gregory asked me to annotate her *Visions and Beliefs* I began, that I might understand what she had taken down in Galway, an investigation of contemporary spiritualism. For several years I frequented those mediums who in various poor parts of London instruct artisans or their wives for a few pence upon their relations to their dead, to their employers, and to their children; then I compared what she had heard in Galway, or I in London, with the visions of Swedenborg, and, after my inadequate notes had been published, with Indian belief. If Lady Gregory had not said when we passed an old man in the woods, 'That man may know the secret of the ages', I might never have talked with Shri Purohit Swāmi nor made him translate his Master's travels in Tibet, not helped him translate the Upanishads. I think I now know why the gamekeeper at Coole heard the footsteps of a deer on the edge of the lake where no deer had passed for a hundred years, and why a certain cracked old priest said that nobody had been to hell or heaven in his time, meaning thereby that the Rath had got them all; that the dead stayed where they had lived, or near it, sought no abstract region of blessing or punishment but retreated, as it were, into the hidden character of their neighbourhood. I am convinced that in two or three generations it will become generally known that the mechanical theory has no reality, that the natural and supernatural are knit together, that to escape a dangerous fanaticism we must study a new science; at that moment Europeans may find something attractive in a Christ posed against a background not of Judaism but of Druidism, not shut off in dead history, but flowing, concrete, phenomenal.

I was born into this faith, have lived in it, and shall die in it; my Christ, a legitimate deduction from the Creed of St. Patrick as I think, is that Unity of Being Dante compared to a perfectly proportioned human body, Blake's 'Imagination', what the Upanishads have named 'Self': nor is this unity distant and therefore intellectually understandable, but imminent, differing from man to man and age to age, taking upon itself pain and ugliness, 'eye of newt, and toe of frog'.

Subconscious preoccupation with this theme brought me *A Vision*, its harsh geometry an incomplete interpretation. The 'Irishry' have preserved their ancient 'deposit' through wars which, during the sixteenth and seventeenth centuries, became wars of extermination; no people, Lecky said at the opening of his *Ireland in the Eighteenth Century*, have undergone greater persecution, nor did that persecution altogether cease up to our own day. No people hate as we do in whom that past is always alive, there are moments when hatred poisons my life and I accuse myself of effeminacy because I have not given it adequate expression. It is not enough to have put it into the mouth of a rambling peasant poet. Then I remind myself that though mine is the first English marriage I know of in the direct line, all my family names are English, and that I owe my soul to Shakespeare, to Spenser and to Blake, perhaps to William Morris, and to the English language in which I think, speak, and write, that everything I love has come to me through English; my hatred tortures me with love, my love with hate. I am like the Tibetan monk who dreams at his initiation that he is eaten by a wild beast and learns on waking that he himself is eater and eaten. This is Irish hatred and solitude, the hatred of human life that made

Swift write *Gulliver* and the epitaph upon his tomb, that can still make us wag between extremes and doubt our sanity.

Again and again I am asked why I do not write in Gaelic. Some four or five years ago I was invited to dinner by a London society and found myself among London journalists, Indian students, and foreign political refugees. An Indian paper says it was a dinner in my honour; I hope not; I have forgotten, though I have a clear memory of my own angry mind. I should have spoken as men are expected to speak at public dinners; I should have paid and been paid conventional compliments; then they would speak of the refugees; from that on all would be lively and topical, foreign tyranny would be arraigned, England seem even to those confused Indians the protector of liberty; I grew angrier and angrier; Wordsworth, that typical Englishman, had published his famous sonnet to François Dominique Toussaint, a Santo Domingo Negro:

> There's not a breathing of the common wind
> That will forget thee

in the year when Emmet conspired and died, and he remembered that rebellion as little as the half hanging and the pitch cap that preceded it by half a dozen years. That there might be no topical speeches I denounced the oppression of the people of India; being a man of letters, not a politician, I told how they had been forced to learn everything, even their own Sanskrit, through the vehicle of English till the first discoverer of wisdom had become bywords for vague abstract facility. I begged the Indian writers present to remember that no man can think or write with music and vigour except in his mother tongue. I turned a friendly audience hostile, yet when I think of that scene I am unrepentant and angry.

I could no more have written in Gaelic than can those

Indians write in English; Gaelic is my national language, but it is not my mother tongue.

III. STYLE AND ATTITUDE

Style is almost unconscious. I know what I have tried to do, little what I have done. Contemporary lyric poems, even those that moved me — *The Stream's Secret, Dolores* — seemed too long, but an Irish preference for a swift current might be mere indolence, yet Burns may have felt the same when he read Thomson and Cowper. The English mind is meditative, rich, deliberate; it may remember the Thames valley. I planned to write short lyrics or poetic drama where every speech would be short and concentrated, knit by dramatic tension, and I did so with more confidence because young English poets were at that time writing out of emotion at the moment of crisis, though their old slow-moving meditation returned almost at once. Then, and in this English poetry has followed my lead, I tried to make the language of poetry coincide with that of passionate, normal speech. I wanted to write in whatever language comes most naturally when we soliloquise, as I do all day long, upon the events of our own lives or of any life where we can see ourselves for the moment. I sometimes compare myself with the mad old slum women I hear denouncing and remembering; 'How dare you', I heard one say of some imaginary suitor, 'and you without health or a home!' If I spoke my thoughts aloud they might be as angry and as wild. It was a long time before I had made a language to my liking; I began to make it when I discovered some twenty years ago that I must seek, not as Wordsworth thought, words in common use, but a powerful and passionate syntax, and a complete coincidence between period and stanza. Because I need a passionate syntax for passionate subject-matter I compel myself to accept those traditional metres that have developed with the language. Ezra Pound, Turner, Lawrence wrote admirable free verse, I could not. I would lose myself, become joyless like those mad old women. The translators of the Bible, Sir Thomas Browne, certain translators from the Greek when translators still bothered about rhythm, created a form midway between prose and verse that seems natural to impersonal meditation; but all that is personal soon rots; it must be packed in ice or salt. Once when I was in delirium from pneumonia I dictated a letter to George Moore telling him to eat salt because it was a symbol of eternity; the delirium passed, I had no memory of that letter, but I must have meant what I now mean. If I wrote of personal love or sorrow in free verse, or in any rhythm that left it unchanged, amid all its accidence, I would be full of self-contempt because of my egotism and indiscretion, and foresee the boredom of my reader. I must choose a traditional stanza, even what I alter must seem traditional. I commit my emotion to shepherds, herdsmen, camel-drivers, learned men, Milton's or Shelley's Platonist, that tower Palmer drew. Talk to me of originality and I will turn on you with rage. I am a crowd, I am a lonely man, I am nothing. Ancient salt is best packing. The heroes of Shakespeare convey to us through their looks, or through the metaphorical patterns of their speech, the sudden enlargement of their vision, their ecstasy at the approach of death: 'She should have died hereafter', 'Of many thousand kisses, the poor last', 'Absent thee from felicity awhile'. They have become God or Mother Goddess, the pelican, 'My baby at my breast', but all must be cold; no actress has ever sobbed when she played Cleopatra, even the shallow brain of a producer has never thought of such a thing. The supernatural is present, cold winds blow across our hands, upon our faces, the thermometer falls, and because of that cold we are hated by journalists and groundlings. There may be in this or that detail painful tragedy, but in the whole work none. I have heard Lady Gregory say, rejecting some play in the modern manner sent to the Abbey Theatre, 'Tragedy must be a joy to the man who dies'. Nor is it any different with lyrics, songs, narrative poems; neither scholars nor the populace have sung or read anything generation after generation because of its pain. The maid of honour whose tragedy they sing must be lifted out of history with timeless pattern, she is one of the four Maries, the rhythm is old and familiar, imagination must dance, must be carried beyond feeling into the aboriginal ice. Is ice the correct word? I once boasted, copying the phrase from a letter of my father's, that I would write a poem 'cold and passionate as the dawn'.

When I wrote in blank verse I was dissatisfied; my vaguely mediaeval *Countess Cathleen* fitted the measure, but our Heroic Age went better, or so I fancied, in the ballad metre of *The Green Helmet*. There was something in what I felt about Deirdre, about Cuchulain, that rejected the Renaissance and its characteristic metres, and this was a principal reason why I created in dance plays the form that varies blank verse with lyric metres. When I speak blank verse and analyse my feelings, I stand at a moment of history when instinct, its traditional songs and dances, its general agreement, is of the past. I have been cast up out of the whale's belly though I still remember the sound and sway that came from beyond its ribs, and, like the Queen in Paul Fort's ballad, I smell of the fish of the sea. The contrapuntal structure of the verse, to employ a term adopted by Robert Bridges, combines the past and present. If I repeat the first line of *Paradise Lost* so as to emphasise its five feet I am among the folk singers — 'Of mán's first dísobédience ánd the frúit', but speak it as I should I cross it with another emphasis, that of passionate prose — 'Of mán's

fírst disobédience and the frúit', or 'Of mán's fírst dís-
obedience and the frúit'; the folk song is still there, but a
ghostly voice, an unvariable possibility, an unconscious norm.
What moves me and my hearer is a vivid speech that has no
laws except that it must not exorcise the ghostly voice. I am
awake and asleep, at my moment of revelation, self-possessed
in self-surrender; there is no rhyme, no echo of the beaten
drum, the dancing foot, that would overset my balance.
When I was a boy I wrote a poem upon dancing that had one
good line: 'They snatch with their hands at the sleep of the
skies.' If I sat down and thought for a year I would discover
that but for certain syllabic limitations, a rejection or acceptance of certain elisions, I must wake or sleep.

The Countess Cathleen could speak a blank verse which I
had loosened, almost put out of joint, for her need, because
I thought of her as mediaeval and thereby connected her with
the general European movement. For Deirdre and Cuchulain
and all the other figures of Irish legend are still in the whale's
belly.

IV. WHITHER?

The young English poets reject dream and personal emotion; they have thought out opinions that join them to this or
that political party; they employ an intricate psychology,
action in character, not as in the ballads character in action,
and all consider that they have a right to the same close
attention that men pay to the mathematician and the metaphysician. One of the more distinguished has just explained
that man has hitherto slept but must now awake. They are
determined to express the factory, the metropolis, that they
may be modern. Young men teaching school in some picturesque cathedral town, or settled for life in Capri or in
Sicily, defend their type of metaphor by saying that it comes

naturally to a man who travels to his work by Tube. I am indebted to a man of this school who went through my work at my request, crossing out all conventional metaphors, but they seem to me to have rejected also those dream associations which were the whole art of Mallarmé. He had topped a previous wave. As they express not what the Upanishads call 'that ancient Self' but individual intellect, they have the right to choose the man in the Tube because of his objective importance. They attémpt to kill the whale, push the Renaissance higher yet, out-think Leonardo; their verse kills the folk ghost and yet would remain verse. I am joined to the 'Irishry' and I expect a counter-Renaissance. No doubt it is part of the game to push that Renaissance; I make no complaint; I am accustomed to the geometrical arrangement of history in *A Vision*, but I go deeper than 'custom' for my convictions. When I stand upon O'Connell Bridge in the half-light and notice that discordant architecture, all those electric signs, where modern heterogeneity has taken physical form, a vague hatred comes up out of my own dark and I am certain that wherever in Europe there are minds strong enough to lead others the same vague hatred rises; in four or five or in less generations this hatred will have issued in violence and imposed some kind of rule of kindred. I cannot know the nature of that rule, for its opposite fills the light; all I can do to bring it nearer is to intensify my hatred. I am no Nationalist, except in Ireland for passing reasons; State and Nation are the work of intellect, and when you consider what comes before and after them they are, as Victor Hugo said of something or other, not worth the blade of grass God gives for the nest of the linnet.

1937

IRELAND AFTER THE REVOLUTION

I ASSUME that some tragic crisis shall so alter Europe and all opinion that the Irish Government will teach the great majority of its school-children nothing but ploughing, harrowing, sowing, curry-combing, bicycle-cleaning, drill-driving, parcel-making, bale-pushing, tin-can-soldering, door-knob-polishing, threshold-whitening, coat-cleaning, trouser-patching, and playing upon the squiffer, all things that serve human dignity, unless indeed it decide that these things are better taught at home, in which case it can leave the poor children at peace.

Having settled that matter I return to more important things. Teach nothing but Greek, Gaelic, mathematics, and perhaps one modern language. I reject Latin because it was a language of the Graeco-Roman decadence, all imitation and manner and other feminine tricks; the much or little Latin necessary for a priest, doctor or lawyer should be part of professional training and come later. D'Arbois de Jubainville worked on old Irish for thirty years because it brought him back to the civilisation immediately behind that of Homer, and when I prepared *Oedipus at Colonus* for the Abbey stage I saw that the wood of the Furies in the opening scene was any Irish haunted wood. No passing beggar or fiddler or benighted countryman has ever trembled or been awe-struck by nymph-haunted or Fury-haunted wood described in Roman poetry. Roman poetry is founded upon documents, not upon belief.

Translate into modern Irish all that is most beautiful in old and middle Irish, what Frank O'Connor and Augusta

Gregory, let us say, have translated into English; let every schoolmaster point out where in his neighbourhood this or that thing happened, or is said to have happened, but teach Irish and Greek together, make the pupil translate Greek into Irish, Irish into Greek. The old Irish poets lay in a formless matrix; the Greek poets kept the richness of those dreams and yet were completely awake. Sleep has no bottom, waking no top. Irish can give our children love of the soil underfoot; but only Greek, co-ordination or intensity.

When I was a very young man, fresh from my first study of Elizabethan drama, I began to puzzle my elders with the question: 'Why has the audience deteriorated?' I would go on to explain that the modern theatre audience was as inferior to the Elizabethan as that was to the Greek; I spoke of the difficult transition from topic to topic in Shakespearean dialogue, of the still more difficult in those long speeches of Chapman; we could not give that close attention to-day. And then I would compare the Elizabethan plot broken up into farce and spectacle with the elaborate unity of Greek drama; no Elizabethan had the Greek intensity. No one could answer my question, nor could I myself, for I still half-believed in progress. But I can answer it now: civilisation rose to its high-tide mark in Greece, fell, rose again in the Renaissance but not to the same level. But we may, if we choose, not now or soon but at the next turn of the wheel, push ourselves up, being ourselves the tide, beyond that first mark. But no, these things are fated; we may be pushed up.

Mathematics should be taught because being certainty without reality it is the modern key to power, but not till the child is thirteen or fourteen years old and has begun to reason. Children before that age are the only born mimics, and they learn all through mimicry and should be taught languages and nothing else, though not so many that they will lose intensity of expression in their own, and these languages should be taught by word of mouth. Greek and Irish they should speak as fluently as they now speak English. If Irish is to become the national tongue the change must come slowly, almost imperceptibly; a sudden or forced change of language may be the ruin of the soul. England has forced English upon the schools and colleges of India, and now after generations of teaching no Indian can write or speak animated English and his mother tongue is despised and corrupted. Catholic Ireland is but slowly recovering from its change of language in the eighteenth century. Irishmen learn English at their mother's knee, English is now their mother-tongue, and a sudden change would bring a long barren epoch.

Let schools teach what is too difficult for grown men but is easy to the imitation or docility of childhood; English, history, and geography and those pleasant easy things which are the most important of all should be taught by father and mother, ancestral tradition, and the child's own reading, and if the child lack this teaching let father, mother, and child be ashamed, as they are if it lack breeding and manners. I would restore the responsibilities of the family.

[1938]

NOTES

THE IRISH NATIONAL LITERARY SOCIETY

p. 18: Duffy's Library a series of Irish books selected by Sir Charles
Gavan Duffy (1816–1903), Irish journalist, founded the Young Ireland
party, became Premier of Victoria, returned to Europe in 1880,
president of the Irish Literary Society. **Thomas of Erceldoune** known
also as Thomas the Rymer (*fl.* 1220–97), Scots seer and poet.
p. 19: Mr. John O'Leary (1830–1907), a Fenian leader, exiled in Paris
for fifteen years for his part in the 1895 rising; he greatly influenced
Yeats as a young man. **Dr. Douglas Hyde** (1860–1949), founder of the
Gaelic League, first President of Ireland; poet, scholar, translator.
Dr. Sigerson Dr. George Sigerson (1838–1923), translator, scientist
and Senator of the Irish Free State. **Count Plunkett** Count George
Noble Plunkett (1851–1948), Irish poet and art critic. **Miss Katharine
Tynan** (1859–1931), Irish novelist and poet, married H. A. Hinkson in
1893. **Miss Maud Gonne** (1866–1953), Irish revolutionary with whom
Yeats fell in love in 1889. Despite repeated proposals from Yeats she
married John MacBride in 1903, separated from him in 1905. He was
shot in 1916 for his part in the Rising. **Mr. Richard Ashe King**
(1839–1932), Irish clergyman and later man of letters. **Mr. Standish
O'Grady** (1846–1928), Irish novelist and journalist, author of *History of
Ireland: the Heroic Period* (1878), important influence on the literary
renaissance. **Strongbow** Richard FitzGilbert de Clare, Earl of
Pembroke (d. 1176) landed in Ireland in 1170, having married Eva,
daughter of Dermot, King of Leinster, whom he succeeded in 1171.

FROM **WILLIAM BLAKE AND HIS ILLUSTRATIONS TO
THE DIVINE COMEDY**

p. 26: Correggio Antonio Allegri da Correggio (1494–1534), Italian
painter. **Bartolozzi** Francesco Bartolozzi (1727–1815), Italian engraver.
Stothard Thomas Stothard (1755–1834), English illustrator and
painter.
p. 29: Young's 'Night Thoughts' a didactic poem by Edward Young
(1683–1765).
p. 30: Blair's 'Grave' *The Grave*, written by Robert Blair (1699–1746),
is similar in character to *Night Thoughts*. **Schiavonetti's** possibly
Andrea Schiavone (1522?–1582) Italian painter whose poems included
'The Adoration of the Magi'. **Thornton's 'Virgil'** Robert John
Thornton (1768?–1837), edited Virgil in a school edition (1812); the
3rd edition in 2 volumes was published in 1821. **Woollett** William
Woollett (1735–1835), English draughtsman and engraver.

Strange Sir Robert Strange (1721–92), Scottish line engraver. **Marc Antonio** Marc Antonio Raimondi (*c.* 1480–1530), Italian engraver. **Linnell** John Linnell (1792–1882), English portrait and landscape painter, friend of Blake.

p. 32: Orcagno a Florentine architect whose real name was Andrea di Crone (1308?–68?). **Giotto** (1266–1336), Italian painter.

A SYMBOLIC ARTIST AND THE COMING OF SYMBOLIC ART

p. 33: AE (George Russell, 1867–1935), poet, essayist and mystic, an active member of the Irish literary renascence and Home Rule Movement, and a founder of the Abbey Theatre. **Miss Althea Gyles** Althea Gyles (1868–1949), symbolic painter, member of the Order of the Golden Dawn, whom Yeats met in theosophical circles in Dublin in the late 1880s.

p. 34: Mr. Whistler James Abbott McNeill Whistler (1834–1903), American painter and etcher who settled in Chelsea in 1863. **Mr. Beardsley** Aubrey Vincent Beardsley (1872–98), black and white artist and editor of the *Yellow Book*. **Sir Edward Burne-Jones** (1833–98), romantic painter and designer, friend of D. G. Rossetti and William Morris. **Mr. Ricketts** Charles Ricketts (1866–1931), painter, sculptor, art critic, stage-set designer. Co-editor of *The Dial* (1889–97). **Degas** Hilaire Germaine Edgar Degas (1834–1917), French painter.

p. 35: Villiers de l'Isle-Adam Comte Villiers de l'Isle-Adam (1838–89), French writer and pioneer of the symbolist movement. **Miss Macleod** Fiona Macleod (William Sharp, 1855–1905), Scottish novelist, essayist and biographer.

THE AUTUMN OF THE BODY

p. 38: 'The Temptation of St. Anthony' *La Tentation de Saint Antoine* (1874), a play by Gustave Flaubert. **Axel** Symbolist drama by Comte Villiers de l'Isle-Adam. See note above. **Maeterlinck** Maurice Maeterlinck (1862–1949), Belgian symbolist poet and dramatist, author of *L'Oiseau Bleu* and *La Mort*. **Flaubert** Gustave Flaubert (1821–80), French novelist, author of *Madame Bovary*.

p. 39: Mr. Lang Andrew Lang (1844–1912), Greek scholar, anthropologist, poet and man of letters, author of *Custom and Myth*, co-translator of the *Odyssey* and *Iliad*. **Mr. Gosse** Sir Edmund Gosse (1849–1928), civil servant, conversationalist, man of letters, author of *Father and Son* (autobiography), poems and various biographies and critical studies. **Mr. Dobson** Henry Austin Dobson (1840–1921), poet and biographer.

p. 39: Mr. Bridges Robert Bridges (1844–1930), appointed Poet

Laureate in 1913, critic and anthologist, author of *The Testament of Beauty* (1929).

p. 40: An Irish poet AE, George William Russell. See note, p. 274. **'Kalevala'** ('Land of Heroes'), national epic poem of Finland.

p. 41: Mr. Symons Arthur Symons (1865–1945), poet and critic who described symbolism to English readers, friend of Yeats with whom he shared rooms in 1896. **Mallarmé's** Etienne Mallarmé (1842–98), French symbolist poet, author of *L'Après-midi d'un faune*.

THE SYMBOLISM OF POETRY

p. 43: Mr. Arthur Symons see note above.

p. 44: Giovanni Bardi Conte del Vernio (1534?–1612), Italian nobleman, scholar and inventor of opera. **the Pléiade** a group of late-sixteenth-century French poets.

p. 46: Nash (or Nashe), Thomas Nash (1567–1601), poet, dramatist, pamphleteer and author of *The Unfortunate Traveller, or the Life of Jacke Wilton*, a romantic tale of adventure.

p. 47: Arthur O'Shaughnessy (1844–81), poet and playwright; author of *Epic of Women* (1870), *Lays of France* (1872), *Music and Moonlight* (1874) and *Songs of a Worker* (1881).

p. 51: Demeter Greek goddess of corn-growing, earth and agriculture, mother of Persephone, who was carried off by Pluto to Hades. So great was Demeter's grief that Jupiter allowed Persephone to spend part of the year with her mother. **Gérard de Nerval** properly Gérard Labrunie (1808–55), French writer. **Maeterlinck** see note, p. 274. **Villiers de l'Isle-Adam** see note, p. 274.

THE PHILOSOPHY OF SHELLEY'S POETRY

p. 53: a group The Dublin Hermetic Society which met in York Street. **Godwin's 'Political Justice'** William Godwin (1756–1836), philosopher and novelist. His best novels are *Caleb Williams* (1794) and *St. Leon* (1799). He had a great influence on Wordsworth, Coleridge and Shelley.

p. 61: the Sidhe the gods of ancient Ireland, the people of the fairy hills.

p. 64: the Echtge hills a range of hills east of Gort, Lady Gregory's home in Co. Galway. **Slieve ná nog** Mountain of the Young.

p. 67: Plato's cave a reference to Plato's *Republic*, Book 7. **Porphyry** (A.D. *c.* 233–304), Neoplatonist. His chief writings include lives of Plotinus and Pythagoras, *Sententiae*, *De Abstinentia*, and the *Epistola ad Marcellam*, addressed to his wife.

p. 68: Taylor's translation Thomas Taylor (1758–1835), known as 'The Platonist'; he translated Plato, Aristotle, Neoplatonists and Pythagoreans. **Mr. Lang's translation** see note, p. 274. **Zoroaster's** Zoroaster was the founder of the Magian religion, probably a Persian living in the sixth century B.C. Zoroastrianism has two spirits, one of light and good, the other of darkness and evil.

p. 72: Maeterlinck see note, p. 274.

p. 74: Oisin . . . in the Gaelic poem probably Michael Comyn's 'The Lay of Oisin in the Land of Youth', on Brian O'Looney's translation of which Yeats partially founded his own poem, *The Wanderings of Oisin* (1889).

p. 77: Proclus (c. 412–485), Neoplatonist, born in Constantinople. **Emilia Viviani** an Italian girl admired by Shelley and the subject of his poem *Epipsychidion.*

FROM MAGIC

p. 81: Bulwer Lytton's Edward Robert Bulwer Lytton, first Earl of Lytton (1831–91), poet and statesman, Viceroy of India. Many of his writings appeared under the pseudonym of Owen Meredith.**geomancy** divination by means of figures or lines, particularly by observing points and lines on the earth or on paper, or by means of figures formed by pebbles or particles of earth thrown down at random.

p. 81: chiromancy the art of predicting events or telling fortunes by examining the hand. **cabbalistic symbolism** the Cabbala or Kabbala are medieval Jewish writings preserved by occultists. They blend cosmogony and explanations of Biblical material.

p. 84: 'Frankenstein' or *The Modern Prometheus*, a tale of terror by Mary Shelley, in which Frankenstein creates a monster which murders Frankenstein's brother and bride and finally Frankenstein himself.

p. 89: 'Carmina Gaedelica' *Ortha nan Gaidheal, Carmina Gadelica* (1900), hymns and incantations with illustrative notes . . . collected in the Highlands and Islands of Scotland and translated into English by Alexander Carmichael. **Finn mac Cumhal** legendary hero of the Fenian cycle of tales. **'Paracelsus'** Paracelsus (1493–1541), magician, alchemist, astrologer, sometimes regarded as the founder of modern chemistry. He once held a Chair of Physic and Surgery in Basle.

FROM AT STRATFORD-ON-AVON

p. 96: Mr. Gordon Craig Edward Gordon Craig (1872–1966), English actor and stage designer, son of Ellen Terry. His aim of simplifying the scene and emphasising the actors was acclaimed in Germany, Italy and Russia. In 1905 he travelled through Europe with Isadora Duncan; settled in Italy in 1906 and founded a theatrical art school in Florence in 1913.

p. 97: Mr. Benson Sir Frank Benson (1858–1939), actor-manager. **Balzac** Honoré de Balzac (1799–1850), French novelist, author of *La Comédie Humaine*, a collection of depictions of French life.

p. 99: Professor Dowden Edward Dowden (1843–1913), first

Professor of English Literature at Trinity College, Dublin. A friend of J. B. Yeats, he did not support the Irish literary revival, and was a Unionist in politics. He wrote a *Life of Shelley*; *Shakespeare, his Mind and Art*; *Puritan and Anglican*, and other critical studies.

p. 100: Verlaine Paul Verlaine (1844–96), French symbolist poet.

p. 101: Gervinus Georg Gottfried Gervinus (1805–71), critic who became Professor of History at Göttingen. His commentaries on Shakespeare were translated into English in 1862. **Bentham** Jeremy Bentham (1748–1832), English writer on law, whose writings affected legislation and the administration of the law.

FROM EDMUND SPENSER

p. 107: Lollards fourteenth-century heretics, followers of Wycliffe and others of similar views. **Langland** William Langland (1330?–1400?), poet, author of *The Vision Concerning Piers the Plowman*. **the other great English allegory** *The Pilgrim's Progress*, by John Bunyan (1628–88).

p. 110: Emerson Ralph Waldo Emerson (1803–82), American transcendental philosopher, poet and lecturer. **Thomas à Kempis's** Thomas Hammerlein (1380–1471), who became a monk and wrote *De Imitatione Christi*.

p. 111: William Morris (1834–96), poet, translator, artist, decorator, printer, manufacturer and socialist, author of *The Life and Death of Jason*, *The Earthly Paradise* and *Sigurd the Volsung*. He founded the Kelmscott press.

p. 113: Hugo Victor Hugo (1802–85), French poet and novelist, author of *Notre Dame de Paris* and *Les Misérables*. He entered politics in 1848, was exiled 1851–70. **Rabelais** François Rabelais (1494?–1553), French humanist, physician and satirical author of *Pantagruel* and *Gargantua* as well as the *Third Book* and *Fourth Book*. Urquhart translated the first three books into English. **Theocritus** Greek poet of the third century B.C., author of the *Idylls*, pastoral poems.

p. 115: the Four Masters Conary and Cucogry O'Clery and Ferfesa O'Mulcrony, who compiled the *Annals of the Four Masters* (also called *Annals of Donegal*) during 1633–36 in the Franciscan monastery of Donegal.

p. 116: The Great Demagogue Oliver Cromwell (1599–1658), Lord Protector. He arrived in Ireland in 1649, sacked Drogheda and Wexford, and was responsible for the 'Act of Settlement' by which Irish gentry were transplanted to Clare and Connacht and their lands handed over to Army officers and men, nine counties being confiscated. **Cairbry Cat-Head** Cairbry Cat-Head led the lower classes in an anti-monarchical revolution, *c*. A.D. 90, but the Irish, still liking monarchy, called him their king. See Thurneysen, *Zeitschirft für Celtisceh Philologie*, XI, 56, and T. F. O'Rahilly 'Cairbre Cattchenn' in Feil

Sgribhinn Eóin Mhin Néill (1940), pp. 101–10. I owe this information
to Mr. Brendan Kennelly.
p. 117: Claude's Claude Lorrain (1600–82), French landscape painter.
p. 118: Smart Christopher Smart (1722–71), English poet.
p. 120: Matthew Roydon (1580–1622), English poet.

FROM **THE HAPPIEST OF THE POETS**

p. 122: an old turreted house Sandymount Castle, Dublin.
p. 123: Habundia's Kin probably a reference to Domina Abundia, a
beneficent fairy whose name occurs in poems of the Middle Ages, who
brought plenty to those whom she visited.
p. 124: Mr. Mackail John William Mackail (1859–1945), British
Classical Scholar; Professor of Poetry at Oxford (1906–11); awarded the
O.M. in 1935.

THE GALWAY PLAINS

p. 127: Lady Gregory Lady Isabella Augusta Gregory (1852–1932),
translator and dramatist, daughter of Dudley Persse, a rich landowner,
and widow of Sir William Gregory. After meeting Yeats she became
interested in the Irish Renascence and was a co-founder of the Abbey
Theatre.
p. 128: Raftery Anthony Raftery (1784–1834), blind Irish Gaelic poet.

FIRST PRINCIPLES

p. 130: Pascal Blaise Pascal (1623–62), French mathematician and
religious philosopher. **Montaigne** Michel Eyqyem de Montaigne
(1533–92), French essayist. **Emerson** see note, p. 277.
p. 131: J. F. Taylor John Francis Taylor (1850?–1902), Irish orator
(Q.C. 1892) and journalist.
p. 132: 'The Rising of the Moon' a play by Lady Gregory included in
Seven Short Plays (1909). **Fenians** originally a semi-mythical,
semi-historical military body said to have been raised for the defence of
Ireland against Norse raids; later an association for promoting the
overthrow of English government in Ireland.
p. 133: Lollard preacher Sir John Oldcastle (*d.* 1417).
p. 136: Cervantes Saavedra Miguel de Cervantes (1547–1616), Spanish
novelist, dramatist and poet.
p. 137: the Fianna see note above on Fenians.
p. 138: Virgil the reference is to *Eclogue IV*, ll. 31–6, where Virgil
prophesies a second Argo and a second Troy. See Yeats's poem 'Two
Songs from a Play', *Collected Poems*, p. 239. **Dr. Hyde** see note, p. 273.
Father Peter O'Leary (b. 1839), Gaelic scholar.

p. 139: Ariosto Ludovico Ariosto (1474–1533), author of *Orlando Furioso*, an Italian romantic epic.

p. 143: Columbanus (or Columban), St. Columbanus (543–615), born in Leinster, founded monasteries in Gaul and died at Bobbio in the Apennines where he had founded a monastery in 612. **Beckford** William Beckford (1759–1844), traveller and novelist; his 'one memorable book', *Vathek*, is an oriental tale. **Prof. Dowden's** see note, p. 276–77. **Lowell** James Lowell (1819–91), American poet and critic.

p. 144: The Well of English Undefiled Geoffrey Chaucer (c. 1345–c. 1400).

p. 144: Sir Charles Gavan Duffy see note, p. 273. **Professor York Powell** (1850–1904), don at Christ Church and Regius Professor of History at Oxford, who wrote poetry and was a friend of J. B. Yeats.

p. 145: Campbell Thomas Campbell (1777–1844), Scottish poet, chiefly remembered for his war songs and patriotic poems.

p. 146: Mr. John Eglinton (b. 1868), pen-name of W. K. Magee, Irish essayist and poet who was at school with Yeats in Dublin. **Flaubert** see note, p. 274. **Björnson** Björnstjerne Björnson (1832–1910), Norwegian novelist and playwright.

p. 149: Villon François Villon (1431–80[9]), French poet, whose chief works are 'Petit Testament' and 'Grand Testament'; his 'Ballade des Dames du Temps Jadis' was translated by Rossetti.

FROM DISCOVERIES

p. 151: 'Little Eyolf' (1894), play by Henrik Ibsen (1828–1906).

p. 152: the hangings of '98 the Irish rebellion of 1798 was savagely suppressed.

p. 153: Villon see note above.

p. 154: Tintoretto's Tintoretto, actually named Jacopo Robusti, was born in Venice where there are many specimens of his art, which includes 'St. George and the Dragon', 'The Last Supper', 'The Crucifixion', 'The Resurrection', etc.

p. 155: 'The Knight of the Burning Pestle' (1613), a comedy by Beaumont and Fletcher. **'The Silent Woman'** alternative title of *Epicœne*, a comedy by Ben Jonson.

p. 157: a Herr Nordau Max Simon Nordau (1849–1923) was born in Budapest, became a physician, wrote some novels and travel books, but is best known for *The Conventional Lies of Society*, *Paradoxes* and *Degeneration*.

p. 159: Balzac see note, p. 276.

FROM POETRY AND TRADITION

p. 161: Charles V (1337–80), called Charles the Wise, was born at Vincennes and reigned from 1364 to 1380; he was a patron of art and

literature and collected a large library at the Louvre. **Duke Guidobaldo**
Guidobaldo de Montefeltro, Duke of Urbino (1472–1508), who built
the magnificent palace at Urbino, which Yeats visited in 1907, and
about which he read in Castiglione's *The Book of The Courtier*. **Duke
Frederick** Frederico de Montefeltro, Duke of Urbino (1410–1482)
father of Guidobaldo.

p. 164: Castiglione Baldassare Castiglione (1478–1529), Italian
humanist, author of *Il Cortegiano* (*The Courtier*).

ANIMA HOMINIS

p. 166: Boehme Jacob Boehme (1575–1624), German theosophist and
mystic. **one close friend** Lady Gregory. **Maeterlinck** see note, p. 274.
Burne-Jones Sir Edward Burne-Jones (1833–98), English painter,
friend of Rossetti and William Morris.
p. 168: Savage Landor Walter Savage Landor (1775–1864), poet and
author of *Imaginary Conversations* (prose). **Beckford** see note, p. 279.
Leigh Hunt (1784–1859), essayist and poet. **Simeon Solomon**
(1840–1905), English painter and draughtsman.
p. 169: Shadwell Charles Lancelot Shadwell (1840–1919), sometime
Provost of Oriel College, Oxford, translated Dante's *Purgatorio* (Pt. I,
1892; Pt. II, 1899) and his *Paradiso* (1915). **Guido Cavalcanti** (*c.*
1230–1300), Italian poet. **Gino da Pistoia** (1270–1336), Italian jurist
and poet, friend of Dante.
p. 170: Giovanni Guirino It is possible that Yeats may be referring
here to *Guerino il Meschino* [the Wretched] an Italian romance by
Andrea of Florence (a contemporary of Dante), first printed in Padua in
1473. Miss Audrey Stead has suggested that Yeats may have come
across this romance in reading John F. Hogan, *Life and Works of Dante
Allighieri* (1899) pp. 336–38, who says Dante may have gained his
knowledge of Irish legend through this romance.
p. 170: Johnson Lionel Johnson (1867–1902), poet and critic. **Dowson**
Ernest Dowson (1867–1900), English poet who spent much of his youth
and later life in France.
p. 171: an old artist probably John Butler Yeats, Yeats's father.
p. 172: Saint Francis St. Francis of Assisi, Giovanni Francesco
Bernardone (1181?–1226), founder of the Franciscan Order, devoted
himself to the relief of the poor and sick. **Caesar Borgia** (1476–1507),
Italian general and administrator.
p. 173: Dodona in Epirus, seat of the oldest oracle (of Zeus) in Greece.
p. 174: Plutarch's precepts Plutarch (*c.* 46–120) was a Greek
biographer. '**Wilhelm Meister**' *Wilhelm Meisters Wanderjahre* (1821)
by Goethe (1749–1832). **Heraclitus** (*c.* 400–440 B.C.), Greek philosopher.
His *Concerning Nature* (*c.* 513 B.C.) contains his view that all things were
in a state of flux.

p. 176: Edwin Ellis (1848–1916), minor critic and poet; he and Yeats edited Blake, the edition appearing in 1893.

p. 178: a woman of incredible beauty see Yeats's note in *Autobiographies* (1956) p. 576 for a full account of this vision or dream. **Balzac's** see note, p. 276. **Christian Cabbala** see note, p. 276.

p. 180: Ariosto see note, p. 279.

A PEOPLE'S THEATRE

p. 181: Romain Rolland (1866–1944), French novelist, dramatist and critic.

p. 182: Swedenborg Emanuel Swedenborg (1688–1772), Swedish philosopher, scientist and mystic.

p. 184: Nietzsche Friedrich Wilhelm Nietzsche (1844–1900), born in Röcken, studied at Bonn and Leipzig. He won distinction for his treatises on tragedy.

p. 187: Henley William Ernest Henley (1849–1903), poet, critic and editor.

p. 190: Mr. Dulac Edmund Dulac (1882–1953), English painter and designer, born in France. **Mr. Rummell** Walter Rummel (b. 1887), son of Franz Rummel; Anglo-German pianist and composer.

p. 191: Chaliapin Fedor Ivanovich Chaliapin (1873–1938), Russian opera singer.

p. 192: the Wild Geese description of Irishmen who left Ireland to fight abroad in continental armies. **D'Annunzio** Gabrielle D'Annunzio (1863–1938), Italian poet, novelist, dramatist and journalist.

p. 193: A certain friend of mine Yeats himself, who had not yet published these poems under his own name.

THE IRISH DRAMATIC MOVEMENT

p. 195: Parnell Charles Stewart Parnell (1846–91), leader of the Irish parliamentary party, repudiated by Gladstone, by the Irish hierarchy and by the Irish party when his relationship with Mrs. O'Shea became public.

p. 196: Lady Gregory see note, p. 278. **a little old tower** Ballylee Castle which Yeats bought in 1917 and named Thoor Ballylee.

p. 197: Raftery see note, p. 278.

p. 198: Mr. Edward Martyn (1859–1923), Irish dramatist, co-founder of the Irish Literary Theatre, interested in church music, lived in Tulira Castle, Galway.

p. 199: Miss Allgood Sara Allgood (1883–1950), Irish actress and sister of Maire O'Neill. **Miss Maire O'Neill** Molly Allgood (d. 1952), Irish actress who was engaged to Synge, later married T. H. Mair, drama critic of the *Manchester Guardian*.

p. 201: Dublin Castle centre of British administration in Ireland.
Cardinal Logue His Eminence Michael Logue (1840–1924),
cardinal archbishop of Armagh. **Miss Horniman** Annie Elizabeth
Frederika Horniman (1860–1937), English theatrical director.
p. 205: Mr. Lennox Robinson's Lennox Robinson (1886–1958), Irish
playwright and manager of the Abbey Theatre from 1910, author of
The White-headed Boy and *Drama at Irish.*

INTRODUCTION TO 'FIGHTING THE WAVES'

p. 207: Hildo van Krop Hildo van Krop (b. 1884), Dutch sculptor.
George Antheil George Antheil (b. 1901), American composer of
Polish descent, born in New Jersey, studied under Bloch and spent some
years in Europe as a professional pianist.
p. 208: Standish O'Grady see note, p. 273. **Parnell** see note, p. 281.
Padraic Colum's Padraic Colum (1881–1972), poet and playwright.
p. 209: Balzac see note, p. 276.
p. 210: Sir William Crookes (1832–1919), English chemist and
physicist.
p. 211: Mr. Sacheverell Sitwell's Sacheverell Sitwell (b. 1897),
English critic and poet. **Dr. Gogarty's** Oliver St. John Gogarty
(1878–1957), Irish poet, doctor and Senator of the Irish Free State,
friend of Yeats. **D'Annunzio** see note, p. 281. **'Sigurd the Volsung'**
(1876), epic by William Morris.
p. 212: 'Tuatha de Danaan' the tribes of the goddess Dana, gods of
ancient Ireland.
p. 213: Professor Richet Charles Robert Richet (1850–1935), French
physiologist awarded the Nobel Prize in 1913.
p. 214: Gemistus Plethon (*c.* 1355–1450), Greek scholar; counsellor in
the Peloponnesus to Manuel and Theodore Palaeologus and went to the
Council of Florence in 1439.

ON D. H. LAWRENCE

p. 216: Twenty Years a-growing autobiographical account of
childhood and youth as the Blasket Islands by Maurice O'Sullivan. It
was originally written in Gaelic and then translated by Moya Davies
and George Thomson.

FROM THE INTRODUCTION TO 'THE OXFORD BOOK OF MODERN VERSE'

p. 217: Verlaine see note, p. 277. **William Watson** (1858–1935), poet
whose *Collected Poems* appeared in 1906.
p. 218: Campbell Joseph Campbell (1879–1944), poet and playwright,
took part in the Ulster theatre movement. **Colum** see note above.

The Shropshire Lad *A Shropshire Lad* (1896), a collection of poems by
A. E. Housman (1859–1936).

p. 219: James Stephens (1882–1950), Irish poet, novelist and
broadcaster, author of *The Crock of Gold*. **Frank O'Connor** (pen-name
of Michael O'Donovan, b. 1903), Irish novelist, short-story writer,
critic and translator. **O'Rahilly** Egan O'Rahilly (*fl.* 1690–1726), Gaelic
poet. **Lady Gregory** see note, p. 278.

p. 220: Davies William Herbert Davies (1871–1940), poet and author
of *The Autobiography of a Super-tramp*. **Binyon** Laurence Binyon
(1869–1943), poet, authority on Chinese art. **Sturge Moore** Thomas
Sturge Moore (1870–1944), poet, artist and art critic, friend of Yeats.
'Michael Field' pseudonym of Katharine Bradley (1846–1914) and
Edith Cooper (1862–1913), English collaborating authors of lyric
poetry and poetic dramas. **Sacheverell Sitwell** see note, p. 282.
Robert Bridges see note, p. 274–75.

p. 122: Aubrey Beardsley's Aubrey Vincent Beardsley (1872–98),
black and white artist, art editor of the *Yellow Book*. **Elinor Wylie**
(1885–1928), American poetess and novelist.

p. 223: Poincaré Raymond Poincaré (1860–1934), French statesman.

p. 224: Manet Edouard Manet (1832–83), French painter. **Rousseau**
Douanier Rousseau (1844–1910), French painter. **Courbet** Gustave
Courbet (1819–77), French painter. **John Gray** John Miller Gray
(1850–1894), Scottish art critic.

p. 225: Francis Thompson (1859–1907), poet, rescued from poverty
by the Meynells, author of *The Hound of Heaven*. **Lionel Johnson** see
note, p. 280.

p. 228: Smart's see note, p. 278. **Stendhal** pseudonym of Henri Beyle
(1783–1842), French novelist, author of *Le Rouge et le Noir* and *La
Chartreuse de Parme*. **Huysmans's** Joris Karl Huysmans (1848–1907),
French novelist.

p. 229: Turner Walter James Redfern Turner (1889–1946),
Australian-born poet, novelist and music critic; friend of Yeats.

p. 230: Pater's Walter Horatio Pater (1839–94), Oxford don and
author of *Studies in the History of the Renaissance*, *Marius the Epicurean*,
Appreciations, etc.

p. 231: Herbert Read Sir Herbert Read (1893–1968), English poet,
critic, publisher and anarchist. **Berkeley** George Berkeley (1685–1753),
Irish bishop and philosopher, author of *Essay towards a New Theory of
Vision*, *Principles of Human Knowledge*, etc. **Grosseteste** Robert
Grosseteste (d. 1253), bishop, poet, philosopher, theologian and author
of *Compendium Scientiarum*.

p. 232: Dorothy Wellesley Lady Dorothy Wellesley (1889–1956),
English poetess. **William Morris** see note, p. 277.

p. 233: Nicholas of Cusa (1401–64), son of a poor fisherman who became Archdeacon of Liège and later Bishop of Brixen. **Ernest Dowson's** see note, p. 280.

p. 234: Florence Farr (Mrs. Emery), member of a group of students of the occult, friend of Yeats, died in Ceylon in 1917.

p. 235: Heraclitus see note, p. 280. **Madge** Charles Madge (b. 1912), English poet and sociologist; Professor of Sociology at the University of Birmingham since 1950.

p. 235: Henley see note, p. 281.

p. 236: Spinoza Benedict Spinoza (1632–77), Jewish philosopher born in Amsterdam, author of posthumous *Ethics* (1677). **Twelfth of July** anniversary of the Battle of Boyne, 1689, celebrated in Ulster.

MODERN POETRY: A BROADCAST

p. 238: Ernest Dowson see note, p. 280. **Lionel Johnson** see note, p. 280.

p. 241: Inigo Jones (1573–1652), architect, designer of masques. **Verlaine** see note, p. 277.

p. 242: Charles Ricketts (1866–1931), English painter and theatre designer. **Delacroix** Ferdinand Victor Eugène Delacroix (1798–1863), French painter. **Sturge Moore** see note, p. 283. **Edith Cooper** see note on Michael Field, p. 283.

p. 243: Miss Bradley see note on Michael Field, p. 283. **Landor's** see note, p. 280.

p. 244: 'A Shropshire Lad' see note, p. 283. **York Powell** see note, p. 279. **Paul Fort** (b. 1872), French writer of ballads and prose poems.

p. 249: Turner's see note, p. 283. **Dorothy Wellesley's** see note, p. 283. **Herbert Read's** see note, p. 283. **Nicholas of Cusa** see note, p. 283.

p. 253: James Stephens see note, p. 283. **Senator Gogarty's** see note, p. 282.

A GENERAL INTRODUCTION FOR MY WORK

p. 256: John O'Leary see note, p. 273. **Thomas Davis** (1814–45), poet, educated at Trinity College, Dublin; called to the Irish Bar in 1838. One of the founders of *The Nation* and of the Young Ireland party.

p. 257: Standish O'Grady see note, p. 273. **O'Curry** Eugene O'Curry (1796–1862), Gaelic scholar, author of *Manners and Customs of Irish People*. **Mitchel** John Mitchel (1815–75), Irish revolutionary, founded the *United Irishman*, transported and escaped to America, returned to Ireland in 1872, became M.P.; author of *Jail Journal*. **O'Donovan** John O'Donovan (1809–61), Gaelic scholar, edited *The Annals of the Four Masters* (1848–51).

p. 258: Hayes O'Grady Standish Hayes O'Grady (1832–1915), Irish scholar who lived 30 years in California as civil engineer before compiling *Catalogue of Irish MSS in British Museum* (completed by Robin Flower); his best work was *Silva Gadelica*, 2 vols, (1892). **Lady Gregory** see note, p. 278. **Lady Charlotte Guest's 'Mabinogion'** Lady Charlotte Guest (1812–95), translated the *Mabinogion* (1838–49). **Rosses Point** district in Sligo where Yeats spent holidays as a child. **Queen Maeve** legendary Queen of Connaught, reputedly buried on Knocknarea, Sligo.

p. 259: Professor Burkitt Francis Crawford Burkitt (1864–1935), English theologian.

p. 260: 'tetragrammaton agla' the four-lettered name for the Hebrew God, pronunciation of which was forbidden. The Kabbalists claimed they knew the name and could, through this knowledge, perform miracles. **Doneraile** market town in County Cork. **James Stephens** see note, p. 283. **George Russell** see note, p. 274. **Pearse** Patrick Henry Pearse (1879–1916), Irish poet and orator, shot for his part in the 1916 Rising, when he was president of the provisional government. **the Red Branch** a cycle of Gaelic legends dealing with the Red Branch heroes. **Cuchulain** the 'Hound of Ulster', hero of Red Branch legends. **Jesse** a genealogical tree representing the genealogy of Christ from 'the root of Jesse', used in the Middle Ages as a decoration for walls and windows. **MacDonagh** Thomas MacDonagh (1878–1916), Irish poet and critic, shot for his part in the 1916 Rising.

p. 261: Mr. Arnold Toynbee (b. 1889), English historian.

p. 262: Parnell see note, p. 281. **Lord Edward** Lord Edward Fitzgerald (1763–98), Irish leader, president of the military committee of the United Irishmen in 1796, wounded and died in prison after leading an abortive rising. **Swedenborg** see note, p. 281. **Shri Purohit Swāmi** an Indian monk with whom Yeats worked on a translation of the *Upanishads* in 1935–6, for whose books he wrote forewords.

p. 262: Lecky William Edward Hartpole Lecky (1838–1903), Irish historian, author of *History of Rationalism*, *History of England* and other works.

p. 264: François Dominique Toussaint Toussaint L'Ouverture (*c.* 1746–1803), commander of forces in San Domingo in 1796, liberated the island and became its president, but was captured by the French and died in prison in France.

p. 265: Thomson James Thomson (1700–48), poet, author of *The Seasons* and *The Castle of Indolence*. **Cowper** William Cowper (1731–1800), poet and letterwriter.

p. 266: Turner see note, p. 283. **Lawrence** D. H. Lawrence (1885–1930), novelist and poet. **Sir Thomas Browne** (1605–82), graduated in Leyden as a doctor; author of *Religio Medici* (1643), *Urn Burial* and *Garden of Cyrus* (1658). **George Moore** (1852–1933), Irish novelist and playwright who wrote maliciously of Yeats in *Hail and Farewell*, an account of Dublin life. **Milton's or Shelley's Platonist** the references are to *Il Penseroso* I and *Laon and Cythna* II, frag. II.

p. 266: that tower Palmer drew an illustration by Samuel Palmer (1805–81), water-colour landscape painter and etcher, in an edition of Milton's *Minor Poems* (1889).

p. 267: Deirdre heroine of the tale of 'The Sons of Usna', one of 'Three Sorrowful Stories of Erin'; she was to marry King Conchubar but ran away with Naoise to Scotland; they returned to Ireland under a safe conduct but Conchubar had Naoise killed on their return. In one version of the legend Deirdre then kills herself. **Paul Fort's** see note, p. 284. **Robert Bridges** see note, pp. 274–75.

p. 269: Mallarmé see note, pp. 275. **Leonardo** Leonardo da Vinci. **O'Connell Bridge** chief bridge over the River Liffey in Dublin.

SELECT BIBLIOGRAPHY

YEATS's criticism occurs in various places in his prose writings, and can be found in his reviews, articles, essays and letters, as well as in *A Vision*, and his Senate speeches. The Introductions and Notes to editions of his own work and to anthologies and selections or editions of the work of other writers also contain his views on life and literature. For fuller details the reader is advised to consult Allan Wade, *A Bibliography of the Writings of W. B. Yeats* (3rd ed., 1968).

A. WORKS CONTAINING CRITICISM

The Collected Works in Verse and Prose of William Butler Yeats (8 vols., 1908)

Letters to the New Island (ed. Horace Reynolds, 1934)

A Vision (1937)

On the Boiler (1939)

Letters on Poetry from W. B. Yeats to Dorothy Wellesley (1940; 1964)

Letters to Katharine Tynan (ed. Roger McHugh, 1953)

W. B. Yeats and T. Sturge Moore. Their Correspondence (ed. Ursula Bridge, 1953)

Letters (ed. Allan Wade, 1954)

Autobiographies (1956)

The Variorum Edition of the Poems of W. B. Yeats (ed. Peter Allt and Russell K. Alspach, 1957). Contains introductions and notes to volumes of Yeats's poetry.

Mythologies (1959)

The Senate Speeches of W. B. Yeats (ed. Donald R. Pearce, 1960)

Essays and Introductions (1961)

Explorations (1962)

The Variorum Edition of the Plays of W. B. Yeats (ed. Russell K. Alspach, 1966). Contains introductions and notes to Yeats's volumes of plays.

Uncollected Prose by W. B. Yeats (vol. 1, ed. John P. Frayne, 1970). This contains Yeats's first reviews and articles from 1886 to 1896, and will be followed by a further volume of similar material.

B. BIOGRAPHICAL AND CRITICAL STUDIES OF YEATS

Joseph Hone, *W. B. Yeats 1865–1939* (1943; rev. ed., 1963)

A. Norman Jeffares, *Yeats: Man and Poet* (1949; rev. ed., 1962)

Birgit Bjersby, *The Interpretation of the Cuchulain Legend in the Works of W. B. Yeats* (1950)

T. R. Henn, *The Lonely Tower* (1950; rev. ed., 1965)

G. B. Saul, *Prolegomena to the Plays of W. B. Yeats* (1958)

F. A. C. Wilson, *W. B. Yeats and Tradition* (1958)

F. A. C. Wilson, *Yeats's Iconography* (1960)

A. G. Stock, *W. B. Yeats. His Poetry and Thought* (1961; rev. ed., 1964)

A. Norman Jeffares (ed.), *A Review of English Literature* [Yeats number] (July 1963)

Peter Ure, *Yeats* [in Writers and Critics Series] (1963)

Peter Ure, *Yeats the Playwright* (1963)

Helen Vendler, *Yeats's Vision and the Later Plays* (1963)

Denis Donoghue (ed.), *The Integrity of Yeats* (1964)

Edward Engelberg, *The Vast Design* (1964)

M. C. Bradbrook, *English Dramatic Form: A History of its Development* (1965)

Curtis Bradford, *Yeats at Work* (1965)

S. B. Bushrui, *Yeats's Verse-Plays: The Revisions 1900–1910* (1965)

Denis Donoghue and J. R. Mulryne (eds.), *An Honoured Guest: New Essays on W. B. Yeats* (1965)

A. Norman Jeffares and K. G. W. Cross (eds.), *In Excited Reverie* (1965)

D. E. S. Maxwell and S. B. Bushrui (eds.), *W. B. Yeats 1865–1965: Centenary Essays* (1956)

Shotaro Oshima, *W. B. Yeats and Japan* (1965)

B. Rajan, *W. B. Yeats: A Critical Introduction* (1956)

Corinna Salvadori, *Yeats and Castiglione: Poet and Courtier* (1965)

Robin Skelton and Ann Saddlemyer (eds.), *The World of W. B. Yeats* (1965)

Alex Zwerdling, *Yeats and the Heroic Ideal* (1965)

Donald T. Torchiana, *W. B. Yeats and Georgian Ireland* (1966)

A. Norman Jeffares, *A Commentary on the Collected Poems of W. B. Yeats* (1968)

Joseph Ronsley, *Yeats's Autobiography. Life as Symbolic Pattern* (1968)

Austin Clarke, *The Celtic Twilight and the Nineties* (1969)